experience

2ND EDITION

WORKBOOK

C1
Advanced

CONTENTS

Listening	Use of English	Speaking	Writing	Review
topic: memory championships **task:** multiple matching	open cloze (p9) word formation (p10)	**topic:** looking back from the future **task:** collaborative task	**topic:** historical drama **task:** review	unit check 1
topic: turning failure into success **task:** sentence completion	open cloze (p19) multiple-choice cloze (p20)	**topic:** disappointment **task:** long turn	**topic:** reality TV talent shows **task:** essay	unit check 2
topic: community kitchen **task:** multiple choice: longer text	key word transformation (p29) word formation (p30)	**topic:** adapting to change **task:** collaborative task: decision question	**topic:** the influence of the media and celebrity **task:** letter	unit check 3 Use of English units 1–3 (p34)
topic: the importance of names **task:** multiple choice: short texts	open cloze (p41) open cloze; multiple-choice cloze (p42)	**topic:** having things in common **task:** collaborative task; discussion	**topic:** globalisation **task:** essay	unit check 4
topic: start-ups **task:** multiple matching	open cloze (p51)	**topic:** learning about money **task:** long turn	**topic:** raising money for a club **task:** report	unit check 5
topic: picture therapy **task:** multiple choice: longer text	open cloze (p61) multiple-choice cloze (p62)	**topic:** truthfulness **task:** collaborative task; discussion	**topic:** working in entertainment **task:** essay	unit check 6 Use of English units 1–6 (p66)
topic: originality **task:** multiple choice: short texts	key word transformation (p73) word formation (p74)	**topic:** news broadcast **task:** long turn	**topic:** school radio station **task:** proposal	unit check 7
topic: nutrition **task:** sentence completion	open cloze (p83) multiple-choice cloze (p84)	**topic:** things of value to health **task:** collaborative task	**topic:** bad eating habits **task:** essay	unit check 8
topic: taking breaks **task:** multiple matching	key word transformation (p93) word formation (p94)	**topic:** work styles **task:** long turn	**topic:** work experience **task:** report	unit check 9 Use of English units 1–9 (p98)
Listening (p112)	Speaking (p116)			

Look ahead, look back

READING

1 Complete the text with these words.

advent   current   cutting-edge   facilitate
flawed   modifying   pave   unnerving

DOCUMENTING MEMORIES

We know that the latest ¹.......................................
technology can be studied and used to
²................................. our understanding
of how memory works, which in turn helps to
³................................. the way for medical
developments. At the same time, however, the
⁴................................. of mobile technology
can actually be damaging the way we make
memories. We used to go on trips, enjoy the view
and then use our camera to take a photo or two.
Our ⁵................................. method is the
reverse – we shoot first and remember later. It's
⁶................................. to think that we have
transformed the function of a photograph – from
something we use to trigger a memory to something we
create a memory from. And then we should consider
the implications of the increasingly popular trend of
⁷................................. our photos. Perhaps it's time
to stop and reflect that this new way of creating memories
is ⁸................................. .

2 Read the article and choose the best description.

1 a series of essays on memory analysis
2 an artistic interpretation of how our memory
   changes from childhood to adulthood
3 a collection of personal accounts of how memory is
   distorted
4 an analysis of the role of memory in distinguishing
   fact from fiction

3 🄴 Read the article again and choose from the
paragraphs (A–G) the one which best fits each gap
(1–6). There is one extra paragraph which you do not
need to use.

A   The root cause of this can often be is simply a case of another
person saying that the events in question either never happened
or else happened very differently from the way they are
remembered and we are persuaded that our memory was faulty.

B   As a result, psychologists have tried to generate false memories
in psychology experiments. They simply get people to imagine
events that never actually happened. This also explains the
phenomenon of non-believed memories, which often involves
people believing things that aren't true because they were led to
believe them by a third party such as a newspaper headline or a
therapy session.

C   You might trust your own memory over theirs, but would you
be right? Unfortunately not always. Feeling convinced that
something was true or having vividly accurate memories that
have no basis in real events is referred to as a 'non-believed'
memory and further highlights the much-discussed fallibility of
human memory.

D   This is just one of several examples in the collection where
there is the possibility that a person's memory was accurate
and that it was the memories of those around him/her that were
at fault, either forgetting an event completely or remembering
it incorrectly. Nonetheless, as **cited** above, there is often
indisputable external proof that the memory cannot be true.

E   Before these studies, we only had access to unsubstantiated
accounts of false memories. One of these is the now
well-known claim by a celebrated singer that aged two she had
encountered a huge black panther in the woods near Exmoor
while walking with her nanny. The story even made the national
press. Although the nanny later admitted to having invented the
sighting in order to get 'into the papers' the singer still has a
vivid memory of the enormous black animal, a memory that she
now knows to be completely false.

F   Alternatively, it could be caused by a difficulty in being able to
differentiate between the memory of something that physically
happened and something that our minds created such as
a dream.

G   This is **reinforced** by one contributor's explanation that he truly
remembers flying when he was a child. The belief that he had
the ability to travel from place to place in the air is so strong
that, although he knows it to have been impossible, he cannot
forget the amazing feeling of freedom that flying brought to him,
even today.

The False Memory Archive

Have you ever had a heated discussion with someone because you remember something from the past **vividly** in one way, yet they remember it in a completely different way? If you've ever been convinced that something happened, only to be told by someone else who shared the same experience that it didn't, how would you know which version of events to believe?

1 ....

Although psychological experiments to manipulate and implant false memories have been carried out for some time, it is only recently that investigations into examples of false memories and why we create them have begun.

2 ....

Theories developed through studying accounts like this demonstrate that the brain can be as creative as it is inaccurate when it comes to memory and is able to transform made-up stories and childhood emotions into remembered fact. This is the subject of a recently published collection made up of diverse real-life examples some of which are at times boring, but at others incredibly strange. It depicts how we end up rejecting 'memories' that we once believed to be true.

3 ....

One contributor recalls the following memory: 'I spent my childhood in a small rural town in Peru, before my family moved to London in my early teens. My brother and I often **reminisced** about our early years in Peru, especially about the succulent pear melons that we used to pick off the tree in the front yard of the house directly across from ours, before racing back home before the owner caught us. Ten years later, my brother returned to Peru and found that the pear melon tree was actually at the end of the road, about six houses down from ours. I was sceptical, but when I went back myself I saw that he was telling the truth. The tree wasn't even visible from our house. Not only that, but the man who lived opposite was delighted to see me.'

4 ....

Another reason for determining a false memory is often quite simply its **implausibility**. For example, it is fairly common for someone to have clear recollections of being invisible or breathing underwater for unlimited amounts of time.

5 ....

Moving on to why we have **subjectively** vivid memories that **contradict** real events, the answer is not entirely clear; however, it could be due to a psychological process in which our memories record events but they don't record accurately the source of the information. For example, we might believe we saw something happen, and in fact we did see it happen, but it was in a film or on TV.

6 ....

Considering that our very identity and the way we see ourselves is a result of the innumerable events and experiences we have accumulated throughout our lives, it is **disconcerting**, to say the least, to find that perhaps some of the memories we treasure most never really happened in the first place.

---

4 Match the words in bold in the article with the phrases in bold (1–8).

1 The artist urged us to look at it **using our own interpretation of it**. ....

2 She can still picture the scene **in detail**. ....

3 Frank **gave** three examples to support his argument. ....

4 The response to the presentation **supported** the organiser's belief that he had made the right decision.

5 The idea was immediately dismissed based on **how impossible it was to prove**. ....

6 The results of the study **are the opposite of** the theory on memory retention. ....

7 Not being able to remember the events leading up to the accident was **uncomfortable** for him. ....

8 We spent a lovely evening when we **remembered and talked about** our schooldays together. ....

GRAMMAR

review of past tenses

1 🔊 **1.1 Listen to Miranda, Sally and Lucas talking about their childhoods. Choose the correct words to complete the sentences.**

1 Miranda **used to / didn't use to** spend a lot of time watching TV.
2 Miranda's parents **had / hadn't** been writing books for a long time.
3 Sally **felt / didn't feel** very alone after Beth had left home.
4 Sally's parents **warned / didn't warn** her that she would miss her sister at first.
5 Lucas **contrasted / didn't contrast** his parent's culture with the British culture as he was growing up.

2 **Complete the text with the correct form of the verbs in brackets. Use** *would / used to* **if appropriate.**

Looking back

Miranda
Add message | Report

Looking back, it seems that most of my childhood consisted of chilling on a sofa, while my parents ¹................................ (work) away writing. From a six-year-old's viewpoint, their work ²................................ (seem) awesome, and my parents ³................................ (be) very laid back about stuff. What was there not to like!

Sally
Add message | Report

After my sisters ⁴................................ (leave) home it dawned on me that the youngest gets a raw deal. I ⁵................................ (share) a bedroom with my sister Charlotte for years and then next thing I knew it was just me. Charlotte and I ⁶................................ (talk) for hours about our plans for the future.

Lucas
Add message | Report

Our parents ⁷................................ (move) here when I was eight years old, but I think my parents ⁸................................ (consider) the move for ages. Our parents were special. They took the time to talk to us and see how we were getting on and if we ⁹................................ (have) a tough time at school they would give us a special treat. They ¹⁰................................ (spoil) us though! Quality time with us mattered to them. That felt good.

3 **Choose the correct answer (A, B or C) to complete the sentences.**

1 When I was younger I .... in my diary every day.
   A used to write   **B** was writing   **C** had written
2 Simon .... before I had time to tell him about the concert.
   A hung up   **B** had hung up   **C** was hanging up
3 I think that my personality has changed over the years. I .... so laid back.
   A didn't always use to be   **B** wouldn't always be   **C** hadn't always been
4 I remember on my sixth birthday party I was sick afterwards because I .... most of my birthday cake!
   A ate   **B** was eating   **C** had eaten
5 When I said that my friends haven't called me recently, I .... about you.
   A didn't talk   **B** hadn't talked   **C** wasn't talking
6 When I was a teenager and I got back home after a party, my parents .... for me.
   A used to be waiting   **B** would wait   **C** had been waiting
7 My sister .... all the information from the hard drive before I had time to tell her not to.
   A deleted   **B** was deleting   **C** had deleted
8 When I was a child we .... an apartment on the coast.
   A would own   **B** used to own   **C** had owned

4 **Complete the text with the correct form of these words.**

apply   become   cross   give   have   work

Moving on

We finished our sixth form studies a couple of months ago and soon after graduation it ¹................ apparent to me that I ²................ enough thought to what I was going to do next.

All my friends ³................ for jobs in a frenzy and some ⁴................ interviews already and were waiting for the results. In my defence, I can say that it ⁵................ my mind because I ⁶................ solidly for the final exams.

VOCABULARY

memory: verbs and collocations

1 Complete the text with the correct form of these words.

block out   jog   memories   memorise   recall   remind

The power of early memories

If you are the nostalgic type who likes to
¹.. events from the past, then you
should carry on! Studies show that people who have
vivid ².. from early childhood are
the fortunate ones. Children whose parents encourage
reminiscing about daily events show better coping
and problem-solving skills later in life. Looking back
over old photos ³.. us about
important milestones and can ⁴..
our memories about happy past events. While we don't
have to go to the extreme of ⁵..
dates and names of people, remembering significant
events is beneficial. They also say that we shouldn't
encourage our children to ⁶..
sad memories as they help to equip them with
a sense of self-continuity
or personal identity.

MEMORY LANE

2 🔊 1.2 Match the first sentence (1–5) with the second sentence (A–E). Listen and check.

1 I can't remember anything from before I was six.

2 I agree that there are some things we just choose to forget.

3 I remember very clearly what my first teacher at primary school said to me though.

4 I have a vivid recollection of both images and smells from my childhood.

5 My brother has got a phenomenal memory though, much better than mine.

A Often I'll come across a scent that triggers a memory from way, way back.

B Loads of times he has to jog my memory because for me it's all a blur.

C I think I blocked out some memories from early childhood, perhaps because my mum was quite ill.

D I guess that's what we call having a selective memory.

E Word for word. I can hear her as if it were yesterday.

3 Choose the correct words to complete the text.

MY GRANDFATHER

My grandfather was a photographer during the Second World War. He says he doesn't remember much about it. I guess he has a ¹**selective / committed** memory because some of the things he saw must have been upsetting. I think it is only natural that the mind sometimes ²**triggers / blocks out** terrible memories when they are too painful. I love his stories and so sometimes I try to ³**jog / trigger** his memory about things that he has seen, but I ⁴**realise / recall** it's difficult for him and so I don't insist.

For anything apart from the war, he has a great memory. He always ⁵**recognises / memorises** people when he meets them in the street and ⁶**reminds / remembers** their names. He ⁷**jogs / commits** phone numbers to memory and can remember long poems word ⁸**by / for** word. He criticises me for keeping all my information on my phone and he says I should ⁹**memorise / recall** the important phone numbers. He's probably right, but I just have a terrible memory. Perhaps I have more of a sensory memory because sometimes smells or images can ¹⁰**trigger / block** memories of childhood. My grandfather would say I'm making an excuse!

Extend

4 Read the text and match the words / phrases in bold (1–5) with the meanings (A–E).

TOP 5 memory hacks

1 Play brain games:
Find brain teasers, do Sudoku or perform **a feat of memory**.

2 Use the power of music:
Ear-worms are annoying, but music can help us remember.

3 Meditate:
Do this **in memory of** Mahatma Gandhi and many others. It's good for focus.

4 Chew gum:
If you have **a vague recollection of something**, chewing gum increases blood flow to the brain.

5 Bundle them:
Bundle the **vivid memories** together with the vague ones.

A extremely clear memories

B in honour of a deceased person

C tunes you keep thinking about after they have stopped playing

D a limited or unclear memory of something or someone

E an extraordinary display of memory

LISTENING

1 🔊 **1.3 You are going to listen to five people talking about competing in the World Memory Championships. Which of these sentences is correct?**

A Some of the speakers' families taught them the memory techniques.

B All of the speakers learnt their memory techniques at school.

C Most of the speakers taught themselves the memory techniques.

2 e 🔊 **1.4 Listen again and complete both tasks.**

Task 1

Choose from the list (A–H) what caused each speaker to develop his / her method for memorisation.

A	health problems	Speaker 1	**1**	☐
B	preparing for a celebration	Speaker 2	**2**	☐
C	needing to occupy free time	Speaker 3	**3**	☐
D	moving house	Speaker 4	**4**	☐
E	helping a teacher	Speaker 5	**5**	☐
F	concentrating on a task			
G	revising for an exam			
H	taking a course			

Task 2

Choose from the list (A–H) the unexpected benefit each speaker mentions.

A	meeting new people	Speaker 1	**6**	☐
B	being able to help others	Speaker 2	**7**	☐
C	turning a hobby into a profession	Speaker 3	**8**	☐
D	developing a training program for companies	Speaker 4	**9**	☐
E	improving physical condition	Speaker 5	**10**	☐
F	setting the world record			
G	achieving Olympic standard in memorisation			
H	realisation that new goals can be achieved			

3 Match the words and phrases (1–6) with the meanings (A–F).

1	link	**A**	interesting and unusual
2	quirky	**B**	give several pieces of information very quickly
3	rattle something off	**C**	naturally find something easy to do
4	reciting	**D**	connection
5	get hooked on	**E**	saying something you have memorised
6	have a knack for	**F**	become addicted to something

> **time** out
>
> **Play Kim's game.**
>
> **1** Look at the picture for one minute.
>
> **2** Cover the picture.
>
> **3** How many of the items can you remember?
>
> **4** What strategies might you employ to help improve your memory?

USE OF ENGLISH 1

1 Complete the blog with these prepositions.

about   at   by (x2)   of   on   to   with

○○○

hello!

Hi! I'm Olivia Vidal, and I confess I am addicted **1**............................ bullet journals! Ask yourself the following questions. Are you ever embarrassed **2**............................ the amount of time you spend on screens? Are you ever concerned **3**............................ the fact that you never actually write anything much off a screen? If so, then visit my Instagram page @gobullet_journals and be inspired **4**............................ my ideas. I think you'll be amazed **5**............................ how bullet journaling can change your life.

Thank you to all my followers 😊. I must confess that initially I was scared **6**............................ starting this blog as it is my first time, but I am really delighted **7**............................ all the amazing comments from you all.

Based **8**............................ what you say, you love bullet journaling just as much as I do!

2 Choose the correct answer (A, B or C) to complete the sentences.

1 Apologising .... his behaviour is the least that he can do in the circumstances.
  A about   **B** for   **C** by

2 Simon is extremely confident and very accomplished .... public speaking.
  A at   **B** with   **C** of

3 Customers concerned .... delays in trains should go immediately to the information desk.
  A for   **B** about   **C** at

4 Protecting animals .... harm is our duty as responsible citizens.
  A for   **B** by   **C** from

5 Prince will always be remembered .... 'Purple Rain'. It's such a well-known song.
  A for   **B** about   **C** by

6 My parents stopped me .... going to the concert as they said it was on too late.
  A for   **B** from   **C** off

7 We're undecided .... where to go on holidays this year. Sea, mountains, culture…I don't know!
  A by   **B** with   **C** about

8 If I were you I'd choose pasta as this restaurant is known .... it's homemade pasta.
  A for   **B** about   **C** with

3 **e** Read the text and complete the gaps with one word only.

HOW TO **DE-CLUTTER YOUR MIND**

It's easy to understand why nowadays people frequently complain about lack of time, about not enough hours in the day and of **1**............................ stressed. We live in times of information overload and we are more often than **2**............................ faced with endless choices to **3**............................ . From the moment we get up in the morning until we go to bed at night we have to make decision **4**............................ decision and each one has a knock-on effect on the next. Exhausting stuff.

Why **5**............................ take a deep breath and take a step back? Perhaps it is time to check what tasks are essential. Start by making a list of all you need to do in the day and from there start to get rid **6**............................ those that are time wasters. Each time ask yourself the question, 'Is this necessary?' **7**............................ the answer is a negative, then simply discard the time wasters. As you gradually de-clutter your day you will start to feel lighter and more **8**............................ to concentrate on those tasks which really require your full attention.

Extend

4 Choose the correct words to complete the text.

My ~~DIGITAL~~ *bullet journal*

Until quite recently I'd been using my bullet journal almost on a daily basis, and it was going really well. But then the routine just went out of the window and I realised that I hadn't used it in days. I was alarmed **1at / by** how quickly I'd tired of using paper and I was quite frankly distressed **2by / with** my lack of discipline. OK, I may be known **3for / by** being impulsive, but this time I was upset **4about / with** myself!

So I've decided to use an app on my phone as an organiser. When I started looking around I was overwhelmed **5by / at** the choice of different apps out there and I refrained **6from / for** grabbing the first app I saw on the market. I think I have found the perfect one! Basically, it's a bullet journal, but on my phone. I'm really adept **7for / at** getting my head around new apps so I'm already loving it! I have all my calendars coordinated with each other and this time I'm committed **8on / to** making this work for me. It's a shame about the paper version, but perhaps this is what will work for me. Let's hope so!

9

USE OF ENGLISH 2

1 Complete the sentences with the correct form of the words in brackets.

1 Some people may find it .... (reassure) to discover there may be a forgetful gene.

2 It can be easier to remember a .... (describe) story than one with fewer details.

3 There is .... (substance) more research available about memory loss than in the past.

4 Many people use .... (memorise) techniques as a way to keep their brain active.

5 Memory is individual and not .... (transfer) between two people.

6 An .... (advice) group of neuroscientists met to discuss their research into memory.

7 .... (repeat) not getting enough sleep can have negative effects on your memory.

8 Research suggests that dogs' .... (recollect) of times and places happens in the same way as humans'.

2 Complete the puzzle with the correct words. Use the example of 'repeat' to help you work out the pattern.

repeat (v)	1	repetitive (adj)	2 ....
describe (v)	repeat (n)	descriptive (adj)	repeatedly (adv)
3	memorisation (n)	different (adj)	4 ....
memorise (v)	5	6	differently (adv)

3 **e** Read the text. Use the word given at the end of some of the lines to form a word that fits in the gap in the same line.

Buy **experiences**, not **stuff**

Think back to your childhood birthdays. If you were asked to give a
1 .... of all the presents you received, would you be
able to do it?
What about the way you chose to celebrate becoming a year older?
Buying material things might give us a rush of 2 ....
at the time, but over the long term, they don't give us as much
3 .... as spending money on experiences, such as
trips, concerts and films.
We end up with a certain level of 4 .... from 'things'
in a way that we don't do with memories. Our 5 ....
of a sweet memory is more likely to make us smile than thinking about
a material purchase, especially when we factor in the excitement of
the 6 .... before the event as well. If the event isn't
7 .... positive, over time we start to remember it
8 .... and our memories of them get sweeter.

DESCRIBE

HAPPY

SATISFY

DETACH
RECOLLECT

ANTICIPATE
PARTICULAR
DIFFER

Extend

4 Read the advertisement. Decide if the highlighted words (1–4) are nouns, verbs, adverbs or adjectives.

> Looking for the perfect gift to spoil someone special? Give them an adrenaline rush with a ride down the world's longest slide, **1restore** their sense of well-being at a serene spa day in a luxurious forest lodge or **2refresh** their cooking skills by giving them a masterclass with a world-renowned chef. Give your loved ones something they will truly treasure – a memory to last a lifetime. Give them an Experience Day*.
>
> *Recipients must book their experience day within one year.
>
> We aim to make our experience days **3accessible** to all and can **4confidently** cater to all special requirements. Contact our customer service team for more information.

5 Put the highlighted words (1–4) from Ex 4 in the correct category in the table. Then complete the table with the words for the other categories.

	verb	noun	adjective	adverb
1				
2				
3				
4				

SPEAKING

1 Complete the phrases with these words.

could exactly more other point putting

1 That's an excellent way of .... it.

2 OK, I agree up to a ....

3 You .... be right, but …

4 I couldn't agree ....

5 That's true, but on the .... hand …

6 That's .... how I feel too.

2 Which of the sentences and phrases in Ex 1 show agreement (A) or partial agreement/polite disagreement (D)?

3 Choose the correct phrases to complete the conversations.

1 **A:** In my opinion you can't really improve your memory.

B: **That's an excellent way of putting it /**
OK, I agree up to a point. There's no way you can get better at recalling things, in spite of all the books out there on the subject!

2 **A:** I think the best way to relax is to sit down with a good book in a quiet place somewhere. Or maybe take the dog for a walk. What do you think?

B: **I couldn't agree more. /**
That's true, but on the other hand I love a good book or a walk in the fresh air when I'm stressed.

3 **A:** What I think is that governments can't really help with this problem – it's up to us as individuals.

B: **I agree up to a point / That's just how I feel too**, but I still think there's a lot they can do.

4 Which comments are true when you're doing the collaborative exam task?

Ada595
The best thing is to take turns when you're speaking. Like, one student thinks about a prompt and says what he thinks, then you say what you think, then you move on to the next one. That's what I do anyway.

Budbot
We've been told to try to make, like, a conversation? So you ask your partner things to get his opinion.

Jam13
What's important I feel is to make sure you listen to your partner and comment on what he or she says by agreeing or disagreeing and then adding what you think.

Saff1
I guess it's better to bounce ideas off each other rather than just one person talk for ages and then the other!

5 Read the collaborative task about what history books in the future might say about life today. Tick (✓) the statement below (1–5) that is true.

education

What do you think a history book in the future might tell people about life today and why?

scientific progress

social issues

world events

popular culture

The students have to:

1 talk about life in the past. ☐

2 say what is difficult about life today. ☐

3 imagine what life in the future will be like. ☐

4 discuss interesting and important things about life today. ☐

5 choose which prompt to talk about for two minutes. ☐

6 🔊 1.5 Listen to two students. Are the statements True (T) or False (F)?

1 They only talk about one prompt. ....

2 They ask for each other's opinion. ....

3 They take turns to give their opinions. ....

4 They refer to each other's comments. ....

5 They use colloquial language. ....

6 They give reasons and examples. ....

7 Look at audioscript 1.4 on page 119. Find words and phrases with these meanings.

1 opinion (1 word) ....

2 focus on (1 word) ....

3 also consider (3 words) ....

4 what you say is really relevant … (5 words) ....

5 is connected to (4 words) ....

6 I wasn't saying … (3 words) ....

7 exactly … (1 word) ....

8 properly, seriously … (2 words) ....

8 🔊 1.6 Listen to two comments made during a discussion of the task in Ex 5. Record your responses. Remember to:

1 answer her question.

2 refer to her comment.

3 add a point of your own.

9 Listen to your recording and check that you included everything in Ex 8.

WRITING

1 Complete the emphatic adjectives to match the synonyms (1–6).

1 very funny: h _ _ _ _ _ _ _ _

2 very scary: t _ _ _ _ _ _ _ _ _

3 very exciting: t _ _ _ _ _ _ _ _

4 very bad: d _ _ _ _ _ _ _

5 unique/very good: e _ _ _ _ _ _ _ _ _

6 very quick: f _ _ _-m _ _ _ _ _

2 Put the letters in the correct order to make emphatic adjectives with similar meanings.

1 The atmosphere in the theatre was **fleiynicertg**.

....

2 She gave a **zizgland** performance. ....

3 The stunts were absolutely **graebtahknit**. ....

4 The plot twist at the end was **triapiannolis**. ....

5 The location they chose was **famegtinnic**. ....

6 The music arrangement was **datustginon**. ....

3 Match (1–5) with (A–E) to complete the recommendations for writing a review.

1 start with	**A**	the present tense.
2 divide the review	**B**	a recommendation.
3 cover	**C**	into clear paragraphs.
4 describe action in	**D**	all the points required.
5 finish with	**E**	an engaging introduction.

4 Read the writing task. Are the statements True (T) or False (F)?

1 Your review will be read all over the world. ....

2 You need to give a detailed outline of the storyline. ....

3 You need to say why it is worth watching. ....

4 You need to give background information about the period. ....

5 You can write as much as you like. ....

You see the following announcement on an international student website.

Many of us love a good historical drama series. Have you watched a really good one recently? Write a review for the website saying what makes it stand-out viewing and how much we learn about the particular historical period.

Write your review in 220–260 words.

5 Read the review of a historical drama TV series and answer the questions.

1 Did the writer follow the advice in Ex 3?

2 Which emphatic adjectives from Ex 1 and Ex 2 has the writer used?

3 List additional emphatic adjectives used in the review.

TABOO

Not all historical drama series are fast-moving thrillers, with heroic characters fighting enemies – or, like *Downton Abbey*, sedate and elegant portrayals of the aristocracy. Some are slow affairs that show the darker side of life of the time. These can have a huge impact when the pace quickens dramatically, sometimes brutally, and take us by surprise. *Taboo*, a recent eight-part series on the BBC, is an example of this.

Taboo traces the consequences of an unexpected inheritance for the enigmatic James Delaney when he returns to London in 1814. From the outset the pace is slow and threatening as we are gradually introduced to the characters who will be significant in this truly intriguing and fascinating story. Two of the main characters are not human; the River Thames and the enormously powerful East India Trading Company overshadow much of the action.

The direction and stunning photography bring a remarkably written screenplay to life. And the outstanding performances of the main actors, including Tom Hardy as the dark and bruised (both physically and mentally) Delaney, make this an electrifying series. What is also superb is how much we learn about the realities of life at that time, from the young children searching for coins in the Thames mud to the decadence of the aristocracy and royalty.

Taboo touches on many topics; corruption, slave trading, the supernatural and patriotism, to name but a few. It is not always easy watching, but this series is most definitely worth taking the time to see.

6 🔊 1.7 Listen to four students talking about planning. Which students have the best attitude:

1 to planning?

2 to checking?

7 🅴 Read the task in Ex 4 again. Plan and write your own review.

8 Read your review and check these points.

1 Have you divided the review clearly into paragraphs?

2 Have you used emphatic adjectives?

3 Have you used the present tense to talk about the plot and/or action?

4 Have you started with an engaging introduction?

5 Have you finished with a recommendation?

UNIT CHECK 1

1 Choose the correct words to complete the sentences.

1 When **did you realise / were you realising** that you had an amazingly sharp memory?

2 I **was trying / had tried** to remember the name of the film all evening, but I had to give up in the end.

3 When I finally got to see the play it **had been running / was running** for over a year!

4 I couldn't get off to sleep last night because I **drank / had drunk** too much coffee.

5 I didn't realise that I **wasn't / hadn't been** invited to the party until after the event.

6 I fell over getting on the train and when I got up, everyone **was staring / stared** at me.

2 Complete the sentences with 'would' or 'used to'. If both are possible, use 'would'.

1 My grandfather .... own a tricycle.

2 I .... have such short hair as I do now.

3 My mother .... take me swimming every Thursday after school when I was six.

4 I .... like playing video games, but I've gone off them now.

5 When my brother was younger he .... spend hours playing the piano.

6 My brother and I .... argue about all sorts of silly things when we were children.

3 Complete the text with the correct form of the verbs in brackets.

While I **1**........................... (wait) at the doctors I read an article about animals and memory. As I **2**........................... (read) the article it occurred to me that in the past I **3**........................... (always / assume) that my dog would remember events from one day to the next. But the article clearly **4**........................... (state) that dogs remember an event for around two minutes. I realised that until this moment I **5**........................... (treat) my dog as if he were another human. Only yesterday I **6**........................... (take) Indie to the beach and I **7**........................... (try) to get her to sit when I asked. I thought that because we **8**........................... (do) this the previous week that she would remember. I **9**........................... (not realise) at the time that I **10**........................... (be) totally unrealistic in thinking that she would remember. Apparently, chimpanzees only remember things for twenty seconds, so perhaps two minutes isn't that bad!

4 Complete the sentences with these prepositions.

about   at   by   from   to   with

1 I was encouraged .... the score I got in the memory test. Not bad at all!

2 My grandfather used to be very accomplished .... playing the piano. He even won prizes.

3 My brother is addicted .... computer games. He plays them non-stop.

4 I ordered some jeans online, but I wasn't satisfied .... the quality of them, so I sent them back.

5 It's sensible to get an anti-virus installed on your computer to protect you .... bugs.

6 I'm not sure what I want to study at university. In fact, I'm completely undecided .... it.

5 Choose the correct words to complete the sentences.

1 I mustn't forget to buy him a present. Can you **remember / remind** me later please?

2 Did you put these pizzas in the fridge? I don't **recall / recognise** buying them.

3 I know it's boring, but the only way to remember French verbs is to **memorise / recall** them.

4 I'm terrible about **remembering / realising** names of people, but I am quite good at **recalling / recognising** faces.

5 Luckily, I **realised / recalled** just in time that I had to renew my passport!

6 We used to live in the USA until I was three years old. I don't **remember / recognise** much of it though.

6 Complete the sentences with the correct form of these verbs.

block out   commit   have   keep   trigger

1 Sometimes .... memories is the only way of coping with painful past events.

2 I am quite good at remembering names, but I have trouble .... passwords to memory.

3 Smells are very evocative and they can .... memories of things we thought we had forgotten.

4 I .... a vague recollection of meeting her before, but I'm not very sure.

5 We all like to hang onto the past and I suppose that .... souvenirs is one way of doing so.

7 Complete the text with these words / phrases.

committing   ear-worms   out of your head   refresh
vague memory   word for word

HOW FIT IS YOUR BRAIN?

Can you remember conversations **1**........................... ? Or do you just have a **2**........................... of what was said? Do you have problems **3**........................... facts to memory? Do you sometimes need someone to **4**........................... your memory when you go shopping? Do you ever get **5**...........................? You know, you can't get a song **6**........................... . You can remember songs, but not the important stuff! If you have answered *yes* to any of the above, try some memory games to improve brain fitness.

2 Winners and losers

READING

1 Match phrases (1–10) with (A–J) to make sentences.

1 After three months off sick, Lee needed to

2 Far from being disinterested, the audience were

3 By refusing to say who was being promoted, the boss was accused of

4 For those not in the know,

5 For a fleeting moment,

6 The students have been warned that

7 Ultimately, the final decision is

8 Despite his nervousness, we're counting on Kevin to

9 Nobody had expected him to

10 You could tell the pressure of

A playing mind games with his team.

B throw a move like that!

C not down to me.

D play catch up.

E hanging on to every word he said.

F it is best to avoid travelling by rail on bank holidays.

G it seemed like he was going to apologise.

H hitting the big time was getting to him.

I the course is not for the faint-hearted.

J rise to the occasion.

2 You are going to read about how four different game show writers work. Read the questions in Ex 3 and underline the key words.

3 🔴 Read the article. For questions 1–10, choose from the writers (A–D). The writers may be chosen more than once.

Which writer:

1 mentions the temptation of limiting questions to a particular topic? ....

2 refers to an overconfidence in their abilities? ....

3 points out the difference between their idea and the reality of writing for quiz shows?

4 says that writing is a group effort? ....

5 mentions a previous intention to put minimal effort into the job? ....

6 cites the need to use different resources? ....

7 describes the difference between the show and the writing? ....

Think being a game show writer is easy? Think again.

8 mentions the players in the studio and at home? ....

9 points out that a lot of general knowledge has already been tested? ....

10 mentions the importance of confirming the validity of facts? ....

Writer A

When I first got offered a **gig** as an assistant game show writer, I was a struggling writer trying, and failing, to get my first novel **off the ground**. Taking on the job seemed appealing if only because it would get my landlord off my back. Honestly, a part of me was hoping that this would be the push I needed for my novel, that a mind-numbing day job thinking up mindless trivia would kick start the creativity I'd been waiting to arrive for months. I also hoped I'd have plenty of spare time to do some of my own writing during the day. The truth? I couldn't have been more wrong. Dashing off trivia questions that are going to be **tricky** for both the show participants and the armchair contestants at home to answer isn't as simple as you think. Especially when TV is **saturated** with game shows so you have to think of questions that haven't been asked before. I had to start actively looking for trivia. A lot of people know that 'facetious' has all the vowels in alphabetical order, but what about words that have the vowels backwards, like 'subcontinental'? Finding good trivia like that is a challenge and as it turns out, I did end up using my creativity, just not in the way I'd expected.

Writer B

I can't remember the exact moment that Google became my best friend, but, if I had to, I'd probably say it was some time in my first few days as a game show writer, which was around the same time I ran out of ideas. I had always been that trivia person, the one always asking, 'Hey, did you know …?' while my family sighed and rolled their eyes. I hadn't expected to **hit a wall** so soon into the job and it was discouraging to discover that my supposedly endless pool of facts dried up so quickly. Falling back on search engines may seem like the easy option, but the truth is you have to be smart. Typing in 'unknown trivia' just won't cut it. Instead, I think about a fragment of a sentence that has the potential to throw up something interesting and let the search engine do the hard work for me. Take the Queen of England. You might think that it would be difficult to discover information about her that isn't commonly known, but I only had to enter 'Every day, the Queen …' into Google to find out that she always has two types of cereal in Tupperware containers on her breakfast table. How many people know that?

Writer C

Continually coming up with new material can be frustrating, especially if your own life experiences have only equipped you with a small stockpile of interesting facts. Although I was fortunate enough to walk straight into the job as assistant game show writer not long after university, the **flipside** is that I didn't get the opportunity to travel so my knowledge of trivia is limited to the few places I have been to. Diversity is key in quiz shows – if you can get the contestant scratching their head because they've never heard of the obscure island in the question, then you're on to a winner because chances are they won't have any general knowledge about it. Revealing facts about little known places is my preferred technique, and I spend a lot of my time searching world maps for tiny archipelagos, headlands and inland towns that could provide cultural or geographical gems for the show. Admittedly, checking this kind of information can be a bit of a nightmare – allowing an incorrect question to make it on air means immediate **dismissal**, but it's worth it when I imagine the contestants thinking 'Well, I never knew that.'

Writer D

Although it is technically a nine-to-five job, I don't really feel that I ever switch off from being a game show writer – everything around me seems like it could be a potential clue or question. The other writers and I are a pretty **tight-knit** group, which means we end up messaging each other at all hours with possible leads – most of our messages start with, 'Hey, did you know that … ' If someone on my team rejects an idea, I know that it's not worth pursuing. For me, that team dynamic is important – we spend a lot of time bouncing ideas off each other. It also stops us getting stuck in a rut. Having other people around you who can point out that you've written twenty questions about the same stretch of ocean stops you from producing a script with the same pattern of questions. Just because one subject has a lot of facts doesn't mean you have to stay with that subject, you need to develop it into different ones. Even though the game show format is formulaic, we have to constantly remind ourselves that the questions can't be!

---

4 Complete the sentences with the words / phrases in bold from the article.

1 The market has become completely .... with cheap copies of designer goods.

2 Rachel was upset at being made redundant, but the .... was that she could invest time in developing her blog.

3 The professor is well known for writing complex questions that her students find .... to answer.

4 Janet had been making great progress with her thesis, but now she's .... and doesn't know what to write next.

5 Even though the event was hard work, it was a pretty lucrative ....

6 After months of struggling to get the project started, they finally got it .... last week.

7 I come from a very .... family and I know that I can depend on my sisters for anything.

8 After working at the company for over a decade, Sam's .... was a shock to everyone.

GRAMMAR

verb patterns: -ing forms and infinitives

1 Match the sentences (1–7) with the rules (A–G).

What does success mean to you?

1 'Having the courage to be myself makes me feel successful.'

2 'Success is having the luxury of time to do what you want.'

3 'Certainly not only money. Some people chase after money, only to find that money doesn't equate to success.'

4 'I was brought up not to be distracted easily. This has made me focused on chasing success.'

5 'Success is to have made the most of all the opportunities presented to us along the way.'

6 'I'd like to think that success is easy, but it isn't. It helps if you like being who you are and having the life you have.'

7 'Success is managing to balance all aspects of your personal and professional life. Having time for it all.'

A verbs which are always followed by the infinitive

B verbs which can be followed by both -ing and the infinitive, but change their meaning

C verbs in the -ing form which are the subject of the sentence

D the to infinitive after nouns

E only + to infinitive after a clause to show result

F (not) to + be + past participle for a passive pattern

G use to + have + past participle for a past concept

2 Choose the correct words to complete the sentences.

✓ Life hacks for success

✓ **Identify your core values:** ¹Create / To create / Creating goals that are in line with your values.

✓ **Choose one goal:** Focus is the key if you want ²succeed / to succeed / succeeding in life.

✓ **Plan daily and weekly goals:** Make a list of what you aim ³get / to get / getting done in the day.

✓ **Learn:** Never stop ⁴learn / to learn / learning. Keep searching for knowledge.

3 Complete the text with the infinitive or -ing form of the verbs in brackets.

The Cheat Code
by Brian Wong

If you have ever struggled ¹............................ (understand) why some people just get ahead faster than anyone else, then try ²............................ (read) my recommendation for this month: *The Cheat Code* by Brian Wong.

Brian is a whiz kid who by the age of twenty-four had created a global mobile advertising giant. His secret? *The Cheat Code*. The book provides seventy-one simple hacks and tips which promise ³............................ (enable) almost anyone to get ahead in life. Wong believes that most people like ⁴............................ (copy) other people and that they need ⁵............................ (follow) a script. He dares us ⁶............................ (throw) aside the script, be more individual and to follow our superpowers! Brian defines a superpower as a passion or pursuit that you're good at and love ⁷............................ (do). He says that we should all endeavour ⁸............................ (identify) our superpowers, use them as often as possible and that success will lead to and generate further success.

4 Six of the sentences below (1–8) contain errors. Find the errors and correct them.

1 Can you imagine to be able to look into the future?

2 What are you doing? I don't recall to have given you permission to read my diary!

3 I'm on a special diet, and at the moment I'm avoiding eating gluten and lactose.

4 This essay doesn't appear be finished. Did you forget to finish it?

5 The job involves organising the social events and exhibitions from now until August.

6 The child denied to have eaten the sweets.

7 The workers voted going on strike for ten days.

8 Will you please endeavour trying harder next time?

VOCABULARY

adjective + noun collocations

1 Choose the correct words to complete the collocations in the text.

A visual feast!

I expect we all remember trips to see the local circus as children. The same acts year after year and the same clowns making **¹futile / resounding** attempts to surprise us with the same jokes. Some fun moments, but they did receive an increasingly **²lukewarm / dismal** response from the public who had seen them a few years running. Then our interest in circus was rekindled by the amazing Cirque du Soleil, which the **³vast / burning** majority of us will probably have heard of. They offered something quite new, a blend of theatre and circus. I recently came across a new group, Cirque Beserk. Initially I was sceptical as I thought that due to the **⁴unprecedented / endearing** success of Cirque du Soleil that no other new circus group could reproduce their sense of drama and spectacle on stage. I went along to see Cirque Beserk and as I am a cynic I predicted a **⁵unmitigated / dismal** failure. I couldn't have been more wrong! The pulsing energy was enthralling and I was on the edge of my seat throughout as I witnessed **⁶futile / formidable** challenges such as four daredevil motorcyclists riding within a cage. Visually, a feast for the eyes. Jugglers, dancers, drummers and acrobats; each act demonstrating yet another **⁷impressive / eternal** accomplishment. Whilst I personally have never had a **⁸burning / colossal** ambition to do anything remotely related to the circus, I can now understand the appeal. A spectacle not to be missed!

2 Complete the sentences with these idioms.

> back to square one   cut their losses   getting there   get the better of
> if all else fails   stay on top of the game   think big   win win

#Oscar night!

→ follow

Talk about low budget! I guess they ran out of money and had to
1 ....

Her performance was abysmal. It's **²** ....
for her. She needs to start from scratch.

He's looking old and jaded. He's not going to be able to
3 ....

The director will have to **4** .... on his
next project if he wants to survive in this industry.

Incredible! Best actress, best film. One success after another. She's in
a **5** .... situation.

Poor thing. She put on a brave face and didn't cry. She didn't let it
6 .... her.

What a disastrous year he is having. Oh well,
7 .... , he can go back to teaching!

Her work isn't as good as it should be, but she's
8 ....

Extend

3 Match the words in bold in the sentences (1–6) with the meanings (A–F).

Steps to a successful career

1 Avoid office gossip if you don't want to be **fair game** for criticism.
2 Have a strategy, but keep it close to your chest. Don't **give the game away**.
3 Keep up the hard work if you want to stay **on top of the game**.
4 Being the boss is a **whole new ball game** compared to being an employee.
5 Watch the competition and work hard to **stay ahead of the game**.
6 Be realistic. No job is **all fun and games**.

A All jobs are a mixture of interesting and uninteresting parts.
B To maintain your current position you need to carry on consistently working hard.
C Don't share your plans with other people.
D Unprofessional behaviour rightly merits criticism.
E This is a different and much more demanding situation.
F In order to be better than the others, you need to put in extra effort.

LISTENING

1 You will hear a data security specialist, Lisa, giving a talk about how she turned failure into success. Read the text in Ex 2 and decide what kind of word should complete each gap: a noun, an adjective or a noun / noun phrase.

2 🅴 🔊 2.1 Listen to the talk. For questions 1–8, complete the sentences with a word or short phrase.

TURNING FAILURE INTO SUCCESS

1 Lisa gives the example of .... as something she regards as a sign of sporting success.

2 Lisa uses the word .... to describe how she felt after a bad injury.

3 Lisa says the worst part of her recovery process was the amount of .... she needed.

4 Lisa mentions that she focused her old .... towards tech.

5 Lisa claims that not being in her .... increases her drive to succeed.

6 Lisa explains that her success has been the result of .... more than other factors.

7 Lisa says that it is .... to work for her current company.

8 Lisa suggests that she wants the listeners to recognise that we can find .... in failure.

3 Match these words / phrases with the phrases in bold in the sentences (1–10).

adversity   braving the elements   cliché   dig deeper   flaw   hunched over   knock-back   resonated   setbacks   visualise

1 His speech had an impact on many people and **stayed with them for a long time**. ....

2 She **forced herself to find the energy to continue**. ....

3 Peter's back was aching from spending all day **bending down to look at** the map on the table. ....

4 The system was almost perfect, except for one **major error**. ....

5 Melanie refused to let the **rejection** stop her from moving forward with her novel. ....

6 Even with all of their **problems and bad luck**, they still have a positive outlook. ....

7 The teacher's inspirational messages have been **used so many times** that the students are tired of them. ....

8 Several **factors have delayed his progress**. ....

9 We went for a walk **despite the torrential rain**. ....

10 The life coach encouraged me to **picture** what I wanted **in my mind** as it would keep me motivated. ....

time out

The IG Nobel Prize is a parody of the Nobel Prize. The prizes are awarded, each year, to obscure and trivial achievements in scientific research. A few are listed below.

Match the first half of the research statement (1–6) with the second half (A–F).

1 Why do old men have
2 Is that me or
3 The brand personality of
4 Swearing as a response to
5 Is 'huh?'
6 Frictional coefficient under

A pain
B a universal word?
C my twin?
D rocks
E a banana skin
F big ears?

USE OF ENGLISH 1

1 Complete the text with these words / phrases.

---

all of   every   half of   less than   little   more   most   no
not enough   other   several   the whole

Global Initiatives. Competitions that make a difference!

At Global Initiatives we are not offering a competition like any ¹.. that you have seen before. We are offering something ².. than the others do – a competition to bridge the gap between education and the workplace.

We believe that ³.. is being done by educators when it comes to dealing with social and environmental change and that current provision is ⁴.. adequate.

At Global Initiatives we delve deep for information because we owe it to our planet to look at ⁵.. picture.

Recent studies revealed that more than ⁶.. the undergraduates interviewed had ⁷.. or no understanding of the most pressing social and environmental issues that we face today. Many confessed that they had ⁸.. real interest in these topics whatsoever.

At Global Initiatives we aim to change this situation. We aim to inform students and recent graduates about ⁹.. these important global issues in the following way. Firstly, participants are given a list of ¹⁰.. social and environmental issues to choose from. ¹¹.. participant is asked individually to demonstrate an understanding of the chosen issue and ¹².. importantly to explore, probe and research all the factors around it.

2 Choose the correct words to complete the text.

Work experience placements

The choice of career path can seem daunting at times and unfortunately ¹**few** / **a few** students are lucky enough to know exactly what they want to do. In fact ²**all** / **most** students at some stage in their lives will find themselves choosing between ³**few** / **several** different options. In my opinion ⁴**too few** / **a little** students take the opportunity to try our work experience placements. I agree that not ⁵**all** / **some** students have access to them and some students have hectic schedules and ⁶**a little** / **little** time to try them out. But for those of you who can, I would recommend them. The experience will open your eyes to the world of work, you'll gain ⁷**plenty of** / **not enough** confidence, and you might even make ⁸**few** / **a few** important contacts who can give you advice about your future career.

3 **e** Read the text and complete the gaps with one word only.

The mental edge

Sportspeople are only truly prepared for optimal performance when they are both mentally and physically prepared. Success in sport is as much to do with mental toughness ¹............................ it is to do with physical strength. In order to perform to your best, whether it be on or ²............................ the sports field, preparation is fundamental and should never be overlooked. It goes ³............................ saying that physical training for a sports event is crucial, but ⁴............................ is mental training. There are various techniques which we can use in order to prepare ourselves mentally for any challenge or confrontation. Visualisation is a well-known form of mental preparation and which consists ⁵............................ the person rehearsing in their mind, or visualising, the competition or the sports event. By imagining different possible scenarios, the person is ⁶............................ to anticipate a variety of potential problems and ⁷............................ he or she may react in any given situation. The key component to mental preparation is self-awareness. Through self-awareness we are able to understand and manage our emotions, and in ⁸............................ so develop levels of resilience which are essential in order to compete.

USE OF ENGLISH 2

1 Read the sentences and insert 'very' before the adjective in bold where possible.

1 It has been .... **wonderful** to rediscover these photos after so many years.

2 They must have been .... **desperate** to have considered committing a crime.

3 We were fortunate with the weather – it was a .... **gorgeous** day.

4 They got a(n) .... **enormous** bill after using their mobile phones abroad.

5 She couldn't believe how they'd left her apartment – it was .... **filthy**.

6 Everyone was .... **surprised** when the teacher left in the middle of the term.

7 Despite being .... **popular** among his work colleagues, Dave didn't have much of a social life.

8 The advertisers were .... **astonished** by the amount of negative publicity they received.

2 Complete the sentences with these words.

believed disappointed enjoyable exaggerated
limited obvious plausible ridiculous

1 It was blatantly .... that he had no facts to back up his argument.

2 It's utterly .... to expect everyone to agree with you.

3 His comments have been wildly .... online.

4 I thought the film was thoroughly ...., even though I didn't understand parts of it.

5 While that idea is perfectly .... there's no evidence to suggest it's true.

6 They are widely .... to have filtered the comments to make themselves look better.

7 I was bitterly .... to see that my comment had been deleted.

8 The powers of the administrators is strictly .... to removing offensive posts.

3 e Read the text and decide which answer (A, B, C or D) best fits each gap.

Can you win an argument on social media?

Winning an argument on social media is a seemingly impossible task; however, recently published research indicates that certain behaviours make it considerably **1**....... to come out of a Twitter or Facebook argument on top. Although the internet can generally be a deceptive place, where strangers can be your best friends one minute and vanish without a trace the next, joining forces with other commenters on a website can **2**....... you an advantage. It's a classic **3**....... in numbers' tactic – multiple challengers can wear down an opponent more easily than just one. **4**....... sure to respond quickly, but avoid sending a stream of messages as this gives the receiver little opportunity to respond and can be seen as **5**....... aggressive. Remember that you aren't strictly **6**....... to just your words – use formatting to your advantage and make your argument more effective with bold font and bullet points. Similarly, provide links to outside evidence to support your argument. It could be that the other person isn't **7**....... informed about the topic so giving real life examples tends to be more powerful than repeating abstract terms. Finally, keep your cool. Even though it's normal to feel passionate, getting involved in **8**....... from behind a screen increases the likelihood of you typing something that you would never dream of saying to someone's face, so take a deep breath so you are absolutely certain before you hit 'send'.

1 A easier **B** longer **C** slower **D** simpler
2 A take **B** offer **C** have **D** give
3 A collaboration **B** teamwork **C** group **D** strength
4 A Make **B** Feel **C** Seem **D** Appear
5 A considerably **B** incredibly **C** virtually **D** entirely
6 A forbidden **B** restricted **C** narrowed **D** true
7 A bitterly **B** widely **C** fully **D** utterly
8 A discussions **B** arguments **C** conversations **D** agreements

Extend

4 Choose the correct words to complete the sentences.

1 It is **reasonably / wholly** unacceptable to make those comments, even in the heat of the moment.

2 Before the televised debate, the reporter was **virtually / expressly** unknown to the general public.

3 We are holding him **dreadfully / entirely** responsible for the comments.

4 She is **reasonably / dreadfully** sorry to have caused so much conflict.

5 Posting offensive comments on articles is **virtually / expressly** forbidden on this website.

6 It is **reasonably / wholly** normal for people to comment on something you post online, but keep in mind that not all comments will be positive.

SPEAKING

1 Choose the correct words to complete the advice.

In the long turn exam task you should:

1 talk about **1 / 2 / 3** picture(s).

2 focus on **describing the picture in detail /
talking about things that are similar and / or different.**

3 finish **well within a minute /
when the interlocutor stops you.**

2 Read the task and tick (✓) the things you have to do.

> Your pictures show people who are disappointed.
> Compare two of the pictures and say why the people
> might be disappointed and what they might learn from
> their disappointment.

1 Give possible reasons for their moods. ☐

2 Say how often they've experienced these moments. ☐

3 Talk about how and when they might cheer up. ☐

4 Say which picture you prefer and why. ☐

5 Say how something good might come out of their
present situation. ☐

3 Complete the extracts (1–6) with these words. You can use
some words more than once.

---

although   both   different   however   major   more   similar
that   whereas

---

1 I'd like to talk about pictures A and B. They're really
interesting pictures because .... the pictures
show people in very .... locations, the theme of
disappointment is evident in each.

2 The people in the first picture are clearly upset because it
looks as if they haven't achieved what they set out to do,
.... the little boy, in the second picture appears
to be disappointed for a completely different reason.

3 A .... difference between the two pictures is
the reason for the disappointment. For the little boy the
disappointment is personal – he's been left out of a game
by his classmates … .... for the sports fans it's
.... that they all feel disappointed for whichever
team they are supporting.

4 The pictures are .... in that they ....
focus on people who are disappointed, as you say.
.... what they might learn from the experience
will be different for each.

5 .... the rowers look very disappointed, they'll
probably get over it quickly and the experience will spur
them on to a better performance in the future.

6 The situations are similar in .... they are
all about disappointment and experiences people can
learn from, but clearly pictures A and B show personal
disappointments .... picture C shows people
who have little control over what can be achieved.

4 Look at the extracts in Ex 3 again. Which one does not
follow the task instructions?

5 Read a different task for the pictures in Ex 2. Plan what you
might say. Remember that you need to:

1 compare the pictures, using words and phrases for
comparing.

2 answer the two questions.

3 talk for up to a minute.

> Your pictures show people in situations they would like
> to change. Compare two of the pictures and say how the
> situations might have been prevented and what might
> make the people feel better.

6 ⓮ Choose the pictures in Ex 2 you want to talk about and
record your answer.

7 Listen to your recording and check.

1 How many words / phrases for comparing did you use?

2 Did you answer both questions?

3 How long did you speak for?

WRITING

1 Read the essay extracts (A–D) and answer the questions (1–5). One extract answers two questions.

Which extract:

1 has the purpose of **persuading**? ....

2 shows the **least formal** style? ....

3 is from a **conclusion**? ....

4 shows the purpose of **informing**? ....

5 gives us an **explanation**? ....

A Reality TV shows can be found on nearly every channel, nearly all of the time. A recent show attracted over ten million viewers mid-week, which is quite remarkable for the UK.

B People enjoy watching these shows because they feature real people in often unusual situations and we are intrigued by their reactions.

C It would surely be better for young performers to get more experience before they are thrust onto a stage in front of millions.

D As far as I'm concerned, the sooner they cut down on the number of reality TV shows the better. There are way too many of them.

2 Are the statements about writing the essay task in the exam True (T) or False (F)?

1 You must use a formal style. ....

2 You must cover all the points in the notes ....

3 You must give reasons for what you say. ....

4 You must use all the opinions provided in the task. ....

5 You must give your opinion and decide which point is most important. ....

6 You must think of at least one more point of your own to write about. ....

3 Rewrite the highlighted sections in the sentences (1–6) using these words to moderate the tone. More than one answer is possible.

can   most   nearly   probably   usually   would

1 It is a difficult time in everyone's life ....

2 We shall definitely .... see changes over the next few years.

3 Competition at school prepares .... us for competition in later life.

4 We all .... want to see more freedom of choice in education.

5 I believe .... changes need to be made in every aspect of local government.

6 It is always .... the parents who want an increase in homework.

4 Read the task and match the extracts (1–5) with the points they are addressing (A–C).

1 Constructive advice is essential for any performer. ....

2 Many suffer as the hectic schedule can take its toll. ....

3 It would normally take many years for performers to be able to reach this point. ....

4 They need to perform on demand as well as fit in interviews and other things. ....

5 It can, however, sometimes be rather humiliating. ....

In your class you have had a discussion about reality TV talent shows. You have made the notes below.

Benefits for contestants:

A showcase talent

B receive feedback and direction

C learn to experience pressure

Some opinions expressed in the discussion:

'It gives people the chance to reach a wide audience.'

'The judges can help pinpoint what needs to be improved.'

'There's a lot of stress involved and if you're not strong, you don't survive.'

Write an essay for your teacher discussing **two** of the benefits in your notes. You should **explain which factor you think is most beneficial** for talent show contestants, **giving reasons** to support your opinions.

You may, if you wish, make use of the opinions expressed in the discussion, but you should use your own words as far as possible.

5 Plan and write your essay in 220–260 words.

6 Check that you have:

1 only covered two points

2 used your own words

3 given reasons and examples

4 used some point-of-view adjectives

5 concluded by giving your own opinion and chosen the most important point

6 written within the word limit

UNIT CHECK

1 Choose the correct words to complete the sentences.

1 I have never really fancied **play / to play / playing** a competitive sport.

2 I recall **want / to want / wanting** to play football in primary, and my mum signed me up.

3 But I was a terrible player and I would forget **take / to take / taking** my kit to the training sessions.

4 I used to deny **have / to have / having** done it on purpose of course!

5 And I couldn't **tell / to tell / telling** my mum about it afterwards!

6 I think in retrospect I preferred **do / to do / doing** individual sports and eventually of course I stopped **play / to play / playing** football!

2 Complete the text with the correct form of the verbs in brackets.

Ready to compete!

Whatever the competition, here are some golden rules you should follow:

- Stay focused and avoid **1** .... (talk) to pessimistic people.

- Don't **2** .... (take) medicines or pills if you are nervous.

- If you struggle **3** .... (calm) your nerves, try breathing deeply.

- If you want **4** .... (socialise) with friends, wait until after the event. You may end up **5** .... (stay out) too late.

- You should try **6** .... (eat) well before the event and you should aim **7** .... (drink) as much water as possible.

- If you have never considered **8** .... (have) a massage before, now is the time! Most people claim **9** .... (feel) much more relaxed afterwards.

3 Complete the sentences with these words.

all   any   little   none   the whole

Students and sports

This is what you told us about your attitude to sport:

1 Most people enjoy team games, but .... of you play team games at a professional level.

2 Some people complained that they have .... free time to play sport. Lack of time is clearly a problem.

3 Surprisingly, we didn't speak to .... fans of martial arts.

4 We were very pleased to find out that .... of you, without exception, do at least some kind of sport.

5 On a really positive note, ... group of people interviewed agreed that playing sport is extremely beneficial.

4 Choose the correct words to complete the sentences.

1 My brother is an **eventual / eternal** student. He is still studying at the age of thirty.

2 I've heard that you can make **colossal / complete** amounts of money from property.

3 Climbing the mountain was the most **phenomenal / formidable** challenge I have ever faced.

4 I didn't get the job and so it's back to **hole / square** one with the job search.

5 After the financial crisis some firms had to **cut / chop** their loses and downsize.

6 I haven't trained enough to compete professionaly yet, but I'm getting **there / here**.

5 Complete the text with these phrases.

burning ambition   dismal failure
futile attempts   get the better of you
impressive accomplishment   resounding success
unprecedented growth   vast number

The competitive world of
game design

Over the past five years there has been an **1** .... in the amount of video games in the market, and surprisingly a **2** .... of them have been designed by quite young designers.

I spoke to eighteen-year-old Jason Bainbridge, whose latest game, 'Scrumble' has been a **3** .... in both Europe and the USA. Jason designed and produced the game in just under a year and on a small budget, which is an **4** .... for a person of any age! Jason told me that he has always loved games. At ten he had a **5** .... to design his own video game. Initially his parents tried to persuade him to choose a different career path, but these were **6** .... and he couldn't be deterred.

Jason advises people his age to be persistent, and that even if your first attempt is a **7** .... , you should try and try again. He says that whilst you will have failures along the way, you shouldn't let this **8** .... , if designing games is what you really want to do.

Choices and changes

READING

1 Choose the correct meaning (A or B) for the words / phrases in bold.

1 They have been **endeavouring** to find a solution for the problem.

    A trying to the best of their abilities

    B not trying hard enough

2 We were hopelessly lost and wandered down an **alley**.

    A narrow, quiet road   **B** large, busy road

3 A **multitude** of issues have been raised as a result of the investigation.

    A a few   **B** significant amount

4 They've been taking measures **to stem the flow** of people visiting the shelter.

    A increase the number of visitors   **B** reduce the number of visitors

5 Perhaps it would be easier to explain if I used an **analogy**.

    A comparison with something else **B** concrete example

6 Working on improving participants' **self-esteem** is an important part of the programme.

    A sense of independence   **B** sense of confidence

7 We've got a **holding operation** in place right now.

    A temporary solution   **B** permanent solution

8 I'm thrilled to be working on such a **groundbreaking** project.

    A the first project of its kind   **B** an ongoing project

2 Read the text about the 'Design for Difference' collection. For questions 1–6, underline the key words / phrases.

1 In the first paragraph, the writer says that

    A the additional elements of Angela's collection were well hidden.

    B the audience was impressed with how waterproof the jacket was.

    C initially, there was nothing to differentiate the jacket from other people's.

    D Angela had previously claimed to be inspired by the weather.

2 In the second paragraph, the writer implies that

    A Angela had specific instructions from the art school.

    B the art school took credit for Angela's collection.

    C Angela's collection interprets the school's policy

    D Angela had to get permission from the school's policy makers.

3 In line 36 *centre-piece* refers to

    A the overcoat.

    B the reflective jacket.

    C the sleeping bag coat.

    D the tent jacket.

4 In the third paragraph, the writer says that Angela

    A uses only recycled materials.

    B throws hardly any material away.

    C gives her unused material to others.

    D uses mass-produced materials.

5 In the fourth paragraph the writer implies that making something the fashion industry likes

    A is a benefit.

    B is an achievement.

    C is profitable.

    D isn't important.

6 In line 55 *closer to home* suggests that

    A the writer is from the USA.

    B the writer lives close to Angela Luna.

    C the writer is writing from a foreign country.

    D the writer is visiting the USA.

3 **e** Read the text again. For questions 1–6 in Ex 2, choose the answer (A, B, C or D) which you think fits best according to the text.

DESIGNING
FOR CHANGE

Returning to New York City for fashion week is one of the highlights of my year, in particular the student fashion shows. This year definitely did not disappoint. Watching the models wearing Angela Luna's senior thesis collection make their way down the catwalk captivated me instantly. The long flowing jacket appeared to be a stunning utilitarian piece of clothing that would be perfect for shielding you from the rain in New York City. What I wasn't expecting was for the art graduate to remove the coat from the model and make it into a tent right there on the catwalk. However, once she had transformed the piece into a portable shelter, it became clear that the young designer had been inspired by something undeniably more **pressing** than a simple desire to keep the wearer dry.

Created with the aim of helping displaced people, Luna's collection, Design for Difference, embodies her art school's commitment to using design for social good. After a documentary made by a fellow arts student **sparked** her interest, the young fashion designer felt compelled to use her expertise to address the urgent issue of millions of people living **precariously** in temporary accommodation. Not only that, but she wanted to make something that was both fashionable and functional, and allowed her childhood memories of annual camping trips in the local countryside to influence her initial designs as a starting point for thinking about **functionality**. Thus, she got to work designing a collection of outerwear that is both multifunctional and transformable to meet the needs of the wearer.

Following months of research, she designed a seven-piece collection of garments that includes a highly reflective jacket that offers complete visibility in low light and has a removable reflective belt and a long overcoat with multiple reversible pockets that transforms into a warm sleeping bag. These are in addition to her centre-piece, **36** which comes in two different sizes and comfortably accommodates five people. In addition to this social commitment is consideration for zero-waste design, which she tackles by drawing cutting patterns that use as much of the section of material as possible, sourcing pieces from sustainable and **repurposed** materials and using natural, environmentally-friendly dyes.

Already, the collection has earned praise from the **notoriously** hard-to-impress fashion industry and was greeted by an enthusiastic reception during a showcase of the collection at the United Nations Global Compact Leaders summit. The adaptability of the pieces means that they can be adopted in different circumstances and used in a range of humanitarian crises involving displacement and extreme poverty. Humanitarian agencies recognise the need for this type of clothing both for the people they assist and the aid workers who travel to help them. The **garments** could be equally useful in societal contexts closer to home, such as in **55** New York City, where the collection was designed, to help keep homeless people warm and safe from the bitter winter nights on the streets in a tent jacket.

With plans in the pipeline to expand the purposes of the garments even further, Luna has recently made some of them available to buy commercially and matches the sale of each garment with an equivalent donation to charity. Although still **in its infancy**, the project is **making great strides** in fulfilling the description of its garments – meeting the needs of the wearer, whether it is for a casual or **strenuous** hike in the woods, strolling through the city or helping someone survive.

---

4 **Choose the correct words to complete the definitions of the highlighted words.**

1 A pressing issue **needs / doesn't need** to be discussed urgently.

2 If something is sparked then it **begins / ends** suddenly.

3 Something that is done precariously means that it **is / isn't** done safely.

4 The functionality of something refers to how it fulfils a **purpose / need**.

5 If something is repurposed, then it **has / hasn't** been used before.

6 A notoriously difficult problem is one that is **well-known / not known** to be difficult to solve.

7 Garment refers to **any / a specific** piece of clothing.

8 If something is in its infancy, it **is / isn't** well established.

9 If someone is making great strides, they are **achieving something / progressing**.

10 If something is strenuous, it **requires / doesn't require** a lot of effort.

GRAMMAR

comparative structures

1 Read the text and match the phrases in bold (1–5) with the descriptions (A–E).

MAKE CROWDFUNDING WORK FOR YOU

Crowdfunding as a fundraising tool is a great way of raising small amounts of money for large numbers of people. Here's how to do it.

› Set yourself up for success: **¹By far the most successful** crowdfunding projects are creative ones. Think outside the box and be courageous.

› Set a financial target: Think low, think high. Then choose **²the more realistic** of the two options.

› Look for support: People are **³much more willing** to give to friends. Build a social media presence and network!

› Prepare your pitch: **⁴The more creative and personal it is, the better chance of success** you have of reaching people.

› Pick a platform: You could **⁵do a lot worse than** choosing one of the main players. Don't waste your time shopping around.

A comparatives showing two things changing or developing together

B comparative instead of superlative when there are only two things in a group

C irregular comparative

D intensified superlative for emphasis

E intensified comparative for emphasis

2 Complete the text with *as*, *like* or *alike*.

Now to make your crowdfunding go viral. Public exposure through platforms ¹.......................... Facebook are crucial ².......................... a way of spreading your message, and your posts here serve ³.......................... your marketing campaign. One person clicks and shares and the loop continues reaching friends and potential backers ⁴.......................... . Examples ⁵.......................... the Ice Bucket Challenge are clear proof of this.

3 Choose the correct words to complete the text.

Blue-sky thinking for Blue Cross

¹As / Like charities go, the UK charity Blue Cross is easily **²the most / the more** inspirational, with a quirky new way of collecting donations. Volunteers and dogs work together **³as / like** a team to collect donations using a contactless payment technology. The dogs wear something **⁴like / alike** a jacket with a card reader on it. Donors can tap their card on the card reader to donate. Blue Cross says people are **⁵much more / most** inclined to give money if it is made easy for them. The growth of cashless societies **⁶alike / such as** ones like the UK is changing the way we use money. This initiative offers a solution to people **⁷as / like** runners or cyclists who don't always carry cash. The charity says that this scheme has been by **⁸way / far** the most lucrative initiative to date and that donations have increased from the young and old **⁹like / alike**. They believe that **¹⁰the more widely / the wider** they can use this method, the more money they can collect.

4 Complete the text with these phrases.

as a way to help   faster this happens   look no further than
more impressive idea   much more creative ways

It's time that charities used entrepreneurial ideas and ¹.. of raising money. Shaking a bucket and asking for coins in shopping centres is sadly out of date. If you want to hear about some real blue-sky thinking then ².. the Blue Cross. They have started this idea of using dogs ³.. boost donations. I'd read about something similar recently, but this was by far the ⁴.. . Organisations such as Blue Cross are changing the way we think about charities, and the ⁵.. the more money our society will be able to raise.

5 🔊 3.1 Listen and check your answers to Ex 4.

6 🔊 3.2 Listen again and choose the correct words to complete the sentences.

1 Charities **have / haven't** developed very quickly over the past few years.

2 The Blue Cross charity **has / doesn't have** to train the dogs.

3 People usually **want / don't want** to give money to charity.

4 **Everybody / Not everybody** carries cash when they are out in the street.

VOCABULARY

verbs with similar meanings

1 Complete the text with these words.

adapt   adjusting   made   modify   re-vamp   transformed   turning   turns

---

Kick start your day
with kindness

I used to be a slob; but that's a thing of the past. I'm a/an ¹.......................... person now! I'm going to ².......................... my diet by shunning all meat products and then completely ³.......................... my cooking repertoire. Some recipes I may just ⁴.......................... by cutting out the meat. I've already ⁵.......................... some sacrifices like ⁶.......................... my salt intake and buying organic. The new me doesn't stop there. I'm ⁷.......................... into a new person. They say kindness makes us feel happier and healthier, and the more the better. I've already changed my daily routine by doing a few good ⁸.......................... , and it feels good.

---

2 There are seven errors in the text. Find the errors and correct them. The first one has been done for you.

How kindness can change the world

Leon Logothetis has ~~made~~ <u>done</u> a lot of good for people by doing a difference to a lot of people's lives and at times even moving them around.

The former stockbroker has travelled the globe on a vintage yellow motorbike giving people a helping hand and generally making acts of kindness. Leon believes that kindness doesn't have to be materialistic and that doing a hug, giving praise or saying a compliment are acts of kindness than can make a difference.

Leon says that kindness is about showing people that they matter and that we can do this by simply making someone a favour and making someone's day a little bit happier.

---

3 Complete the tweets with the correct form of 'do' or 'make'.

#be kind   → follow

The school library closes at 19.00, but the librarian ¹.......................... an exception for me and let me stay until 19.15.

Someone in the park left a box of tennis balls for dogs to play with today. I ².......................... a double take. I couldn't believe my eyes!

I failed my exams: my mum left me a note saying '³.......................... the best of the rest of the day' and a huge box of chocs. She's a star!

Alice bakes wonderful birthday cakes for her friends. They are delicious and they really ⁴.......................... a mockery of my baking skills.

Chloe is so sweet. We had an argument the other day and then to ⁵.......................... amends she sent me some flowers.

My parents are the BEST. They let me ⁶.......................... my own thing, come and go as I like and they give me no hassle.

---

4 Find the words / phrases in Ex 3 to match these meanings.

1 look twice at something because you are surprised ....

2 improve a bad situation ....

3 exempt someone from a general rule ....

4 compensate for a bad situation ....

5 be obviously superior to something else ....

6 do what you want to do ....

LISTENING

1 You are going to listen to an interview with Jason and Carol who are involved in a community development programme called Community Kitchen which provides food for those in need. Read each question (1–6) in Ex 2 and underline the key words.

2 ⓔ 🔊 3.3 Listen to the interview. For questions (1–6) choose the answer (A, B, C or D) which fits best according to what you hear.

1 Why did Carol set up Community Kitchen?
   A because people were having financial difficulties
   B because the local supermarket warehouse closed
   C because people didn't know how to cook nutritious meals
   D because parents had to work long hours

2 How does Carol feel about asking people to pay for the meals?
   A It is acceptable because of the low price.
   B It is necessary because of the high demand.
   C It is important to teach people the value of money.
   D It is the only way to run the project.

3 What does Jason like most about his job?
   A working in local government
   B developing educational programmes for the local government
   C improving relationships between local government and communities
   D seeing projects come to life

4 How does Jason feel about being an outreach worker?
   A pleased to provide meals to young people in the community
   B excited to be able to help young people learn how to cook
   C privileged to give young people more opportunities
   D honoured to make a difference to young people's nutritional habits

5 What do Jason and Carol both think about the future of the project?
   A It can sell different products.
   B It can be financially independent from investors.
   C It can be expanded into other communities.
   D It can offer jobs to more people in the community.

6 How does Carol feel about the families who have meals at the community kitchen?
   A They should come to the community centre to meet other people.
   B They should eat meals at home together.
   C They should improve their communication between family members.
   D They should play an active part in helping the project expand.

3 Match the words from the recording (1–8) with the definitions (A–H).

1 unsettling   5 empower
2 touch on   6 rewarding
3 insight   7 on board
4 liaise   8 engage

A in agreement with a plan or situation
B briefly mention or refer to something
C something you find satisfying and makes you feel happy
D something that makes you feel upset or worried
E exchange information between people or organisations to be more effective
F be involved with something
G clear understanding of a difficult situation / topic
H give people power or control over their life or a certain situation

4 Complete the text with the correct form of some of the words from Ex 3.

Introduction to community development

Community development has long been considered a ¹............................. , if not financially, but at least morally, career. In recent years, projects have changed from ones that are top-down to ones that focus on community involvement and ensuring that members of the community are ²............................. in decision-making. This aims to ³............................. and give them a voice so they feel heard and that their opinions matter. Using ⁴............................. gained from research in various community development projects, this article describes the importance of ⁵............................. with all levels of the community so that channels of communication are always open, and ⁶.......................... common strategies for doing this effectively.

USE OF ENGLISH 1

1 Complete the text with the correct form of these verbs.

allow (x2)   get   have   help   let   make (x2)

Generational labels

Sociologists use labels as a way of **¹**........................... us to understand the subtle generational characteristics of groups of people. One of the most talked about generations are the Millennials, born between 1980 and the millennium of 2000. In comparison with their predecessors, Millennials are more educated as educational grants **²**........................... them access to university over the past few years. They were raised by doting parents who **³**........................... them discover the world at their own pace. Parental authority was less prominent than before and children **⁴**........................... to have greater freedoms, and not **⁵**........................... to comply with the rules applied to previous generations. Millennials are skilled negotiators, great in teams and proficient at **⁶**........................... people to do things for them. The next generation is Generation Z. They are more entrepreneurial and, rather than having decisions **⁷**........................... for them, they focus on individuality. They prefer to resolve their own problems as opposed to **⁸**........................... things done for them.

2 Choose the correct words to complete the sentences.

1 The Ice Bucket Challenge **allowed / made / helped** to promote awareness of ALS.

2 A recent report **made / let / allowed** people re-evaluate the current situation for Millennials.

3 Millennials don't **make / let / help** current unemployment statistics get them down.

4 Recent social change has **made / got / had** millennials apprehensive about stability.

5 Reports reveal that Generation Z is **made / let / allowed** to feel welcome by the Millennials.

6 Generation Z doesn't believe in **having / getting / letting** others to do their work for them.

3 Complete the text with the correct form of these verbs.

allow   get   have   let   make

→ follow

I think that our generation has a very positive outlook on life and, personally, I don't **¹**........................... things get me down.

I prefer working independently. I can always **²**........................... help if I need it from my colleagues.

I chose psychology because it's what I'm passionate about. I certainly wouldn't choose a course because somebody **³**........................... me do it.

Our generation is definitely the most individualistic. Just look at us! You should **⁴**........................... your eyes tested if you can't see that.

I'd like a job which **⁵**........................... me to travel around the world.

4 e Complete the second sentence so that it has a similar meaning to the first sentence using the word given. Do not change the word given. Use between three and six words.

1 According to reports, Generation Z are more entrepreneurial than the Millennials.
   REPORTED
   Generation Z .... than the Millennials.

2 Teachers predict problems if young people's use of social media is not closely monitored by parents.
   RESULT
   Teachers predict that young people's use of social media .... unless it is closely monitored by their parents.

3 'Some careers advice would do all of you a lot of good,' the teacher said to the students.
   BENEFIT
   The teacher told the students that they .... careers advice.

4 'You should stop your students from making the mistakes we made,' my brother told me.
   LET
   My brother advised me .... make the same mistakes we made.

5 A recent report claims that the number of successful young entrepreneurs has reached an all-time high.
   EVER
   The number of successful, young entrepreneurs today is the .... according to a recent report.

6 After students made several complaints about the marking scheme, examiners were persuaded to re-mark their papers.
   GOT
   Students .... about the marking scheme.

USE OF ENGLISH 2

1 Complete the table with the adjective form of these words.

autumn courage destroy eat globe humour
instruct literature negotiate reverse

-ary	
-ive	
-al	
-able	
-ous	
-ible	

2 Complete the sentences with some of the adjectives from Ex 1.

1 The decision isn't .... so think long and hard before you make it.

2 Most of the conditions are .... so we can ensure that we meet your expectations.

3 Requiring employees to have a health check was a(n) .... decision made across the organisation.

4 They have some good speakers at the .... event for aspiring authors.

5 The video showed the .... power of the tornado.

6 We decided on .... name badges as a fun gimmick for the participants.

7 He left us an .... note that made it very clear what we had to do.

8 He made a very .... decision and everyone admired him for it.

3 e Use the word given in capitals at the end of some lines to form a word that fits in the gap in the same line.

Your decision making

Have you ever noticed how senior politicians and CEOs appear to be wearing the same outfit in different photos?

Occupying positions of power means making
¹ .... decisions on an hourly basis. By taking away the option of what to wear, they are removing a decision from the long list. This ² .... seems logical; take away basic decisions in order to be able to make others more ³ .... This strategy is especially ⁴ .... for people who have difficulty because they are naturally ⁵ .... This kind of thinking can easily be applied to different aspects of life.

Nonetheless, although ⁶ .... of simple tasks and fixing a routine may be ⁷ .... in that it helps to focus on key decisions, some psychologists warn that ⁸ .... rejecting different options means that you might miss enjoyable new experiences.

NUMBER

EXPLAIN

EFFECT
BENEFIT
DECISION

PRIORITY
ADVANTAGE

CONSCIOUS

Extend

4 Choose the correct answer (A, B or C) to complete the sentences.

1 The board requested a ...... audit of all budgetary decisions in the last year.

A comprehend **B** comprehension **C** comprehensive

2 Everyone agrees that Peter's ...... nature will take him far in life.

A enquire **B** inquisitive **C** enquiry

3 I had a ...... lapse and couldn't remember what I had just said.

A moment **B** momentary **C** momentum

4 The changes were so dramatic that they were barely ...... by the staff.

A tolerated **B** tolerable **C** tolerance

5 After such a lengthy review, it was ...... that they wanted to change things again.

A outrage **B** outrageous **C** outraged

6 Checking with the owner before repainting the flat isn't obligatory, but getting ...... is advisable.

A permissive **B** permit **C** permission

SPEAKING

1 Are the statements about the decision question in the collaborative exam task True (T) or False (F)?

1 You have less time to discuss the decision question than for the main discussion phase.

2 The decision question always asks you to choose a prompt that is the 'most' difficult, important, interesting, etc.

3 The decision question always refers to the prompts on the word map.

4 You must make a decision within the time given.

5 You need to agree with your partner.

2 Put the words in the correct order to make phrases that introduce a justification.

1 that's / and / because / …

....

2 that / because / say / main / is / I / the / reason / …

....

3 is / if / point / that / my / …

....

4 start / for / well / a / …

....

5 example / is / good / a / …

....

6 at / if / look / got / you've / to / just / happens / what / …

....

7 that / got / what / remember / to / is / we've / …

....

8 about / if / it / think / you / …

....

3 🔊 3.4 Complete the comments (1–6) with phrases from Ex 2. Listen and check.

1 It's hard to make a decision about this and the .... is because there are pros and cons to all the options.

2 We can't change the planning laws! You've .... people are allowed to extend their houses without any consultation! It's a nightmare.

3 People need to eat less sugar. If ...., one biscuit contains huge amounts.

4 Buying from websites you don't know can be dangerous. My .... that you don't know how secure your payments are.

5 In my opinion it's important to save money every week. For ...., you never know when you might really want to buy something big.

6 There are lots of benefits of sharing a flat. A .... that there's always someone to chat to or to ask advice from.

4 🔊 3.5 Listen again and underline the word in each phrase in Ex 3 that is stressed.

5 Match the instructions (1–3) with the extracts from the student answers (A–C).

1 Now you have about a minute to decide which of these changes you think would have the most lasting effect on our lives. ....

2 Now you have about a minute to decide which of these changes you think would be easiest to implement. ....

3 Now you have about a minute to decide which of these changes you think we would need most outside advice about. ....

A All things considered it has to be the lifestyle change – surely? Fruit and vegetables instead of cakes and biscuits. Not expensive – could do that tomorrow.

B For me, it would definitely be about my future career – I really respect the opinions of my friends and family and they know me very well!

C I guess it depends on the individual, but I would say work is such a big part of our lives and initial decisions have a long-term impact.

6 Read the collaborative task about adapting to changes and think about the question and the options. Then read the decision question and plan what you might say to a partner in this phase.

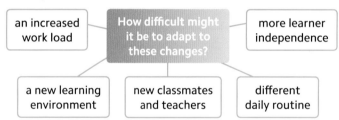

an increased work load

How difficult might it be to adapt to these changes?

more learner independence

a new learning environment

new classmates and teachers

different daily routine

Now you have a minute to decide which of these changes might take the longest time to adapt to.

7 🔊 3.6 Listen to a student's opinion of the task in Ex 6. Record your response. Remember to:

1 comment on what the other student says

2 use phrases to give your opinion

3 use phrases to show agreement or disagreement

4 give justification for your opinion with reasons and examples

5 finish by giving the other student opportunity to comment on what you've said

8 Listen to your recording. Did you include all the points in Ex 7?

WRITING

1 Are the comments about the email or letter writing exam task True (T) or False (F)?

1 'You can use an informal style for all the letter/email tasks in Part 2.' ....
2 'You always need to give some sort of reason for writing at the beginning of your letter.' ....
3 'If you're writing to complain or disagree with a point of view, you should always say what action you want the reader to take.' ....
4 'If it's an email, you don't need to follow the normal letter conventions.' ....
5 'You need to support your opinions with reasons or examples.' ....

2 Match the extracts (A–E) with the comments (1–5) in Ex 1.

A I think it would be beneficial to everyone if you could … ....
B I really think your comments were a load of rubbish … ....
C Editor – my opinions about the … ....
D I disagree with the new proposals because … ....
E I read your comments today in the early edition and I feel I must say that … ....

3 Complete the sentences with these words.

case   consider   discover   incorrect   insist   worth

1 You make out that all young people follow these trends. However, this is not the ....
2 It is .... pointing out that very few people actually act as you suggest.
3 In my view what you're saying is ....
4 I .... that you publish my letter in the next edition.
5 I strongly believe that you should .... how this affects us all.
6 I was shocked to .... that your point of view was so biased.

4 Rewrite the phrases so they are more formal using the words in brackets.

1 I've got to write to you because … (feel)
....
2 I know that you've got to give both sides of the question, but … (appreciate)
....
3 You must retract your statement. (think)
....
4 You need to print an apology … (if)
....
5 I think you're wrong. (mistaken)
....
6 I don't agree. (different)
....

5 Read the task. Which points might you include in your answer?

1 it's wrong to focus only on young people
2 family influences on young people
3 other facts referred to in the article
4 the patronising tone taken by the writer
5 a request for another article, redressing the points

You read this extract from an online magazine article.

The decisions and choices that young people make today are far too easily influenced by the media and the way so-called celebrities behave. They need to think more for themselves.

Write a **letter** to the Editor of the magazine explaining your views on the points raised in the article, giving reasons for your opinions.

6 **e** Plan and write your letter in 220–260 words. Remember to:

1 use the correct format and style
2 start by giving a reason for writing
3 moderate your language by using polite phrasing
4 give your opinion and support it with reasons and examples
5 indicate clearly if there is any action you would like the reader to take.

UNIT CHECK

1 Choose the correct words to complete the text.

FUNDRAISING THE FUN WAY

Fundraising doesn't have to be dull. In fact, people are
¹much more likely / most likely to want to take part in
something which is creative. If you are interested in fundraising,
then look no further **²as / than** here for some great ideas!

- Outdoor events are always popular and adults and children
  ³like / alike love a sponsored mountain hike.
- A sponsored treasure hunt. See this **⁴like / as** an opportunity
  to get to know your own town. The more clues you find, the
  ⁵better / best you get to know your town.
- Cook an enormous pizza. The larger your pizza, the **⁶more /
  most** money you raise for charity.
- Let your imagination fly **⁷further than / as far as** it will go.
  Be creative. A body painting competition, anyone? Easily the
  ⁸more / most creative idea of them all.

Remember it is people **⁹as / like** you that can make a difference.
So, spread the word. Be vocal. Working **¹⁰as / like** part of a
team is fun.

2 Complete the text with the comparative or superlative form of the words in brackets.

Community gardening

If you are looking for a new hobby, you could do a lot
¹ .... (bad) than joining a community
gardening project. Maria and Jo of 'Community
Gardeners' explained that community gardening
projects are the ² .... (good) way
of re-utilising urban waste land in inner cities to grow
vegetables, be outdoors and to have fun. Maria said that
the ³ .... (challenge) thing for them is
to get young people interested. Generally young people
are ⁴ .... (not prepared) adults to
spend time gardening. But working outdoors with other
people is much ⁵ .... (healthy) than
sitting in front of a computer, and consequently much ⁶
.... (good) for our mental and
physical wellbeing.

3 Complete the sentences with the correct form of these verbs.

allow	force	get (x2)	have	help	let	make

1 I managed to .... a really high mark in the exam.
  Such a surprise!
2 You've .... your hair cut! It really suits you like
  that.
3 Please don't .... me tell you who did it. I
  promised not to tell anyone.
4 The teacher .... the students go home early
  after the exam, as a special treat.
5 She is so lazy! She's always .... people to do
  things for her.
6 The rules of the school are that you are not ....
  to wear jewellery or make up.
7 I really didn't want to have tennis lessons, but my parents
  .... me to. .
8 If you have time later, can you .... me to make a
  cake for the school fundraising event?

4 Choose the correct words to complete the sentences.

1 I want to **alter / revamp** my wardrobe. I'm so sick of
  wearing the same clothes all the time.
2 I love your haircut! It has completely **transformed /
  modified** your face.
3 I haven't handed my essay in yet because I have to **adjust /
  amend** the conclusion still.
4 When I stayed in England I found it hard to **evolve / adapt**
  to eating lunch so early.
5 I've **altered / transformed** the screen saver on my phone. It
  looks so much better.
6 Technology is constantly **evolving / amending** and
  changing the way we live our lives.
7 The teacher told him to **modify / adjust** his language in the
  essay because it was too informal.
8 I've had a sort through my old clothes and I'm going to
  donate / lend a load to charity.

PART 1

Read the text and decide which answer (A, B, C or D) best fits each gap.

Living the DREAM

To most people the idea of living on a **0**desert island sounds instantly appealing. Just imagine, you could **1**....... your life by exchanging your dull flat for white sands and crystalline waters. Most of us at some point in our lives have roughed it on camping expeditions, but because we have quite **2**....... memories, we only remember the best bits. The moments of cold and hunger are generally not the ones which we are most likely to **3**....... the most, which is perhaps why some people decide to **4**....... their lives around by moving to remote locations.

According to real-life accounts of people who, driven by some **5**....... ambition, have actually exchanged their comfy lives for island life, it can be tough, very tough. There are some accounts of idyllic lives which have clearly been a **6**....... success, but there are also stories which can be only classified as **7**....... failures. Sadly, some of these people end up having to cut their **8**....... and return home.

0	**A** solitary	**B** desert	**C** lonely	**D** single
1	**A** transform	**B** swap	**C** adjust	**D** alter
2	**A** choice	**B** selective	**C** discerning	**D** discriminating
3	**A** remind	**B** memorise	**C** recognise	**D** recall
4	**A** make	**B** get	**C** turn	**D** move
5	**A** endearing	**B** burning	**C** colossal	**D** eternal
6	**A** resounding	**B** challenging	**C** mitigating	**D** running
7	**A** eternal	**B** lukewarm	**C** futile	**D** dismal
8	**A** failings	**B** losses	**C** damages	**D** casualties

PART 2

For questions 9–16, read the text and complete the gaps with one word only.

The dangers of sugar

We are all aware **0** ....that.... sugar is bad news for our health, yet most of us are addicted **9** .... a little bit of sugar a day, whether it be added to coffee or an illicit bit of chocolate. However, are we really aware just **10** .... harmful sugar can be? Figures from last year show that whilst we were consuming less sugar than we **11** .... been doing the previous year, sadly obesity in the Western world is still **12** .... the increase.

Recently we have seen a sugar tax introduced on most soft drinks **13** .... a way of encouraging people to take the issue seriously and to cut **14** .... on the amount of sugar we all consume. Doctors say that the sooner that this is extended to other items, the better.

If you are concerned **15** .... the amount of sugar that you are eating, then you should visit your doctor. Put your health first and don't **16** .... the sugary temptation get the better of you.

PART 3

For questions 17–24, read the text below. Use the word given in capitals at the end of some of the lines to form a word that fits in the gap in the same line.

Small changes make a big difference

Deciding to make a change in your life, **0** ...regardless... of whether it's related to your **REGARD**

fitness, career or personal life, usually comes after months, and maybe years, of growing

17 .... until you declare that you can't go on any longer. **SATISFY**

Although this can help you address what is **18** .... affecting your happiness and **NEGATIVE**

needs to be changed, that doesn't **19** .... mean that will finally push you into **NECESSARY**

making any real changes.

Too many people fall into the trap of making changes that are **20** .... over a long **SUSTAIN**

period. Rather than make **21** .... changes to your lifestyle, most life coaches **DRAMA**

advise that you should aim to make small **22** .... to your daily routine that you can **ADJUST**

gradually build up into more **23** .... ones. **SIGNIFY**

An example of this might be **24** .... quitting your job because you've decided you **IMPULSE**

need a career change rather than switching careers gradually by dedicating some time in

each day to studying something new.

PART 4

For questions 25–30, complete the second sentence so that it has a similar meaning to the first sentence, using the word given. Do not change the word given. Use between three and six words, including the word given.

0 Recording my notes is something that I used to do after each lesson.

WOULD

I ....would record my notes........ after each lesson.

25 William tried to forget falling over in front of the whole school.

BLOCK

William tried to .... of falling over in front of the whole school.

26 I have to say that I found your behaviour at the event extremely embarrassing.

BY

I have to say that I .... your behaviour at the event.

27 When we checked our bank account, we found that all the money had been spent.

ONLY

We checked our bank account .... all the money had been spent.

28 The doctor's suggestion was that we eat less fatty foods.

ADVISED

The doctor .... so many fatty foods.

29 How much effort to do you need to make to become an Olympic athlete?

INTO

How much effort do you have .... an Olympic athlete?

30 Despite all of her hard work, she got a poor grade on her essay.

ENDED

Despite all of her hard work, she .... a poor grade on her essay.

READING

1 Complete the summary of a documentary about the loss of individual identity with these words / phrases.

---

diehards   disdain   norms   pretentiousness
purport   spot-on   stance   ushering

Part of an award-winning series that is praised for its **1**............................ analysis of modern culture, *Have we all got the same tastes now?* is a documentary that investigates the new society **2**............................ that mean we wear the same clothes, listen to the same music and take the same photos whatever our age or social group. Taking a neutral **3**............................ , reporter Rachel Robbins investigates experts whose studies **4**............................ to show that the removal of divisions in such categorisations as age, social class and gender is **5**............................ in a new era of blandness. Does the globalisation of culture spell the end for **6**............................ and individualism? Or will there always be **7**............................ with a **8**............................ for blending in with the crowd?

2 🅴 Read the online comments about the documentary. For questions 1–4 choose from the commenters (A–D).

Which person:

1 has a different opinion to Adam about why we wear similar clothes? ....
2 holds the same opinion as Eva about consumers being controlled? ....
3 expresses a similar view to Helena about how the documentary represented the future? ....
4 has a different opinion to the others about the tone of the documentary? ....

A Luke Eddison

Honestly, the assumption that we are all losing our individualism is offensive and I didn't like the **condescending** attitude of the documentary. Only the second section got me thinking. As it pointed out, it's no secret that websites and apps **tailor** their search results based on your browser history for things from T-shirts to holidays. I'd always assumed that the whole point of the internet was to be able to access anything, so it was interesting that the documentary pointed out how filtered searching can make it seem like only our self-interest exists. That being said, that's about the only thing it got right! I think the rest of its claims were exaggerations. In particular, the **doom and gloom** it spreads about how things might be in years to come.

B Helena Jefferies

The premise of the documentary was basically that instead of all becoming the same we are actually all finding our own way to be different, but the evidence it presented contradicted itself. While the documentary claimed that we are becoming more **narrow-minded** because computer algorithms are predicting what we might like to buy, watch or listen to online based on our previous choices, at the same time, it said that we have never had more choice and power over what we choose. I found the second part of the documentary really quite condescending, especially as it was implied that we were being pushed around online at the command of large companies. Although I found it light-hearted and verging on amusing at times, on the whole, I came away feeling quite disappointed. Instead of a thought-provoking documentary, it was just another ninety minutes of depressing speculation on what we can expect.

C Adam Yoon

Having worked in the **retail** industry for years, I found the second part of the documentary fascinating, particularly its predictions about online advertising, and presented in an accessible manner, without being overly intense. Retail branding used to be all about identifying a specific customer and pursuing them, while ignoring other demographics. With the **shift** to online advertising, this has largely been **scrapped** and the same shop will market products to everyone. As identified in the documentary, the key difference is that different products are marketed to different people. If only I'd had such an insight when I worked on the shop floor! While I'm not convinced that it's completely down to the way that we are targeted online by companies, I do think that the documentary got one thing right: you are more likely to see someone wearing the same thing as you because of this.

D Eva Lyon

It goes without saying that the overriding feel of the documentary was tongue in cheek, quite funny really, and I'm frankly surprised that so many people don't seem to have understood that. Although we may share music preferences or fashion choices, that's really down to passing trends. Alternatively, maybe that's just because they are better, not because we are **manipulated** to do so by some rogue computer programmers or power-hungry corporations. What I took away from the documentary was a light warning not to limit ourselves to what we are shown. If anything, it was a reminder not to get lazy. Just because an ad pops up next to your social media recommending something you have been looking for, doesn't mean you shouldn't look around and check out other options. Nonetheless, I found the facts and figures presented in the second part a little disconcerting; I had no idea just how much of what we see online is driven by our browser history and we do need to be aware of this in the future.

---

3 Replace the highlighted words in the sentences with a word in bold from the comments.

1 The department store cancelled its plans to offer only unisex clothing. ....

2 Millie didn't like the teacher's arrogant and superior assumption that she was arguing just to be different. ....

3 Saying that you belong to a subculture and refusing to accept other views is quite intolerant. ....

4 Both my brother and sister decided to work in a shop when they finished school. ....

5 I'm looking for someone to adjust this dress for me so that it fits perfectly. ....

6 It's typical of an older generation to make predictions full of unhappiness in the future based on the actions of the younger generation. ....

7 The change in the perception that there are divisions between tastes is a recent one. ....

8 It's shocking how much they have controlled us for their advantage. ....

4 Same or different?

GRAMMAR

present tenses

1 Match the phrases in bold (1–5) with the descriptions (A–E).

Dressed to shop?

Visualise an upmarket supermarket. **¹I'm thinking** delicatessen goodies, top of the range brands and well-dressed customers leisurely doing the weekly shop … Not wearing pyjamas! But **²as the weather gets warmer, so the shoppers bother less** about dressing to shop. There are those who **³criticise** such behaviour. 'Those who shop in pyjamas **⁴are trying** to cause offense.' 'Take yesterday for example, I **⁵go to the supermarket, buy the milk, queue up**. The only customer properly dressed!'

A colloquial use of stative verb

B events following a natural or expected order

C result of a regular activity or habit

D reference to attitude / purpose

E a sequence of dramatic events in the past

2 Correct the sentences that are incorrect. Sometimes both sentences (A and B) are correct.

1 A I look forward to hearing from you.
  B I look forward to hear from you.

2 A I'm loving this dress. It's so you!
  B I love this dress. It's so you!

3 A I'm depending on you to help me revise for this exam.
  B I depend on you to help me revise for this exam.

4 A The woman walks in wearing pyjamas and the other shoppers look on aghast.
  B The woman walks in wearing pyjamas and the other shoppers looked on aghast.

5 A I'm thinking white walls, minimalist furniture and bold colours for this room.
  B I think white walls, minimalist furniture and bold colours for this room.

6 A Is this bill including the wine and deserts?
  B Does this bill include the wine and deserts?

3 Match the sentences (1–6) with the contexts (A–F).

1 It's well worth taking the necessary precautions before leaving.

2 The guy leaves his wallet on the table and looks away for a split second.

3 We are seeing the results of the hard work which has been put into the last few weeks.

4 You are always using the same lame excuse.

5 He uses a backhand and slams the ball over the net.

6 Armed officers arrive at the border.

A school report

B sports commentary

C travel advice

D story

E news article

F argument

4 Complete the text with the correct form of these verbs.

begin   complain   find   get   lead   leave   portray
shake   think   wear

A SPLASH OF COLOUR FOR WORK

The headline on the front page grabbed my attention. It read 'Colours ¹............................ to pay rise and promotion'. It certainly got me thinking. I am a bit of a diehard classic grey suit sort of person and I ²............................ it difficult to step out of my comfort zone. In fact, my wife is always ³............................ that I am too conservative in my choice of colour. Only this morning Susie takes one look at my attire, ⁴............................ her head with a look of desperation, and ⁵............................ for work. Am I doing something wrong? Am I ⁶............................ the right image at work? Isn't that guy ⁷............................ those ridiculous socks just being pretentious?

According to the article vibrant colours shout confidence, lift your mood and ⁸............................ you noticed. As you wear more colour, so the bosses ⁹............................ to notice you more. Perhaps I am making a big mistake. OK, so let me re-think. Right, so for tomorrow it's checked shirt and red tie. Or am I ¹⁰............................ green and yellow striped shirt? This is fun!

VOCABULARY

clothing adjectives

1 Complete the text with these words.

bootcut designer embroidered five-inch flared loud pleated ripped
shabby skimpy

How stylish was the decade?

1950s The neat and tidy look. Simple cardigans and ¹............................ skirts.

1960s Flower power. Miniskirts and ²............................ trousers.

1970s Show the midriff with a ³............................ crop top.

Black make-up, safety pins and ⁴............................ tights.

1980s In-your-face fashion. Shoulder pads and ⁵............................ colours.

New romantics wore ⁶............................ jeans and heavily ⁷............................ silk shirts, for the pirate look.

1990s Welcome back platform shoes! We totter about treacherously on ⁸............................ heels.

2000s Dress down for the grunge look. Oversized ⁹............................ clothes for that worn-in look.

Anything goes for the today's trendsetters. From the 'couldn't be bothered' scruffy image to the chic ¹⁰............................ look.

2 Choose the correct words to complete the sentences.

1 I wear clothes which are eco-friendly and **consistent / compliant** with my beliefs.

2 Fashion is an expression of our **individuality / individualism**.

3 All trends are repeated and they all become **indistinguishable / incomparable** from each other.

4 Right now a lot of people look the **spitting / splitting** image of scarecrows.

5 Talking about fashion is **equivalent / equal** to a conversation about biscuits.

6 Fashion victims are **cardboard / carbon** copies of each other.

3 Match the sentences in Ex 2 (1–6) with the sentences (A–F).

A You know, with that trend for wearing their jackets halfway down their backs.

B It is our way of making a statement about who we are.

C They just want to follow each other like sheep and fit in with the crowd.

D I don't know why we keep trying to re-invent the wheel.

E My clothes are an expression of who I am.

F I'm not interested in the slightest in trends.

4 🔊 4.1 Listen and check your answers to Ex 3.

5 🔊 4.2 Listen again and decide if the statements are True (T) or False (F).

1 Vicky is studying Marine Biology at university. ....

2 Vicky enjoys being creative in her choice of clothes. ....

3 Vicky sometimes follows the current fashion trends. ....

4 Noah believes other subjects should take precedence over fashion. ....

5 One reason that Noah dislikes fashion is because it is so short-lived. ....

6 Noah has no sympathy for followers of fashion. ....

similarities and differences

6 Complete the article with these words.

anonymity difference far fit rebellious stood
synonymous take uproar wavelength

● ● ●

Have tattoos lost their cool?

During the 90s tattoos were everywhere and were ¹............................ with being cool and hip. They seemed to blossom overnight and anyone and everyone who wanted to ²............................ in with the in-crowd got one. Some people abstained, possibly craving ³............................ , however ironically, more often than not they ⁴............................ out from the crowd for being different.

The thinking used to be that they were only for the ⁵............................ , but fast forward and the activity no longer causes an ⁶............................ . Today the tattoo industry in Britain is estimated to be worth £80 million; a ⁷............................ cry from the money made in small tattoo shops years ago.

Recent figures show a change in the tide. Tattoo removal is the fastest growing cosmetic treatment and figures suggest there is a world of ⁸............................ between the appeal of tattoos in the 90s and of today. Today's teenagers seem to be on a different ⁹............................ and they don't seem to be so interested in getting tattoos. Perhaps they simply have a different ¹⁰............................ on life and tattoos really have lost their cool.

LISTENING

1 You are going to listen to three different extracts. For questions 1–6, underline the key information.

Extract 1

You are going to listen to two presenters talking on a radio show about names.

1 Why does the woman mention the court case in the USA?

  A to provide evidence for the link between names and confidence

  B to clarify her feelings about names and personality traits

  C to explain a commonly held belief about names and achievements

2 What do they both think about the process of choosing a name?

  A It should involve more people than just the parents.

  B It is a decision that shouldn't be made under pressure.

  C Its importance is often underestimated.

Extract 2

You are going to listen to a teacher talking to a new student.

3 How does the student feel about having to bring up this topic with the teacher?

  A determined to be treated fairly

  B uncomfortable about bringing the topic up

  C frustrated that nobody is listening to him

4 Why doesn't he want to use an English name?

  A It's too difficult for him to pronounce.

  B It doesn't reflect his personality.

  C It still wouldn't help him fit in with the other students.

Extract 3

You are going to listen to a radio interview between a chat show host and a blogging expert.

5 How did the man feel about his own name when he was younger?

  A embarrassed that it was unusual

  B lucky that people remembered it

  C difficult to explain to people

6 What advice does the man give about choosing a name to work under?

  A Check that it hasn't been used before.

  B Make sure it isn't too unusual.

  C Think carefully about the spelling.

2 🄴 🔊 4.3 Listen to the extracts. For questions 1–6 in Ex 1, choose the answer (A, B or C) which fits best according to what you hear.

3 Choose the correct definition (A or B) for the words in bold in the phrases (1–8).

1 a **sense** of identity

  A reason

  B understanding or feeling

2 an effect our name can have on **shaping** our personality

  A forming

  B losing

3 being **ridiculed** by his peers

  A laughed at in an unkind way

  B told he was ridiculous

4 **get to grips** with the way school works here

  A do something (difficult)

  B understand something (difficult)

5 didn't want to **make** too much of **a fuss**

  A talk about something for too long

  B complain about something unnecessarily

6 I don't like being **singled out**

  A chosen out of a group for a particular reason

  B made to speak in front of a group

7 an **obscure** name

  A difficult to understand

  B not well-known

8 a **budding** blogger

  A beginning to develop

  B having difficulty

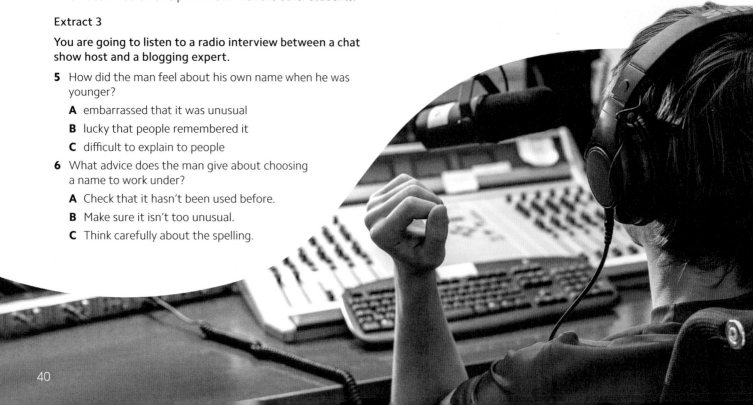

USE OF ENGLISH 1

1 Complete the sentences in the quiz with these words / phrases.

> any   do too   doing so   each one   ones   so

● ● ●

How well do you know yourself?

How many of these questions can you answer?

1 Are you living the life you want? And in .... does it make you happy?

2 What are your two greatest wishes? If you have ....

3 Crying is healthy. Women cry, and men .... Do you believe in the healing power of tears?

4 Some people believe that humans are essentially good. Do you think .... ?

5 Describe your three best qualities. What adjectives would you use to describe .... ?

6 What is your favourite food? Do you like traditional meals or exotic .... ?

2 Replace the highlighted words / phrases in the text with these words / phrases.

> am too   any   did too   doing so   neither do I   one   ones   so

● ● ●

Don't ask me if I have made a decision today – I don't think I have made ¹a single decision .... !

The process of selecting alternatives and choosing the best ²of the alternatives available .... should be straightforward. I have friends who love making decisions and in ³making decisions .... they build more confidence. Others agonise whether it is a big decision or a small ⁴decision .... If you suffer from chronic indecision it could be that your parents ⁵also suffered from indecision .... In my case, my mother has always been very indecisive and I ⁶am also indecisive .... She never knows which dish to choose from a menu and ⁷I never know which dish to pick either .... Am I indecisive? Aagh, I have to make a decision! Yes, I think ⁸that I am indecisive .... !

3 Choose the correct words to complete the sentences.

◄ **Keys to making good decisions** ►

> › Identify the problem: Decide whether you have a problem or ¹don't / not / isn't.

> › Gather information: Research information if you need some and you don't have ²either / any / all.

> › Develop options: Ask yourself if you have all the facts and, ³do too / if so / doing so, plan your options.

> › Evaluate alternatives: Which is the best ⁴one / each / ones?

> › Select one alternative: Eliminate some of the alternatives and, in ⁵doing so / doing it / so, your decision will become clearer.

> › Act on the decision: Act quickly. ⁶If not / If so / Doing so, you will waste valuable time.

4 Correct the highlighted words.

1 I enrolled for a course in psychology and my sister did so ....

2 I am very bad at making decision and too .... is my brother.

3 Jon and I can't agree and none .... of us wants to admit we are wrong.

4 If I finish the book in time I'll lend it to you. If so ...., I'll send it to you by post later.

5 I made a decision about the colour of the paint, but I'm not sure that it was the right ones ....

6 I'm not certain I heard Pam come in, but I think some ....

5 🄴 Read the text and complete the gaps with one word only.

┌───┐
│ 🧠 **Male and female brains** 🧠   │

Men are good at putting up shelves and map reading and other tasks synonymous ¹........................... being the provider, and women are the sociable ones, good at housework and making lists. I can already hear the roar ²........................... disapproval from each and every one of you, and quite rightly ³........................... . According to researchers who have conducted studies on 14,000 male and female brains, and analysed seventy-six papers on the subject, there is no clear difference between ⁴........................... . Studies show that the part of the brain called the hippocampus (which controls memory and emotions) is indistinguishable, which disproves the gender stereotyping we are so familiar ⁵........................... . So, whilst men and women may not always be on the ⁶........................... wavelength, we can scientifically say that neither men ⁷........................... women have the edge when it comes to certain tasks. Men might not enjoy reading a map or doing the washing up ⁸........................... more than women do!
└───┘

USE OF ENGLISH 2

1 Complete the three-part phrasal verbs.

1 I need to .... **up on** the topic ahead of next weekend's seminar.

2 I'm surprised they **got** .... **with** it. They'll have to be more careful in future.

3 I haven't **got** .... **to** fixing that shelf yet.

4 If she doesn't .... **up for** herself, things will never improve.

5 Nobody can stand listening to people **go on** .... their time away!

6 It's a struggle to .... **up to** people's expectations after that talk.

2 Match the sentences (A–F) with the phrasal verbs in Ex 1.

A I've been meaning to do it, but I haven't had time. ....

B Rob's presentation was so good that the others didn't think they could do as well. ....

C She has to put her point of view across more firmly. ....

D I'll have to spend some time researching the economic situation in the country. ....

E The children blamed the broken vase on the dog and their parents believed them. ....

F He didn't realise that he had been talking about his holiday so much until Neera mentioned it. ....

3 **e** Read the blog post and complete the gaps with one word only.

It's now my third week being stuck at home after my operation. Fortunately, just when I thought I'd ¹ .... out of things to watch, my streaming subscription was renewed, so I've been able to ² .... up on some series that I missed and see a few new films, too. I've just watched *All This Noise*, which was described as 'the most realistic teen movie of all time'. Ordinarily, I'd ignore a film with a title like that because it often means that the director has ³ .... up with what he or she imagines will relate to teens, not what teens actually like. In the end, though, I was pleasantly surprised. The film does ⁴ .... with stereotypical teenage characters who only care about superficial things and includes scenes that made me stop and think, 'I feel like that, too.' Unfortunately, it wasn't all perfect. The soundtrack was a bit cheesy, though I could just about ⁵ .... up with it. I really think the costume director should have ⁶ .... up on what teenagers wear because some of the styling was awful.

4 **e** Read the article and decide which answer (A, B, C or D) best fits each gap.

Hidden messages in animated films

Who doesn't love animated films? Sure, people may claim that they are only for children, but ¹......... down everyone has a soft spot for at least one animated film. It's understandable; animation technology has ²......... on leaps and bounds in recent years. But, have you ever noticed that a lot of animated films present similar messages? The characters may change but they always inhabit the human world. Although we have to give ³......... imagination a little to believe that non-humans can talk, we are still firmly based in our reality. Secondly, while the characters always come up ⁴......... some kind of problem, there is often no magic wand to provide a solution. ⁵........., problems are shared and solved by the forming of a ⁶......... between characters with different abilities. There's often a more intelligent character in the steering wheel, but the less intelligent one also ends up playing a vital role. This ⁷......... mirroring of real life promotes the idea of ⁸......... together to defend what is right.

1	**A** far	**B** deep	**C** somewhere	**D** low
2	**A** developed	**B** increased	**C** moved	**D** come
3	**A** into	**B** up	**C** off	**D** out
4	**A** for	**B** with	**C** against	**D** opposite
5	**A** Even	**B** Although	**C** Whereas	**D** Instead
6	**A** partnership	**B** group	**C** relationship	**D** cooperation
7	**A** clear	**B** subtle	**C** open	**D** complicated
8	**A** being	**B** putting	**C** working	**D** talking

Extend

5 Choose a verb and complements from A, B and C to form phrasal verbs for the definitions (1–6).

A catch put come get run do

B out (x2) up (x3) away

C of (x2) with (x4)

1 .... : avoid having to do something that you don't want to do

2 .... : have none left of something

3 .... : get up to date on something

4 .... : tolerate someone or something that you don't like

5 .... : remove something

6 .... : invent something

SPEAKING

1 Which two pieces of advice about the discussion task questions are correct?

1 You have to answer questions in turn. Look interested in what your partner is saying, but don't worry – you don't have to answer it too!

Reply   Like

2 With the discussion task questions it's OK to jump in and say something when your partner pauses – it might be a good question that you've got something to say about. The examiner wants to hear you talk as much as possible.

Reply   Like

3 You might get a question that you can both have a discussion about. That's a great opportunity to show how you interact well.

Reply   Like

4 Sometimes your partner gets a question you can answer, so when he's finished you can add something.

Reply   Like

5 The examiner always asks both students the same question, so while your partner is speaking – you can prepare what you're going to say.

Reply   Like

2 Match the sentence halves to make useful phrases.

1 That's something
2 There are several ways to
3 Well, there is
4 I'm so sorry,
5 Would you mind

A repeating that please?
B no one answer to that.
C I haven't considered before.
D come at this question.
E did you say that people think it's … ?

3 Match the phrases in Ex 2 with these follow-up sentences.

1 Firstly from the point of view of the employers and then from the point of view of the employees.
2 What an unusual and interesting question. Let me think …
3 I'm afraid I didn't quite catch what you said.
4 I guess it really depends on who you ask. Some people might say that …
5 Only if so, I'm not sure that I quite agree.

4 🔵 🔊 4.4 Read the collaborative task about things that are important to have in common with friends. Listen to a student starting the discussion. Record your response and move the discussion on to another point.

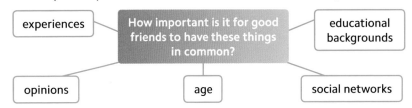

Now decide which of these things might have the greatest effect on the length of a friendship.

5 Read the discussion questions and think about how you would answer them.

1 Some people say that the friends we make when we're very young remain our best friends. Do you agree? Why / Why not?
2 In a close relationship, such as marriage, do you think it's better to have similar or different opinions and interests? Why?
3 People often expect children to have similar personalities to their parents, but they don't. Why might this be?
4 Do you think you can make really good friends online, without ever meeting them? Why / Why not?

6 🔊 4.5 Listen to three of the questions in Ex 5. There are three different interaction patterns. Match the questions 1–3 with the patterns A–C.

A You will need to respond to another student.
B You will need to answer the question directly.
C You will need to add your points after the other student's.

7 🔵 🔊 4.6 Listen again and record your responses.

8 Check your recording. Did you remember to:

1 use one or two of the useful phrases?
2 refer to the other student's contribution when following on?
3 bring in the other student who will follow you?
4 give reasons / examples to justify your answer?
5 give a relevant answer to the question?

WRITING

1 Read the exam task. Match the comments in the task (1–3) with the rewritten forms (A–C).

A We can buy the same items from global retail stores worldwide.

B People get ideas from what they learn happens or is popular in other countries.

C Communities are affected by the people from other countries who visit or make their lives there.

Your class has had a discussion about the reasons why countries and cultures are becoming more similar. You have made the notes below.

Reasons why countries and cultures are becoming more and more similar:

• influence of the internet
• international chains selling the same products
• people working and studying in different countries

Some opinions expressed in the discussion:

1 'We see what's going on all over the world and think – that's a good idea, we can do that.'

2 'Most of us can get international fast food, for example, from places like MacDonald's.'

3 'A lot of people work abroad and take their cultures with them.'

Write an essay in 220–260 words for your teacher discussing **two** of the reasons in your notes. You should **explain which reason is more important** for explaining why countries and cultures are becoming more similar, **giving reasons** to support your opinion.

You may make use of the opinions expressed in the discussion, but you should use your own words as far as possible.

2 Read the answer below and say which points have been addressed and which is considered the most important.

3 Read the answer in Ex 2 again and complete gaps 1 and 2 with the correct phrases (A, B or C) from Ex 1.

4 Read the second writing task and plan your essay. Decide which two points to include and make notes on what you could include for these points.

Your class has had a discussion about the possible dangers of globalisation. You have made the notes below.

Possible dangers of globalisation:

• conflict between generations
• decline of interest in traditions
• loss of minority languages and dialect

Some opinions expressed in the discussion:

1 'Parents and grandparents often don't understand or like the new habits young people are taking up.'

2 'Local customs and even skills are getting lost.'

3 'It's terrible how some languages are dying out completely!'

Write an essay for your teacher discussing **two** of the possible dangers in your notes. You should **explain which danger is more important, giving reasons** to support your opinion.

You may make use of the opinions expressed in the discussion, but you should use your own words as far as possible.

5 Write your essay in 220–260 words.

In the past there used to be very marked distinctions between the cultures and lifestyles of different countries, but it seems that now people all over the world are getting much closer in how they lead their lives. It's interesting to ask why this is happening.

Firstly, I believe it's important to consider the effect of the internet. We are all in constant contact with people from different countries and share news, music, opinions and a host of other diverse things with each other. **1**............... This is bound to reflect in the choices we make regarding our own lifestyles and decisions.

Another crucial point is the number of chain stores and organisations that operate worldwide. **2**............... This means that we see people wearing the same clothes or even changing their habits because of what is available in these stores. Another example would be that in many hotels across the world, the bedrooms are remarkably similar with exactly the same facilities.

Although both these factors contribute to bringing cultures closer together, I would say that the internet is by far the more powerful. It takes us directly into people's homes all over the world and also affects our views and opinions about how we live our lives and what is important.

People vary in their points of view about whether becoming closer is good or bad, but overall I believe that anything that brings people closer together has to be a positive step to global understanding.

UNIT CHECK

1 Choose the correct words to complete the text.

Taking the *perfect selfie*

OK, here we go. Today I **¹think / 'm thinking** hippie chic: floaty dress, beads, pale face. So, strike the pose, glance at the camera, **²press / pressing** the button. That's more like it. I **³love / am loving** the way this selfie has turned out. I ask myself, **⁴'Am I wearing / Do I wear** the right clothes today?', **⁵'Do I project / Am I projecting** the right image?' My mum **⁶is always telling / always tells** me that I spend far too much time posing with my phone. But apparently **⁷have / having** a good selfie is important for prospective employers. You never know who **⁸looks / is looking** at your profile page.

2 Replace the highlighted words with these words / phrases.

> any   did too   doing so   not   ones   so

1 A: Are you going to be late? **B:** I think I will be ....

2 Some people say that we take too many selfies, but I love taking selfies ....

3 She asked me if she could borrow my skis, but I don't have skis ....

4 Call me as soon as you finish class. If you don't call me .... , then I'll call you later.

5 I bought an iPhone and my best friend bought one, too ....

6 Do you want the green grapes or the red grapes .... ?

3 **e** Read the blog and complete the gaps with one word only.

My friend Irene and I are doing this project at the moment and we have to post stuff daily. I thought it would be a difficult job finding things to post, but it's actually turned out to be an easy **¹**..................... . I also thought we would get some bad comments, but I didn't really get **²**..................... . At the beginning, I expected to get some negative comments, but we never **³**..................... . In fact, most of the comments were complementary and the **⁴**..................... that weren't, I simply deleted. I think it's going to be a great success and Irene thinks **⁵**..................... , too. But if **⁶**..................... , then it doesn't matter because we've had fun.

4 Put the letters in the correct order to form adjectives to go with the nouns.

1 pyksim .... shorts

2 edboermirde .... shirt

3 adelfr .... jeans

4 ffcysur .... hair

5 ootbtcu .... trousers

6 teldeap .... skirt

7 vfei-cihn .... heels

8 dluo .... pattern

5 Complete the sentences with these words / phrases.

> cause an uproar   equivalent to   indistinguishable
> individuality   rebellious   spitting image
> · wavelength   world of difference

1 My friend and I get on really well, we are on the same ....

2 She looks so like her mother, she's the .... of her.

3 I can't see the difference between the two. To me they are ....

4 He likes wearing different clothes and he says it an expression of his ....

5 He ate two pizzas for supper. That's .... 2,000 calories!

6 I think he's just trying to draw attention to himself with his .... behaviour.

7 The service in this hotel is so much better than in the other. There is a .... between them.

8 If you wear that ripped T-shirt to school, it will really .... with the teachers.

6 Choose the correct words to complete the sentences.

1 This is the life! This beach is a **far / distant** cry from the classroom!

2 Sam is a **carbon / calcium** copy of her sister. They are so similar, it's unbelievable.

3 These marks are **consistent / constant** with my expectations.

4 Flared jeans and ethnic tops are synonymous **with / about** 60s fashion.

5 She is quite eccentric and likes to stand **out / up** from the crowd by wearing loud colours.

6 I can't understand why you bought those boots. They are identical **with / to** your brown ones.

All or nothing

READING

1 Complete the text with these words / phrases. There is one word / phrase you do not need.

buy into bulk defining generated initial
prospective spouses

Time to get away from stereotypes

From the **1** .... scene of the grandmother's sadness as she peeled potatoes in the kitchen to the closing shot of the men laughing around the table as their **2** .... served them dinner, your latest advertising campaign reinforced stereotypes and didn't reflect modern family structures. It seems foolish that you really believed that **3** .... customers would **4** .... the ideas presented in your ad. Having long considered your company's campaigns to be outdated and offensive, I was pleased to see the discontent that this campaign has **5** .... online and in the press. I hope that this represents a **6** .... moment for your company and that you use it to change your approach.

---

2 Read the first paragraph of the article, then read paragraphs (A–G). Underline information in the paragraphs that is similar to the first paragraph in the article to help you decide which option goes in the first gap.

3 🅔 Read the text. Six paragraphs have been removed. Choose from the paragraphs (A–G) the one which best fits each gap (1–6). There is one extra paragraph which you do not need to use.

A Even if an influencer's audience never grows above the tens of thousands, that doesn't automatically mean that they will have less of an impact than one with hundreds of thousands as larger followings can sometimes result in reduced engagement.

B This type of attitude from an influencer may be frustrating and even surprising to company executives who are used to focusing on the bottom line. However, the freedom to choose what they will **endorse** results in a level of authenticity that is important in ensuring the marketing campaign is successful, making it more worthwhile in the long run.

C Knowing who and what you are working with is key. It's important for the brand to have a history of interaction with the influencer in order to understand factors such as how they respond to negative feedback, how often they post new content and whether it is of consistent quality.

D So, why this return to the promotional basics? These pop culture personalities are so effective precisely because of how much influence they have over their audience; they are so **engaged** and responsive to the people that follow them that these followers are more likely to trust something that they endorse.

E One such successful blogger is Daniella Barbosa, who writes about healthy eating. She says that, the most effective campaigns she has worked on were those that allowed her to help determine the content. 'I once worked with a supermarket chain who turned up with a list of recipes for me to cook; I felt they just wanted to use me for my skills and audience. On the other hand, another whole food brand told me which products they wanted to promote and asked me to use them in the way I though best. It was a much more enjoyable experience.'

F The key is to find someone who is 'on brand', whose own personal brand and audience aligns with the target market of the company's products. Many influencers will readily turn down an offer that doesn't fit with their ideology, even if it means rejecting a large fee.

G There are so many social media personalities and bloggers nowadays that it's hard to stand out from the crowd. Influencers have to believe in their own potential to sell a product or a brand.

Influencer marketing promotes products and services using people that consumers admire and respect. Called 'influencers', these people are usually prominent users of social media platforms such as Facebook, Instagram and YouTube, with impressive audiences. Social media influencers are seen as an authentic and trusted source – and using them can be an effective strategy. In a somewhat paradoxical twist, the most forward-thinking brands are relying on the simplest, most traditional form of advertising: word-of-mouth.

1 ....

This could also **be indicative of** a certain level of cynicism from consumers, who get tired of having products pushed on them by companies. Think about it this way: are you more likely to buy something that your friend recommended or something recommended by the company making money off that product?

2 ....

Celine Leroy, a fashion and lifestyle blogger, claims to only accept offers from companies whose products have something to do with her brand identity, saying, 'For example, I recently reviewed some rainbow-coloured nail varnishes on my vlog. It made sense because my logo has a rainbow in it. On the other hand, I turned down some **lucrative** offers to advertise products because they had nothing to with what I stand for. I'm not just going to push any old product onto my followers.'

3 ....

Eric Woodward, a video game YouTuber, confirms this need for caution. 'A lot of my followers have been watching my videos since they were the poorly-edited ones I made with bad lighting in my university halls,' he says. 'They helped me get to where I am now, by liking and sharing my videos, so I don't feel it's fair to **exploit** that to make some quick cash. There is so much competition nowadays that I feel protecting my brand is the most important thing. Otherwise people will just unfollow me and follow someone else.'

4 ....

In addition to freedom over who they work with, most influencers prefer to have freedom over how they work. One of the crucial mistakes brands make when approaching influencers is to assume that they know best. It's easy to forget that although an influencer may have limited tools at their disposal, those tools were enough to enable them to become powerful marketing force.

5 ....

As with most things in business, timing is everything. While **bidding** for a well-known influencer to represent your product might get a brand immediate coverage, building a relationship with someone with fewer followers could bring bigger returns **in the long run**.

6 ....

So, at the same time as brands are moving into a future of social media-based advertising strategies, they are also leaning on the age-old adage of quality over quantity.

---

4 Match the highlighted words and phrases in these comments from social media influencers to the words in bold in the text.

1 'I have to admit, it was a good feeling to know that several well-known companies were competing to offer me more money to be part of their campaign.' ....

2 'I don't prepare a script before recording videos and I only edit them lightly; I want my followers to get to know the real me.' ....

3 'It's a misconception to think that all advertising deals make bloggers a lot of money.' ....

4 'Being in direct contact and involved with my followers is what I love most about making these videos.' ....

5 'Building my follower base has been slow going, but in the future I know I'll appreciate having had this time to perfect my editing skills.' ....

6 'Allowing you to make decisions about the direction of a campaign is usually a sign that the company respects your voice.' ....

7 'I'm always wary of companies who only want to use my name for their own advantage.' ....

8 'I try to promote only products that I would use myself.' ....

GRAMMAR

ways of talking about the future

1 Match the examples (1–7) with the descriptions (A–G).

Global luxury slowdown

It's official! We are spending less money on luxury goods and our consumer behaviour is changing. Here are some examples.

1 We holiday in other people's houses. Predictions say that this **will have completely changed** the way we holiday.

2 We hail taxis by smartphone apps and people say that on-demand business models **will become** more common.

3 We choose to buy online over the high street, and in 2020 and beyond we **are to see** global e-commerce conferences.

4 We like niche advertising and Berlin **will be hosting** a trade fair on this next spring.

5 We shop with our mobile and tracking means we **are going to see** more tailor-made advertising.

6 We love second-hand shopping apps and by 2020 we **will have been using** them for over ten years.

7 Don't take your eye off the ball. The next future consumer global conference **starts** on 6 September.

A something that is inevitable or unstoppable

B something that will be completed before a certain time limit

C something that will have been in progress up to a time limit

D something that is considered or believed to be a future fact

E something that is arranged officially

F something that is organised or timetabled

G an action in progress, repeated in the future, or part of the anticipated programme

2 Choose the best answer (A, B or C) to complete the sentences.

TOP 5 CONSUMER TRENDS FOR 2030

1 It is clear that social media .... consumption in 2030.
   A will be driving   B will have driven   C drives

2 Marketeers .... upon advanced analytics.
   A will have relied   B will rely   C will have been relying

3 Sales indicate that by 2030 the majority of us .... an electric car.
   A will have bought   B will buy   C are going to buy

4 Experts say that we .... virtual reality glasses as commonplace gifts.
   A will be seeing   B are going to see   C see

5 By 2030 we .... shopping online for thirty-five years.
   A will be have shopped   B will be shopping
   C will have been shopping

---

3 Put the words in the correct order to form sentences.

1 was / the / about / invest / intelligence / in / artificial / company / to / .

....

2 knew / society / impact / a / we / that / technology / would / mobile / on / have / massive / .

....

3 by / big data / become / have / will / key / a company's / 2030 / success / to / .

....

4 take / in / to / I'm / next / advanced / course / robotics / month / a / .

....

5 years / have / here / five / September / will / working / by / I / been / for / .

....

6 everyone / used / will / by / banking / soon / online / be / very / .

....

4 Choose the correct words to complete the text.

Minimalism. A trend to stay?

The economic recession had an impact on people's attitude to money, but perhaps we never realised it **¹would / was going / will** lead to minimalistic lifestyles. Young people now buy 'green' and it is predicted that we **²are to / going to / will** see more of this in the future. Tendencies to recycle and repurpose mean that in the future people **³are to live / are going to be living / will have been living** well for less. Hopefully this mindset **⁴will have created / will have been creating / is to create** a more conscientious approach to spending for future generations, and we can say with confidence that in the future we **⁵will be spending / will have spent / are to spend** less on luxury goods. It looks like the concept of living 'light' **⁶will be / will have been / is to be** here to stay.

VOCABULARY

buying and selling

1 Use the clues to complete the crossword.

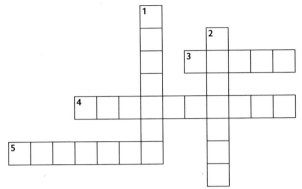

Down

1 To use something or use up / finish something (7)
2 To bring or gather things together from different places and sources, over a period of time (7)

Across

3 To store something away out of sight, typically in a secretive way (5)
4 To get an increasing number or quantity of things (10)
5 To obtain something by buying it or being given it (7)

2 Insert one of these words to complete the sentences.

out   onto   up (x3)   without

1 I could have gone mad in that shop. It was so me, I could have bought the shop.
2 My mum is a bit low so I'm going to splash and buy her something nice.
3 I'd love some new clothes, but I'll have to go until I get my allowance.
4 I'm going for the minimalist look and I'll throw away anything that clutters my flat.
5 Those jeans don't fit anymore, but I'll hang them in case I lose some weight.
6 I love a bargain and I never pass the opportunity to go sales shopping.

3 Match the sentence halves.

1 The design of the shop pushes all the right buttons
2 The salesman was so insistent that it really put me off buying it;
3 I've already spent most of my allowance this month,
4 My sister is really mean when it comes to spending,
5 I just couldn't resist buying it
6 I have this insatiable desire

A for a pepperoni pizza.
B I hate it when they give you the hard sell.
C because it's such a lovely place to wander around.
D at such a knock-down price.
E so I'm going to have to watch my money.
F and never wants to part with money.

4 🔊 5.1 Listen to the conversations and check your answers to Ex 3.

5 🔊 5.2 Listen again and answer the questions.

1 Why isn't it the man's favourite shop?
2 What does the woman want to buy?
3 Where does the woman want to go?
4 What is the present for?
5 Where is he going to put the rose bush?
6 Has she eaten a takeaway this week?

6 Complete the text with these words / phrases.

a soft touch   buy up   easy prey   go without
hanging onto   hoard   insatiable desire
sentimental value

A year without luxuries

It may sound amazing, but Michelle McGagh decided to [1] .... luxuries for a year. She realised that she had a tendency to [2] .... things, including things that she didn't need, and so she decided to give them away. She made a selection of items, only [3] .... things which were either valuable or that had a special [4] .... She decided that for a whole year she would only spend money on the mortgage, utility bills and food. Her friends were sceptical saying that she had always been [5] .... when it came to luxury goods and that she wouldn't be able to resist temptation. Michelle also thought that at the end of the year she would have an [6] .... to spend money as fast as possible and that she would want to go on a shopping spree and [7] .... the shops. But it didn't happen. Whilst before the experiment she had been [8] .... for most salespeople, she now felt indifferent to their hard sell.

LISTENING

1 You are going to listen to five short extracts in which people are talking about beginning start-up companies. Look at the two tasks and underline the key words in the options (A–H) in both tasks.

Task 1

For questions 1–5, choose from the list (A–H) the reason each speaker gives for starting their company.

A	encouragement from friends and family	Speaker 1	**1** ☐
B	reassessing priorities	Speaker 2	**2** ☐
C	experience living abroad	Speaker 3	**3** ☐
D	listening to an expert	Speaker 4	**4** ☐
E	raising money for charity	Speaker 5	**5** ☐
F	meeting people with the same problems		
G	talking with a foreign friend		
H	getting advice from peers		

Task 2

For questions 6–10, choose from the list (A–H) the advice each speaker gives to new entrepreneurs.

A	don't overreact to embarrassing situations	Speaker 1	**6** ☐
B	don't shut out the people around you	Speaker 2	**7** ☐
C	don't get too comfortable	Speaker 3	**8** ☐
D	don't expect to still have a social life	Speaker 4	**9** ☐
E	don't worry too much about mistakes	Speaker 5	**10** ☐
F	don't accept every piece of advice you're given		
G	don't lose your enthusiasm		
H	don't listen to your careers department's advice		

2 🄴 🔊 5.3 Listen and complete the two tasks in Ex 1.

3 Complete the definitions with these words / phrases.

cliché   embrace   intuition   on the backburner   overwhelmed
prototype   retreat   seek out

1 .... : not dealing with something for a while because it's not considered a priority

2 .... : the first example or production of something

3 .... : ask or look for something in particular

4 .... : know something because of the way you feel, not based on a fact

5 .... : something that has been said so often that it's not considered useful anymore

6 .... : accept an idea, opinion or event willingly

7 .... : move away from something or someone, usually after a negative experience

8 .... : feel that something is too much or too difficult to deal with

time out

The UK TV show Dragon's Den is a very popular business format that has been replicated in many countries all over the world.

Below are some business ideas, some are real ideas that appeared on the show and some are fake. Write 'R' in the box for the ones you think are real and 'F' for the ones you think are fake.

1 Umbrella vending machine ☐
2 Money mouse trap ☐
3 Egg boiling machine ☐
4 Collapsible water bottle ☐
5 Dog grooming vacuum ☐
6 Storytelling teddy bear ☐

One of these businesses ideas received £140,000 in investment on the show. Which one do you think it was?

USE OF ENGLISH 1

1 Complete the sentences with the correct form of these verbs.

> establish   examine   have   impose   investigate   take

We all 🖤 second-hand
#welovemarkets

Is it my imagination or are we loving second-hand? If we ¹............................ the evidence of flea markets and junk shops, it seems we do.

I wanted to ²............................ attitudes towards buying second-hand and here's what you told me.

'It's worth ³............................ a chance on markets. You never know what you'll find.'

'I ⁴............................ an aptitude for finding a bargain. I always find knock down prices!'

'It is important to ⁵............................ a relationship with the seller, it makes parting with money easier!'

'I don't have to watch my money! I ⁶............................ a limit on myself and I never go over.'

Based on your comments, I'd say second-hand pushes all the right buttons!

2 Correct the highlighted word in each sentence.

1 The article provides information of .... the growth of second-hand shopping.

2 People who sell second-hand goods usually develop a relationship of .... their customers.

3 There is evidence on .... an increasing tendency to buy second-hand as opposed to new.

4 It would be interesting to identify the cause on .... the boom in second-hand markets.

5 One way of obtaining information would be to investigate attitudes of .... buying used goods.

6 The findings should be based with .... data about people's attitudes and shopping habits.

3 Choose the correct words to complete the text.

Here at *Shopping Hub* we asked you about your attitudes to e-shopping. We decided not to ¹**impose / identify** a time limit on the survey, but to keep it open for as long as needed. What a response! So far, more than 1,000 people have taken part and have ²**let / made** comments on our blog. You only have to ³**provide / examine** the evidence, your comments, to see that *Shopping Hub* is a hit! Our customers ⁴**play / make** an essential part in shaping the future of *Shopping Hub* and your responses have ⁵**provided / given** us with essential feedback. We will use your feedback to ⁶**create / play** new ways to deliver even higher quality products.

Here are just a few things you told us ...

'Commerce is evolving and I think that *Shopping Hub* ⁷**takes / has** an aptitude for creative thinking.'

'⁸**Take / Create** a chance on shopping at *Shopping Hub*. You won't regret it!

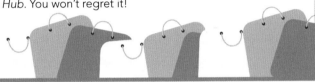

4 🅔 Read the text and complete the gaps with one word only.

The revival of markets

Street markets around the world are being forced to evolve and reinvent ¹............................ as the pressures from hypermarkets and e-commerce are being felt. It would seem that street vendors are rising ²............................ the challenge and a more creative vision of trading ³............................ before is evident. The regeneration of urban inner city areas has created the opportunity ⁴............................ more vibrant market stalls. Young people are also rising to the challenge with markets organised and run ⁵............................ teenagers. Giving young people the opportunity to exhibit their entrepreneurial skills as either a trader ⁶............................ a performer; offering locals an eclectic range of products ⁷............................ second-hand clothes, food products and crafts through to performances of music, magic or theatre. An incredibly successful scheme with clear benefits for all. Whilst these are still challenging times for market vendors, these initiatives are having a positive impact ⁸............................ the health of market commerce.

USE OF ENGLISH 2

1 Read the clues (1–6) below and complete the notes about a problem at a college using these words. You do not need two of the words.

breakthrough cover-up crackdown drawback
fallout intake setbacks turnover

Problem: staff ¹ ....

College head's solutions:

² .... of the problem and

highlight ³ .... of students

Reaction

From the teachers: anxious about the

⁴ ....

From the college head: no ⁵ ....

From the college board: ⁶ ....

1 More teachers have left the college in the last year than the previous five years.

2 The college head has decided not to tell the college board the reasons why and instead has said that he is going to implement a new organisational structure.

3 There have been record number of applications to the college this year, so the head will emphasise this in his reports.

4 The teachers are concerned that there will be negative consequences to the college head's plan of action.

5 According to the college head, however, he has experienced no obstacles in implementing the new structure.

6 What the college head doesn't realise, is that the college board has decided to investigate all the colleges in the area to learn more about staffing rates because it is determined to identify and resolve all the current problems.

Extend

2 Match the nouns in bold in the sentences (1–8) to the meanings (A–H).

1 I can't believe what a **show-off** Daniella has become since she got her new job.

2 The recent **cutbacks** mean there isn't enough money for the teachers' association.

3 It's important that we keep these details to ourselves so there isn't an **outbreak** of panic.

4 Unfortunately, her arrogance about her abilities contributed to her **downfall**.

5 No matter what happens, Mark continues to have a positive **outlook** on life.

6 Negotiations stopped after a **breakdown** in communication.

7 Is it true that women are expected to wear **make-up** to work in some companies?

8 Although the college **set-up** was a little unusual, most of the students preferred it to a traditional one.

A something that causes loss or failure

B something you put on your face to enhance your appearance

C a person who tries to make others admire them

D the failure of a system or relationship

E reductions in expenses

F a general attitude towards something

G the way something is arranged or organised

H something that happens suddenly

3 Look at the phrasal verbs in bold in the sentences (1–8). Do they have a similar (S) or different (D) meaning to the nouns in Ex 2?

1 The organisers spend all day **setting up** the hall in preparation for the ceremony.

2 Sadly, nobody believed Fern because she is known for **making up** stories about her life.

3 Everyone is tired of Dan **showing off** about his talents and accomplishments.

4 She let the issue **fall down** her list of priorities and will address it as soon as possible.

5 We should **break** the session **down** into two parts to ensure that people don't get bored.

6 We need to **cut back** on administrative costs as far as possible.

7 The company prides itself on **looking out** for its' teachers' well-being.

8 Despite the security measures, some of the suspects managed to **break out** of the police station.

SPEAKING

1 Tick (✓) what you should do in the long turn exam task.

1 speak on your own for a minute ☐

2 comment on your partner's long turn ☐

3 discuss issues raised in the long turn with your partner ☐

4 choose two out of three pictures to talk about ☐

5 describe the pictures you choose in detail ☐

6 answer one question about the pictures ☐

7 use words and phrases to talk about what is similar and different about the pictures ☐

8 choose your favourite picture ☐

2 Which student is correct, A or B?

A: Listen carefully to the questions because you'll need to remember them and they're sometimes quite long. You can always ask the examiner to repeat them though.

B: Don't only talk about what's happening in the pictures, you've got to use your imagination and do some guessing too!

3 Complete the phrases for speculation with these words.

all	faint	gather	highly	likelihood	may
	pure	right	well	would	

1 It's .... likely that … ☐

2 It's a .... guess on my part, but … ☐

3 In .... probability … ☐

4 There's a .... chance that … ☐

5 I .... be wrong, but … ☐

6 As far as I can .... … ☐

7 I think I'm .... in saying that … ☐

8 It could .... be that … ☐

9 I .... say that … ☐

10 There's a strong .... that … ☐

4 🔊 5.4 Read the examiner's introduction to a long turn task below and look at the pictures. Listen to a student doing the task and answer the questions.

1 Which pictures does the student choose to talk about?

2 Which of these questions does she answer?

   A Why might they be learning about money in these ways?

   B How useful might these ways of learning about money be?

   C How might the people be feeling?

   D How memorable might these situations be?

Examiner: Your pictures show people learning about money in different ways.

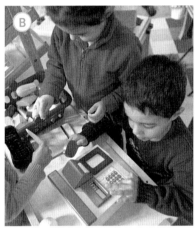

5 🔊 5.5 Listen again and tick (✓) the phrases from Ex 3 that the student uses.

6 🔊 5.6 Look at the pictures again. Listen to the instructions for a different task and record your response.

7 Listen to your recording and check.

1 Did you talk for a minute?

2 Did you use language for comparing?

3 Did you use language for speculating?

4 Did you avoid giving detailed descriptions?

WRITING

1 Are the statements about writing a report True (T) or False (F)?

1 It should be informal. ....

2 It should be objective. ....

3 It is usually for someone official or in authority. ....

4 It often contains passive forms. ....

5 It is usually one long piece of text with the heading 'Report'. ....

6 It should start by outlining its purpose. ....

7 It sometimes includes a complaint. ....

8 It should include some form of recommendation. ....

2 Read the extracts (1–5). Which are inappropriate for a report?

1 We really enjoyed the fashion show and would like to congratulate the organisers on their efficient planning.

2 I feel a future event such as this would benefit from more effective advertising, such as better placement of posters and even short radio advertisements.

3 It is hoped that the next show will be equally as successful as this one.

4 The auction got off the ground at about 4.30 which was way too late as loads of visitors had got fed up and left by then.

5 This report aims to describe and evaluate the success of the recent charity event held at Barton School.

3 Read the task. How many sections do you think the report should contain: 1, 2, 3, 4, 5 or 6?

An art club you belong to recently organised an activity to raise money for the club. You have been asked to write a report for the club organiser outlining the event, evaluating the outcomes and making recommendations for the next time the activity takes place.

Write your report in **220–260** words.

4 Read the report and check your answer to Ex 3.

Report on Art Club Sale

The aim of this report is to describe an event the art club organised to raise money for the club and to offer recommendations should the event be repeated in the future.

The sale
Members of the club were asked to donate paintings or drawings on the topic of 'animals' to be displayed in the town library for a fortnight in June. The artworks were priced by the committee and the prices indicated beneath each piece. People visiting the library could contact the Art Club to buy a piece. Posters advertising the sale were displayed by local shops.

The results
The sale proved very successful and seventy percent of the artwork on display was sold, raising over £2,000 for the Art Club. The money will be invested in paint supplies for members and visits to art exhibitions in London. Buyers were very impressed by the standard of the artwork, and many commented that the art sale had attracted them to the library where they had then discovered other library services. So, it appears that the sale benefitted both the library and the Art Club.

Recommendations
The success of this sale would indicate that we should definitely repeat it next year and we could consider extending the two-week display to a full month. I would also suggest that we have additional paintings and drawings to replace those that are sold. It may also be a good idea to offer to draw or paint library visitors' pets. In this way, we would maximise the amount of money raised for the club.

5 Replace the highlighted words in the sentences with these synonyms.

by doing this   consider   indicate   might   outlines   purpose   recommend   to sum up

1 The aim .... of this report is to ...

2 The report describes ....

3 The results show .... that ...

4 We should bear in mind ....

5 It may .... be a good idea to ...

6 In conclusion .... I should say that ...

7 I would suggest .... that ...

8 In this way .... we would ...

6 e Read the task in Ex 3 again and write your own report for another club. Make notes about what you will include. Think about:

1 including all the points in the task

2 which style you will use, who will read the report

3 being objective, using passive forms

4 dividing your report into sections with clear headings

5 using phrases from Ex 5

UNIT CHECK

1 Complete the sentences with the correct form of the verbs in brackets.

1 A month from now I .... (stay) at a campsite with my friends in Italy.

2 By the end of this month I .... (know) my neighbour for exactly a year.

3 I have been told all students are .... (attend) the interview.

4 I love dancing. By the end of this term I .... (go) to classes for three years.

5 The doctor .... (see) you in ten minutes. Apologies for the delay.

6 The shop .... (close) at 19.00, so I don't think I'm going to make it in time.

7 This time next week I .... (fly) over the Alps.

8 In April I .... (live) here for three years exactly. Doesn't time fly!

9 Don't be late. The concert .... (start) at 21.00.

10 Don't worry about forgetting your lines tonight. Nobody .... (notice).

2 Choose the correct words to complete the text.

Tiny **dwellings**

I'm desperate to get my own place. I knew that I **¹will / would** never be able to get a mortgage, so I've been looking for a rented flat. I **²am / was** going to ask my friend Sally if I could stay with her, then I heard about 'tiny dwellings'. Just in time, because I **³was about to / would never** give up the search and stay with my parents.

'Tiny dwellings' are these cheap micro apartments designed for single people like me. I am so pleased because by the end of this month I **⁴will have been looking / will have looked** for a flat for nearly six months! And by then I **⁵will have seen / will have been seeing** more than fifty!

I have a meeting with the agency on Monday and I **⁶am to see / will see** a flat the same day. I am really excited about it and I'm sure that it **⁷will be / is to be** the one for me. So, friends, stay tuned, I **⁸'ll be having / 'm going to have** a flat warming party in no time!

3 Complete the text with the correct prepositions.

Trends in shopping

Most people's attitude **¹**........................... online shopping is that in time it will replace the high street. However at certain times of the year the high street shops are still flooded **²**........................... customers, so I'm not sure whether there is enough evidence **³**........................... a decline in high street spending. I don't think we have enough information **⁴**........................... spending patterns to be able to make this assumption, and theories should be based **⁵**........................... more reliable data than we currently have. It is true that some of the larger department stores are in financial difficulty, but the causes **⁶**........................... this could be many. It could be due to people's dissatisfaction **⁷**........................... the current offer on the high street or it could be that their relationship **⁸**........................... the customer needs to change.

4 Choose the correct words to complete the text.

Enough is enough!

I had **¹accumulated / consumed** so much stuff that it was almost impossible to get into my bedroom. It didn't help that I would **²hoard / acquire** anything at all that people passed onto me, rather than throwing it away. So, I decided that I had **³acquired / consumed** far too many things. I've thrown away over ten pairs of shoes, but I did keep my first ever running shoes for their **⁴sensitive / sentimental** value! I'm keeping away from the shops, because I'm easy **⁵prey / ploy** when it comes to a bargain. I'm such a **⁶soft / gentle** touch, I can't say no! It doesn't even have to be **⁷hard- / soft-** sell marketing to tempt me. I think it's the knock- **⁸down / up** prices that are so irresistible for me. But I am determined not to fall back on bad habits and **⁹consume / collect** things that essentially just take up space. I'm also going to take a long hard look at what I **¹⁰consume / acquire** in terms of food each week because I am sure that I buy far more than I need. Enough is enough!

5 Complete the sentences with the correct prepositions.

1 It's not a good idea hanging .... clothes, because they always go out of fashion.

2 Try not to clutter .... your room with too many things.

3 Don't pass .... the opportunity to try rafting. It's a great experience.

4 I splashed .... on the gorgeous sandals for the summer. I just couldn't resist.

5 In fact I could have bought .... the whole shop. I loved it all.

6 I've decided to go .... a summer holiday because I want to get away in November.

6 Image and reality

READING

1 Match the sentence halves.

1 The review very plausibly explains
2 Criticism from readers is part and parcel of putting
3 The amount of praise received really puts
4 The audience's disappointment
5 Some novels, especially trilogies, have such dedicated fans
6 Her novel is a typical hybrid of
7 Her ability for conjuring up
8 The critics made a lot of

A complex characters is incredible.
B the complaints into perspective.
C was tangible.
D how the film is better than the book.
E that they are almost like disciples.
F the changing of the ending, but it made sense to me.
G your work in the public domain.
H science fiction and teen romance.

2 Read the article and decide if these sentences are True (T) or False (F).

1 Film isn't always the most effective medium for a book adaptation.
2 Screenwriters need to accept that they won't please everyone.
3 Fans of the book can be unreasonably critical of adaptations.
4 It is relatively easy to adapt a book into a play, film or television show.

3 ⊜ Read the article again. For questions 1–10, choose the answer (A, B, C or D) which you think fits best according to the text.

1 What point does the writer emphasise in the first paragraph?
 A the power of the written word
 B the unique characteristics of the written word
 C the difficulty of creating believable characters in books
 D the links between characters in stories

2 What does 'as such' refer to in line 15?
 A a difficult process
 B a different entity
 C a loyal interpretation
 D an effective piece of art

3 What does the writer imply in the third paragraph?
 A Publicity for adaptations is less expensive than for original films.
 B People always perceive the adaptation to be different from the book.
 C There is a pattern in the way adaptations are received by the public.
 D Adaptations receive more publicity than original screenplays.

4 What restricts a book adaptation into a film?
 A regulations about inappropriate content
 B potential complaints about the changes
 C length of the original story
 D number of locations

5 What considerations does the writer imply in the fourth paragraph?
 A Choosing the type of media depends on the type of story being adapted.
 B The choice of media is irrelevant because the audience understands it is fiction.
 C Adapting a book into a play is usually less complex than adapting into a film.
 D The limitations of the book affect the choice of media for an adaptation.

6 According to the writer, what are the benefits of adapting a book into a television series?
 A It doesn't cost as much money to make and can include more detail.
 B It encourages viewers to read the book.
 C It allows the writer to reduce events in a more natural way and caters to fans' expectations.
 D It can be more faithful to the book and doesn't have to assume the audience has read it.

Are adaptations
always a disappointment?

Reimagining a book as another form of media is a complicated process in which writers and producers not only have to take into consideration the enjoyment of the potential audience, but also that an audience has invested in the story. There is perhaps nothing more personal and difficult to define than a reader's relationship with a story; writing possesses a special power to **evoke** different emotions and create vivid connections with fictional characters, which can prove a difficult obstacle to **overcome** in an adaptation. How the screenwriter interprets a character's personality, reactions and even physical appearance is likely to differ from an individual reader's interpretation; and both of these may be in disagreement with the author's original intentions.

15 Ultimately, an adaptation of a story deserves to be treated as such, and should be judged **on its own merits**, especially considering the practicalities that come into play when transforming something that is read into something visual. What, therefore, are the main ways of adapting a book and what considerations should be made for each one?

The most obvious adaptation form is film. Cinematic adaptations of books have long been **a staple of** the film industry, particularly in recent years. A film version of a popular book usually generates huge amounts of publicity in the lead up to its release and is more often than not followed by an outcry that it is different from the book. That a film will be different from the original story is undeniable; films are subject to a wide range of restrictions that a book is not. The lack of a rating system for books means that authors can put characters in a variety of situations that would not be permitted on screen. Similarly,

'filler' characters or events, which add to the richness of the story and allow you to be part of the character's world, fit into the leisurely pace of a book, but would be **tedious** in a film that has to **condense** a complex story arc into a ninety-minute time frame.

Books with more narrated scenes are more suited to adaptations for the theatre, they make more sense on the stage than on the big screen. The way in which theatre requires the audience to suspend reality means that internal **musings** and monologues transfer to stage in a way that would seem odd or unnatural on the screen. If a book is action-heavy or falls into certain genres, such as science fiction, it can be difficult to adapt them to the stage due to the limitations of spacing and set design. However, these limitations actually cater perfectly for novels set in one place.

Books that switch between different moments in time or flick backwards and forwards between different moments in the characters' lives don't translate smoothly to either films or plays. This level of detail would force adapters to choose between cutting out large amounts of the story, thus angering fans of the book, or expecting the audience to have read the book before the film or play, and therefore potentially confusing viewers who hadn't read it. In this case, an adaptation into a mini television series is most appropriate. Although more expensive to produce, the nature of television series allows the inclusion of side stories that help **piece together** the story naturally, as in the original source material.

---

4 **Complete the sentences with the words in bold from the article.**

1 I'm thinking about publishing a book of essays, but I don't know how many people will be interested in my ....

2 I've never sat through anything so .... ; I was almost asleep by the end of the film.

3 Famous actors are a .... blockbuster films.

4 The play is completely different and deserves to be considered ....

5 The cinematography and costumes .... memories of the golden era of cinema.

6 Let's .... the clues and work out what happened.

7 The screenwriter struggled to .... his lack of confidence in what he was writing.

8 It's difficult to see how they will .... so much information into one paragraph.

GRAMMAR

mixed conditionals

1 Match the sentences (1–6) with the descriptions (A–F).

Choosing a **profile picture**

Questions you should ask yourself before uploading your new profile picture:

1. If you hadn't used a filter would the quality of your photo be better?
2. Were you to wear different clothes, would you cause a better impression?
3. Had you had a better camera on your phone, do you think the quality would have been better?
4. Wouldn't you have included friends in the photo if you had thought about it?
5. If this weren't such an important occasion, would you have spent so long getting the photo right?
6. Should you get loads of 'likes', will you remember how you chose it for next time?

A the future result of a hypothetical situation in the past

B the (possible) result in the present of a hypothetical action in the past

C the past result of a hypothetical situation in the present

D inversion

E *Should* to replace if

F *Were to*

2 Choose the correct words to complete the sentences.

1. If only I **hadn't put** / **wouldn't have put** that picture on my wall, this would never have happened!
2. I wouldn't have been able to take such good-quality pictures if I **hadn't had** / **had** a new phone.
3. Supposing your mother commented on your feed, what **do you do** / **would you do** about it?
4. If I were to say that I **didn't like** / **hadn't liked** your haircut in this picture, what would you say?
5. Were you to have taken his advice, the picture **would have turned out** / **would turn out** quite different.
6. If I **had had** / **had** your help, I wouldn't have got into this mess.
7. If it hadn't been for the social media course, I **wouldn't know** / **wouldn't have known** all that I do now.
8. You know what the celebs say: 'If you didn't get a selfie, it **didn't happen** / **hadn't happened**!'

3 There is one mistake in each sentence. Find the mistakes and correct them.

1. If it isn't for my brother, I would never have met my best friend.

   ....

2. If you didn't tell me, I would never have remembered it was his birthday.

   ....

3. If I knew you hated cheese, I wouldn't have put it on the pizza.

   ....

4. But for your help, I would have never had taken such a good photo.

   ....

5. Supposing you failed the exam, will you re-take it?

   ....

6. If only I have enough money, I would go on holiday with my friends to Greece.

   ....

4 Complete the text with the correct form of the verbs in brackets.

More than just **a picture**

If you are thinking of changing your profile picture then
¹.. (read) on. Your choice of photo tells a lot about you.

Timid: If you claim that you ².. (use) a picture of yourself if you ³.. (have) time … , we don't believe you! Were you to ⁴.. (have) time, I'm sure you would have still opted for your cute pooch or kitten. Be honest!

Serious: If you think that wearing smart clothes and frowning at the camera ⁵.. (get) you further in life, then we have news for you: that's not the case. If you would only ⁶.. (smile) a bit, the camera ⁷.. (love) you.

Sociable: You love hanging out, and should we ⁸.. (need) a friend we know where to find you!

Assertive: You love to strike a pose, to cause an effect. Had you ⁹.. (be able) to create a more spectacular image, I'm sure you would have.

So, if you ¹⁰.. (read) this earlier, would you have changed your photo?

VOCABULARY

words with similar meanings

1 Use the clues to complete the crossword.

Across

1 a mistaken belief in something (8)

3 a deceptive or false belief (7)

5 aspirations, ambitions or hopes (6)

8 something which you can see or hear, but which is not really there (14)

10 a pleasant situation that you imagine, but which is unlikely to happen (7)

Down

2 the ability to have creative ideas (11)

4 something that is not what it seems to be or looks like (8)

6 a truthful or accurate way of showing things (7)

7 the real world as opposed to an imaginary one (7)

9 a picture in your mind of what something looks like (5)

2 Complete the sentences with a preposition.

Be a stand-up comedian! 😄

1 Be creative. Vary your act because people aren't taken .... by the same joke time after time.

2 Be brave. Step out of your comfort zone and put .... a different voice.

3 Be convincing. You should make .... that this is the first time you have ever told this joke.

4 Be inventive. Make it .... as you go along, nobody will know!

5 Be a chameleon. Take .... a different role at each performance.

6 Be assertive. If you are confident then people will take you .... a professional.

3 Complete the text with these words / phrases.

> delusion   fallacy   get into character
> give us the impression   go to great lengths
> put on a brave face   semblance
> through and through

The benefits of clowning

Clowns are clumsy, they fall over and
1 .... to entertain us. They also **2** .... that clowning is easy, and you may be surprised to know that there is an art of clowning. I always thought that clowns were just for kid's parties, but that's a
3 .... They are much more.

Clowns accept failure and success in equal measures; they are not perfect and we love them for it. Anyone who thinks that clowning is easy is suffering from a serious
4 .... It is anything but easy. I recently did a course in clowning and I found out the hard way!

I took me a while to **5** ....
.... and I had to shed any
6 .... of scepticism which I had about clowning. The course was a thrilling experience and I learnt so much about myself. It taught me that I don't always have to
7 .... and that I can be vulnerable. It also helped me to know myself
8 .... in a way I never did before.

59

6 Image and reality

LISTENING

1 You are going to listen to an interview in which illustrator Patrick Hampton and psychologist Melanie Rowles talk about using pictures as therapy for children. For questions 1–6, underline the key words. Think of different words and phrases to express the ideas.

1 What does Patrick say about his previous work?

  A He tended to paint rather than draw.

  B He didn't consider drawing for his sister.

  C He wasn't enthusiastic about doing children's illustrations.

  D He preferred to illustrate comic books.

2 How does Patrick feel about the way his idea developed?

  A proud that he can now run a successful business

  B surprised that it happened so quickly

  C pleased that he can help so many people

  D overwhelmed by the number of purchases

3 For Melanie, what should be avoided?

  A depending on the owl to teach children how to behave

  B telling the owl how they feel instead of their parents

  C leaving children alone for too long with the owl

  D allowing children to spend too much time talking to the owl

4 What does Melanie think about telling children made-up stories?

  A It has a negative impact on their creativity.

  B It isn't the same as lying.

  C It can be disappointing for children.

  D It is something that parents do too often.

5 When asked about imaginative play, both Patrick and Melanie express

  A sadness that it is being replaced by technology.

  B nostalgia for childhood memories.

  C a desire to promote it in schools.

  D frustration that it isn't taken seriously.

6 What do Patrick and Melanie both think about electronic games?

  A They make life more enjoyable.

  B They can't replace the power of make-believe.

  C They are better because they are more realistic than other games.

  D They are ruining modern children's childhoods.

2 🔊 6.1 **Listen to the interview. For questions (1–6) in Ex 1, choose the answer (A, B, C or D) which fits best according to what you hear.**

3 🔊 6.2 **Listen again and complete the extracts (1–8) with the correct words.**

1 It actually gained .... pretty quickly, and I was able to …

2 I realised that I'd .... something special when …

3 … given that the .... is uncomplicated, I suppose it makes sense that …

4 This can also be exploited by parents as a tool for .... positive behaviour, …

5 Children actually learn to .... between …

6 … children benefit .... from games of make-believe …

7 If you ask me, there's .... in indulging …

8 … especially when real life can be so .... sometimes …

4 Match the words in Ex 3 with the synonyms (A–H).

  A supporting ....   **E** make a distinction ....

  B greatly ....   **F** discover ....

  C idea ....   **G** driving force ....

  D not a bad thing ....   **H** hopeless ....

time out

Which of these famous characters do you know? Match the characters (1–8) to the dates these characters were first aired / published (A–H).

1 Snoopy   **A** 1997
2 Mafalda   **B** 1964
3 Dora the Explorer   **C** 1974
4 Scooby Doo   **D** 2000
5 Mickey Mouse   **E** 1958
6 Pikachu   **F** 1928
7 Paddington Bear   **G** 1969
8 Hello Kitty   **H** 1950

USE OF ENGLISH 1

1 Complete the text with these words / phrases.

---

coupled with   most notably   or rather   provided that   since
so as to   then again   under these circumstances

The gender colour gap

There are studies, **1** ....
examining colour blindness, which indicate differences in
vision between men and women. Colour blindness affects
one in twelve men as opposed to one in 200 women, and
it is generally considered to be a male condition. Research
suggests that there may be other differences in visual perception
2 .... colour blindness. Tests
have been carried out **3** ....
discover the nature of these differences, and the results show
that **4** .... men have a
higher count of testosterone they have difficulty distinguishing
between similar hues of colour. It would seem men are
at a disadvantage, **5** ....
women are at an advantage when it comes to seeing
colours. There is no resoundingly clear scientific proof
and so **6** .... we
can't yet say that there is a significant gender difference.
At the moment, the proof is at times contradictory,
but **7** .... it
often takes years to build up conclusive evidence.
8 .... scientists consider this
to be an interesting area of research, I'm sure we will have
further information about this topic in the next few years.

2 Match the sentence halves.

1 There are differences in vision between men and women,
2 The professor decided to continue the lectures,
3 Scientists devised an experiment
4 Men have difficulty distinguishing between certain colours,
   most notably
5 Since men have higher levels of testosterone,
6 Coupled with problems with night-time vision,

A provided there was no problem with the timetabling.
B between bluey green and green.
C or rather, they perceive colours differently.
D this may account for the difference in visual perception.
E he is sensitive to bright light.
F so as to establish the cause of the infection.

3 Choose the correct words to complete the text.

Tetrachromacy

Most humans can perceive millions of colours **1since /
in other words** we have three types of cone cells in our
eyes and each cell can detect one hundred different
colours. People who are colour blind have two cone cells
as opposed to three, **2for instance / or rather** they have
two that function and a third which is a mutant cone
cell. **3Under these circumstances / Then again** people
with colour blindness usually have difficulty discriminating
between red and green. Some organisms have four cone
cells and they are known as tetrachromats. There are
some mammals, **4most notably / coupled with** reindeers
and apes, which are also tetrachromats. Scientists now
believe that some women may also be tetrachromats,
5provided that / coupled with they have a fourth cone
cell. Recent studies have been carried out **6in order to /
or rather** determine whether these women exist. It is
thought that the mothers and daughters of colour blind
men may possess the three cone cells **7most notably /
as well as** a fourth mutant cone cell. **8In other words /
Having said that**, the results of this research haven't yet
been verified.

4 **e** Read the text and complete the gaps with one word only.

The trickery of yellow

Were you to look around your house, you may well find
different shades of yellow and interestingly this may be
1 .... to the fact that you chose those items at
different times of the year. Apparently, we all see four colours,
yellow, red, blue and green, known **2** .... 'unique
hues', which are pure, unmixed colours.

At York University they carried out research **3** ....
order to ascertain whether our colour vision changes according
to our surroundings. The experiment consisted **4** ....
a group of volunteers in January and in June using a dial
5 .... a colorimeter to find a unique yellow which
they felt contained no hint of red or green.

The remarkable thing **6** .... the findings was that the
volunteers adjusted their perception of yellow depending on
the time of the year.

In the summer we are surrounded by green foliage, and under
7 .... circumstances the eye does something amazing
and compensates **8** .... filtering out the green hue.
This gives us the false impression that the yellow we see in the
summer is the same as in the winter.

61

USE OF ENGLISH 2

1 Underline the odd word out in each group.

1 impersonate   mock   fake   forge

2 hoax   scam   above-board   fraud

3 authentic   falsehood   lie   bluff

4 make-believe   candid   mythical   fictitious

5 honest   above-board   authentic   disguise

2 Complete the post with these words.

believe   cheat   disguising   fib   honest   mocking   play   scam

Last week, while I was on a trip to the beach resort, I decided to ¹........................ a prank on one of my friends by making him ²........................ that I had met a famous actor. The photo was real, but I took it from some distance away as there were too many security guards around to actually approach him. I hardly ever lie; I'm usually very ³........................ and I never ⁴........................ at games or anything like that. It was only a little ⁵........................ because I was just so tired of my friend boasting about what she does at weekends and ⁶........................ me over my supposedly 'boring' life. I mean, it's only a small lie; it's not like ⁷........................ myself as someone else online or making her fall for a ⁸........................ . After all, little white lies aren't really lies, are they?

Extend

3 Read the sentence pairs and match the words in bold to the meanings (A and B).

1 **1** His application for extra funding was **legitimate**. ....

   2 His application for extra funding was **authentic**. ....

   A based on facts   **B** allowed by law

2 **1** Fran's claim about the accident was **phony**. ....

   2 Fran's claim about the accident was **fictitious**. ....

   A imaginary   **B** fake.

3 **1** We discovered that Sam had **forged** the money. ....

   2 We discovered that Sam had **concealed** the money. ....

   A illegally imitated / copied   **B** hidden

4 **1** The presenter's **gags** caused a lot of upset. ....

   2 The presenter's **scam** caused a lot of upset. ....

   A dishonest scheme to make money   **B** jokes

5 **1** The threats in the email were just a **bluff**. ....

   2 The threats in the email were just **fabrications**. ....

   A attempt to deceive someone into thinking that something is going to happen

   B invention / lies

4 **e** Read the article and decide which answer (A, B, C or D) best fits each gap.

What's wrong with a little white lie?

On the surface, little white lies are seemingly insignificant untruths that we tell to avoid hurting someone or having to give a long, unnecessary explanation for something that seems innocent. However, recent studies have shown that regularly ¹........ fibs can make us less likely to stop ourselves from telling bigger lies. We all have a chemical in our brain whose ²........ is to be our moral guide, helping us understand right from wrong and preventing ³........ behaviour. The more we lie, the less effective this chemical is in ⁴........ the morality of our actions. Case studies involving eighty volunteers discovered that telling lies becomes easier over time as we become desensitised to the feelings of guilt. ⁵........ like the snowball effect, where something small quickly builds into something significantly bigger, the way we portray facts changes over time. Our negative feelings about lying impacts our ability to ⁶........ the ⁷........ to which we are prepared to lie, thus allowing small acts of dishonesty to escalate into more significant lies. So, think ⁸........ before telling that small untruth.

1	**A** giving	**B** saying	**C** telling	**D** speaking
2	**A** part	**B** role	**C** act	**D** code
3	**A** wrong	**B** inappropriate	**C** boring	**D** irrelevant
4	**A** prohibiting	**B** determining	**C** resolving	**D** hiding
5	**A** Indeed	**B** Just	**C** Even	**D** Instead
6	**A** diminish	**B** damage	**C** deepen	**D** limit
7	**A** amount	**B** extent	**C** frequency	**D** size
8	**A** second	**B** finally	**C** twice	**D** initially

SPEAKING

1 Read the collaborative exam task about how important it is for certain things to be truthful and match the students' comments (1–3) with three of the prompts.

Here are some things which people do not always trust to be truthful.

photographs of celebrities   autobiographies

How important is it for these things to be completely truthful?

food advertisements   weather forecasts   historical films

1 It depends which accounts or records they're based on. Some are really informative. But I'd say most people don't expect the full truth really – after all, it's fiction. On the other hand, if we're told that they're based on fact then the facts should be accurate.

2 They make so many promises and claims, and legally they're supposed to be upfront and honest about everything, but in reality I think they get away with a lot, or really skirt the edges of the truth! Personally, I think it's irresponsible and people are easily influenced by them.

3 You can't really tell what's been airbrushed out! And in my opinion it's really dangerous – because people try to achieve that image and can end up damaging themselves.

2 🔊 6.3 Think about the prompt 'autobiographies' and note down things you might say about this. Then listen to a student talking about it. Does she mention any of your points?

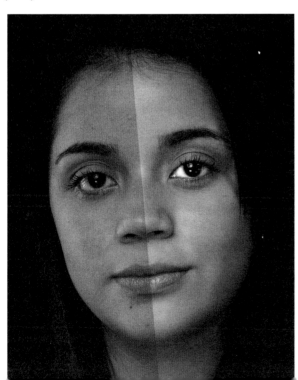

3 e 🔊 6.4 Listen again then record your response. Remember to:

1 refer to the other student

2 make a different point yourself

3 invite the other student to agree, disagree or comment further.

4 e 🔊 6.5 Read the discussion question for the task in Ex 1. Listen to the other student's comment and record your own.

Which of these things do you think the public trusts the least?

5 Put the words in the correct order to make introductory phrases.

1 say / the / is / because / this / I / reason / ...

....

2 is / think / because / this / I / way / why / ...

....

3 behind / the / is / reasoning / this / ...

....

4 an / let's / example / take / ...

....

5 got / you've / remember / to / only / ...

....

6 mean / what / if / I / is / ...

....

6 Complete the sentences with these words. For some sentences there is more than possible answer.

also   basically   instance   mean   prime   take

1 Advertising is a .... example.

2 I ...., look at the claims they make.

3 That's .... because they don't feel responsible to the public.

4 For ...., think about the recent film about the Queen.

5 .... the celebrity's story about meeting his agent, for example.

6 This is .... because they don't really know the truth about it.

7 Read the discussion task questions. Make notes about what you would say. Record your responses. Try to use some of the phrases from Ex 5 and Ex 6.

1 People often tend to trust what they see in print. Why do you think this is?

2 Do you think people are right to believe health advice they read on the internet? Why / Why not?

3 There's a saying 'It's too good to be true'. What might this refer to and do you agree? Why / Why not?

4 Some people never read the terms and conditions for things they sign. Why might this be?

8 Listen to your recordings. How many phrases to introduce reasons and examples did you use?

WRITING

1 Are the statements about writing an essay True (T) or False (F)?

1 You must include all the points in the task. ....

2 Your essay is written to give information to people of your age group. ....

3 You will give your opinion at certain points in the essay. ....

4 Your essay will usually have four paragraphs. ....

5 You can quote the opinions included in the task. ....

6 You need to add one more point of your own. ....

2 Read the writing task to check your answers to Ex 1.

Your class has had a discussion about the attractions of choosing a career in the entertainments industry. You have made the notes below.

Attractions of choosing a career in the entertainment industry:

- non-routine nature of the work
- possibility of fame
- opportunity to influence other people's moods

Some opinions expressed in the discussion:

'You would never get stuck in a nine-to-five routine job and risk getting bored and fed up'.

'There's the chance of becoming really successful, winning awards and having everyone in the world know your name!'

'It must be great to help people forget their problems for a while.'

Write an essay for your teacher discussing **two** of the attractions in your notes. You should **explain which attraction is more influential** for choosing a career in the entertainment industry, **giving reasons** to support your opinion.

You may make use of the opinions expressed in the discussion, but you should use your own words as far as possible.

3 Read the model answer for the task in Ex 2 and answer the questions.

1 Which two points are included?

2 Which point is considered to be the most influential?

3 Did the writer use the ideas from the quotes? If so, were they rephrased?

Increasing numbers of creative and imaginative people are considering a career in the entertainment industry, a career which, in the past, parents often tried to dissuade children from following. Why then is this type of career becoming more popular?

One of the major attractions is undoubtedly the desire to engage in work that can be different day-to-day, or week-to-week. It is important to realise that many people are horrified by the thought of a regular eight-hour day with a fixed timetable. It is equally important to understand that for people like this, doing the same tasks day in, day out could be extremely boring and even depressing. In light of this, it is unsurprising that the entertainment industry is so attractive.

A second attraction is, unsurprisingly, the possibility of becoming famous. Although would-be actors or singers might profess a dislike of fame and what it brings, it is nevertheless true, in my opinion, that the idea of becoming a household name, with the associated benefits, is basically what many strive for. After all, when you are performing, you want your performance to touch as many people as possible, and fame and popularity certainly allow that to happen.

Whereas both attractions are unquestionably important, I believe the more significant is the chance to become famous. This also brings the opportunity to select projects that best suit the artist and their lifestyle. Who wouldn't embrace that alternative to a comparatively unexciting daily routine job?

4 Read the task. Plan and write your essay in 220–260 words. Remember to link your ideas using some phrases from the unit and give your opinion with adverbs.

Your class has listened to a radio discussion on the drawbacks of working in the entertainment industry. You have made the notes below.

Drawbacks of working in the entertainment industry:

- insecurity of employment
- potentially low rates of pay
- impact on family life

Some opinions expressed in the discussion:

'It isn't that easy to get a job in entertainment – and people are never sure that when one job finishes another is going to come along quickly.'

'Unless you're really lucky you're not going to make a fortune working in entertainment – lots of people have to accept very low fees.'

'The irregular hours and the need to go where the work is – sometimes on the other side of the world – can disrupt relationships.'

Write an essay for your teacher discussing **two** of the drawbacks in your notes. You should **explain which drawback is more significant** for people hoping to work in the entertainment industry, **giving reasons** to support your opinion.

You may make use of the opinions expressed in the discussion, but you should use your own words as far as possible.

UNIT CHECK

1 Complete the text with the correct form of the verbs in brackets.

✚ Morris dancers ✚

This summer I went to visit England for the first time. If I **1**............................ (know) it was going to be such fun, I **2**............................ (visit) years ago! I stayed with my friend Alice in Somerset and I came across this unusual traditional dance called Morris dancing. If I **3**............................ (see) it with my own eyes I don't think I **4**............................ (believe) anyone who described it to me. It consists of a group of men dancing around a pole wearing bells tied to their ankles. Had I **5**............................ (realise) that it was going to be so entertaining, I **6**............................ (pay) more attention when my friend was telling me about it. So, should you **7**............................ (need) some traditional entertainment when you are in southwest England, I would recommend this. Were I **8**............................ (choose) one of the most memorable things about this holiday, it might well be this dancing.

2 Complete the second sentence so that it has a similar meaning to the first sentence using the word in brackets.

1 I read the book thanks to my friend Marina. (read)
   If it hadn't .... the book.
2 I'm not brave enough to go sky diving, but I'd like to. (braver)
   If .... sky diving.
3 Seeing such a strange event makes me want to film it. (see)
   If .... to film it.
4 I didn't bring sun cream because I didn't think it would be sunny. (known)
   Had .... sun cream.
5 The mystery was resolved thanks to the detective. (for)
   If it hadn't .... resolved.
6 I didn't pass chemistry so I couldn't study medicine. (able)
   If I .... to study medicine.

3 Complete the sentences with these words.

fantasy   hallucinations   illusion   image   imagination   realism

1 I have this .... that one day I'll get the lead in a film and of course go on to win lots of Oscars.
2 I read an article about a dress that changed colour. I think it was really an optical ....
3 Once I got sun stoke; I had a really high fever for about two hours and I had ....
4 You need to have a good .... in order to be able to write poetry.
5 I'm not keen on abstract art, I think I prefer ....
6 I have this .... in my mind of us lying on a beach in the Caribbean.

4 Choose the correct words to complete the sentences.

1 My mother went to **great / long** lengths to give me a wonderful party.
2 She seems very happy, but occasionally the facade **slips / moves** and I can see that she isn't.
3 Sometimes it takes actors a while to get **into / about** character, especially if it's a difficult part.
4 She got an Oscar because she gave such a **convincing / striking** performance.
5 He gives the **idea / impression** that he loves his job, but I'm not sure.
6 There wasn't much food, but he managed to make some **shadow / semblance** of a meal for the family.

5 Complete the text with these phrases.

make out   making it up   put on   take on   taken her for   taken in

We have a new girl in our class who apparently is a real princess! I was so surprised when she told me because I certainly wouldn't have **1**............................ a princess! At first most people in the class thought that she was **2**............................ . I believe her though. I'm not the sort of person who is **3**............................ by people easily and I think she's telling the truth. Also, why would she want to **4**............................ that she's a princess if she isn't? It just doesn't make sense. I asked her the other day to **5**............................ a princess type voice and she did. It was hysterical! When she is in class she just seems the same as the rest of us. I guess that out of class she is different because sometimes people do **6**............................ different roles in different contexts.

PART 1

For questions 1–8, read the text and decide which answer (A, B, C or D) best fits each gap.

The power of magic

We all love magic. We only have to **0**reflect on the runaway success of *Harry Potter* to see this. The haunted mansion of Hogwarts and the tales of power and corruption have all created a classic which really does **1**...... from the rest when it comes to fantasy. The *Harry Potter* books and films really did **2**...... all the right buttons with young and old alike and we were transported to a wizard school where children **3**...... supernatural powers. Why did we love it? Perhaps because for a few minutes the idea seemed real and not just a **4**...... of our imagination. Or perhaps, we all **5**...... onto memories from our childhood of bewitching adventures into the unknown.

I believe our fascination with magic is understandable. Why would anyone **6**...... up the opportunity of escaping from our day-to-day lives to that of a **7**...... world?

An interesting **8**...... on why magic intrigues us is that believing in fate and superstition makes us feel that we have a greater control over our lives. Perhaps. Who knows.

PART 2

For questions 9–16, read the text and complete the gaps with one word only.

Silence please!

Technology dependence, social media and mobile phones use **0**......up...... precious time. Recent theories show that **9**........................... we were to limit our screen time and to dedicate less time to technology, then we would free **10**........................... time to daydream. Yes, daydream! You heard it correctly. It may sound **11**........................... madness, but it is becoming clear that whilst daydreaming our minds are creatively active. In **12**........................... words, by limiting the time we spend in front of a screen we give our minds the opportunity to switch **13**........................... from the constant barrage of information and to be truly creative.

Recent social experiments confirm, not surprisingly, that the people can boost their creativity by limiting their access to social media. Statistics currently suggest that in five years' time we will **14**........................... spending even more screen time than now. So, perhaps it's time to reflect. I, for one, don't want to look **15**........................... with regret in five years' time, and think that I could **16**........................... used my time more inventively.

0	**Ⓐ** reflect	**B** recall	**C** remember	**D** remind
1	**A** stand out	**B** stand up	**C** stand over	**D** stand away
2	**A** touch	**B** pull	**C** push	**D** bang
3	**A** possess	**B** collect	**C** own	**D** hoard
4	**A** piece	**B** fabrication	**C** creation	**D** figment
5	**A** suspend	**B** hang	**C** keep	**D** clutch
6	**A** give	**B** break	**C** let	**D** leave
7	**A** fantasy	**B** illusion	**C** delusion	**D** fallacy
8	**A** look	**B** take	**C** vision	**D** stand

PART 3

For questions 17–24, read the text. Use the word given in capitals at the end of some of the lines to form a word that fits in the gap in the same line.

Standing out from the crowd

The easiest way for a company to separate itself from its ⁰ ....competitors....... **COMPETE**
is to have something unique. Simple factors such as providing excellent
customer service, speaking **17** .... about the capabilities **TRUTH**
and **18** .... of your product and demonstrating a **LIMIT**
19 .... to social responsibility can build a good reputation **COMMIT**
among consumers. In a world **20** .... dominated by **INCREASE**
competition, some companies prefer to rely on gimmicks to grab consumers'
attention and turn it into cash.

Gimmicks largely depend on natural human **21** .... to be **CURIOUS**
effective. For example, when Copenhagen Zoo wanted to increase its visitor
numbers, it counted on the **22** .... of passers-by stopping **PROBABLE**
to look at buses that had been painted so that they looked like they were being
crushed by a huge snake.

However, things don't always go to plan. One company made the
23 .... decision to build the world's largest ice **DISASTER**
cream and display it in New York City on a hot summer's day. It was a
24 .... mistake that the company will always be remembered **FOOL**
for, rather than for their range of drinks.

PART 4

For questions 25–30, complete the second sentence so that it has a similar meaning to the first sentence using the word given. Do not change the word given. Use between three and six words, including the word given.

0 The garage is full of old newspapers that my grandma has collected over the years.

AWAY

The garage is full of old newspapers that my grandma ....has put away....... over the years.

25 Just thinking about flying made Peter break out in a sweat.

THOUGHT

Just .... flying made Peter break out in a sweat.

26 Erin sees life in a very different way to other people.

ON

Erin's .... is very different to that of other people's.

27 I can't concentrate on my work if there is too much noise.

HARD

I find .... on my work if there is too much noise.

28 Fred didn't want to clean the car so he decided to do it later.

OFF

Fred .... the car until later.

29 'I'll leave the office very soon,' said Jenny.

ABOUT

Jenny said that she .... the office.

30 To make a complaint fill out this form.

SHOULD

You need to fill out this form, ... make a complaint.

7 Be seen, be heard

READING

1 Complete the sentences with the correct form of these words.

accommodate entice galvanise inaccessible profess
refrain successive unashamedly

1 Films and plays bring us close to events that might otherwise be ....

2 Although the singer .... to care about poverty in his lyrics, he doesn't help anyone.

3 Vouchers were offered as a way to .... people into the restaurant.

4 The company were .... trying to promote their products at the entrance to the exhibition, even though they hadn't hired a stand inside it.

5 His novel is the result of two years of .... research in local communities.

6 The poet had to change some of his lyrics to .... his editor's requests.

7 She found it difficult to .... from including her personal opinion in the report.

8 His powerful speech .... the audience into action.

2 Read the introduction to the article.
Which of these things is not mentioned?

1 dance routines
2 lighting
3 storylines
4 costumes
5 characters

3 e Read the whole article. For questions 1–10, choose from the musicals (A–D). The musicals may be chosen more than once.

Which musical:

1 exemplifies problems faced by poor people at the time? ....

2 contains moments of optimism? ....

3 uses a variety of devices to show social issues? ....

4 has been exploited for educational purposes? ....

5 isn't based on an existing story? ....

6 contributed to the development of a particular genre? ....

7 raises questions about the importance of family? ....

8 features references to criminal activity? ....

9 is set against the background of a real historical event? ....

10 has a musical style that is surprising considering the subject matter? ....

The Power of the Musical

Musicals have traditionally been depicted as feel-good productions that gloss over any problems and negative experiences and exploit raw emotions for a show-stopping musical number, rather than dig deeper and explore their causes and effects. Nevertheless, behind the flashy clothes and breath-taking choreography is a potential to tackle darker, more realistic subject matter. Here are four musicals whose plots address social issues.

Musical A

One of the best-known musicals, mainly due to the award-winning feature-length film version, *Les Miserables* paints a vivid picture of the cycle of despair and poverty in which many French citizens were trapped in France in the early 1800s. The climax is set in the 1832 June Rebellion in Paris. Based on the influential nineteenth-century novel by Victor Hugo, the musical has touched theatregoers for decades with its **harrowing** ballads and rousing choruses, which evoke the characters' current desperation and hope for a better future. Despite the questionable morality of some of the characters' actions, setting them to music doesn't **trivialise** them, but rather clarifies the complexity of decision-making for people who find themselves in a constant struggle to achieve a basic standard of living.

Musical B

Dealing with the **bleak** topic of child labour in nineteenth-century Britain is *Oliver!*, a musical based on Charles Dickens's gritty classic novel *Oliver Twist*, which has enjoyed several successful runs on London's West End over the past half a century. The musical follows the story of orphan Oliver from his hard days living in the tough workhouses to an equally difficult life as a street boy under the watchful eye of an older boy who is skilled in pickpocketing. While the music portrays the issues facing abandoned children living in poverty, such as the upbeat 'Food, glorious, food', which captures the characters' excitement at satisfying their hunger, the costume design also highlights the difference between rich and poor. The former are clothed in **opulent** costumes and the latter in **rags** with dirt on their faces. While the reality of life in capital cities is different nowadays, the musical still emphasises the vulnerability and loneliness of children without a support network.

Musical C

Perhaps less known to modern audiences, but no less ground-breaking in the way it **tackles** relevant social issues, is *The Cradle Will Rock*. First hitting the stage on Broadway in the 1930s, and having at least five subsequent revivals, its operatic score underlines lyrics addressing the struggles of working-class America. Using a groundbreaking original script, it explores a small town's attempt to put together a workers' union to fight against the corruption of a local businessman who controls most of the town's business dealings. The contrast involved in telling a tale that focuses on working-class people through a genre generally associated with the upper classes makes this musical truly original and it is said that it helped pave the way for other playwrights to write stories based on related subjects.

Musical D

A popular choice for high-school drama clubs, due to its handling of multiculturalism and identity, *West Side Story* is a melodramatic musical set in New York City in the 1950s. Borrowing the central theme from the ever-popular Shakespearean romance, *Romeo and Juliet*, the musical focuses on the relationship between two teenagers who belong to rival gangs in a working-class neighbourhood. The two gangs are separated not only by their intense dislike of each other, but also by their ethnic backgrounds with one gang being first- and second-generation Puerto Ricans and the other white Americans. The songs are catchy and the choreography impressively energetic, alongside a storyline that explores hatred and discrimination as barriers to **social cohesion** between different ethnic groups. In spite of changes in society since the first performance in 1957, the themes at the forefront of the musical haven't **dated** and can be seen in modern societies around the world.

---

4 Match the words in bold in the article with these meanings.

1 luxurious ....

2 deals with something ....

3 make seem less important ....

4 become old-fashioned ....

5 old, used cloth ....

6 without hope ....

7 upsetting ....

8 unity amongst a group of people ....

GRAMMAR

past modals

1 Match the modals in bold in the sentences (1–6) with these words.

| certainty (x2)   criticism   necessity   possibility (x2) |

1 You **may well not** know that forty-three percent of the world's population is under twenty-five. The future is ours! ....

Reply   Like

2 Today's social problems **could have been** avoided, if we'd been more informed. ....

Reply   Like

3 I **needed to** feel that I was contributing to society, and so I joined a local youth group. ....

Reply   Like

4 The Youth Forum event **must have been** amazing because there were people from over 200 countries! ....

Reply   Like

5 World poverty **should have been** eradicated by now. We must make it our goal. ....

Reply   Like

6 You **will have** heard about us on social media. Everyone is talking about us! ....

Reply   Like

2 Choose the correct answer (A or B) to complete the sentences.

1 We ought to have known that social media .... the key to success.

  A would be   **B** hadn't been

2 I wouldn't have thought about doing voluntary work .... for my friend Sam.

  A if it hadn't been   **B** if it wasn't

3 If I'd written to my political representative, I .... put a stop to this earlier.

  A must have   **B** could have

4 I was needlessly .... that people wouldn't take me seriously.

  A worried   **B** thinking

5 We only got one response so we .... just as well have not bothered.

  A should   **B** might

3 🔊 7.1 Listen and check your answers to Ex 2. Are the statements True (T) or False (F)?

1 Mark isn't that impressed by social media. ....
2 Alexia's parents supported her in her decision. ....
3 Simon is a keen cyclist and has been cycling for years. ....
4 Sally thinks that parties on the beach should be banned. ....
5 Joanna got advice before starting the petition. ....

4 Choose the correct words to complete the text.

●●● ◁ ▷   🔍 🏠

Supporting local projects ↑

Detroit Soup was set up by a group of people in Detroit who felt that small-scale community projects **¹needed / had** to have a voice in the local area. The idea was quite innovative and the events **²would / could** have been a failure, but they were a great success. I'm sure you **³will / might** have heard of the name 'Detroit Soup', but you **⁴may / could** well not be familiar with how they work, so I'll try to explain. Detroit Soup is a crowdfunding event for local people and local projects. You pay a small entry fee for a bowl of soup and local groups spend five minutes explaining why they need the funding. You vote for the best idea and the winners take the money. So simple! This **⁵may / could** not have hit social media yet, but it will soon because the events are gaining momentum around the country. I spoke to a couple of participants. This is what they said:

'I came here tonight to get funding for my start-up. I **⁶should / ought** to have prepared my pitch a little better, I think, as I didn't get many votes. I'll be back though as it's been such a fun evening!'

'Such a great way of encouraging local ideas and local businesses. I **⁷would / could** have come to these events before if I had known they were going to be such fun.'

'If you'd told me a few years ago that soup would be a way of raising money I **⁸might / should** not have believed you. But seeing it with my own eyes today, I can see that it can be.'

VOCABULARY

communicating

1 Complete the text with these phrases.

a way with words   for want of a better word
have your say   hold back   in a word   say it as it is
sit up and take notice   tongue-tied

Is graffiti vandalism? Vote now!

What do you think about graffiti? Tell us what you really think, don't ¹.. . Write in now and ².. .

Graffiti is vandalism and I wish people would ³.. , and see what's really happening. Jack.

Good for you Jack! ⁴.. , that's what I say. I'm sick of this nonsense about self-expression. Doris

Graffiti is creative, graffiti is expression, graffiti is inspirational. Graffiti is, ⁵.. , art. Sally

Sally you've got ⁶.. ! I couldn't have said it better myself. Graffiti IS art. Jim

Speaking from personal experience, I'd say that graffiti is positive. My son Alex used to be painfully shy and would get ⁷.. at any social event. He found graffiti, or graffiti found him and, ⁸.. , graffiti saved him. Sarah

2 Choose the correct options to complete the paragraphs about Banksy.

Who is Banksy?

Banksy has always striven to remain anonymous and it looks as if he **¹has got his own way / is on his own way**. What do we know about him? **²In a word / For want of a better word**, little. We know he's a graffiti artist often hailed as the most exciting British artist in decades and who has made the art world **³sit up and take notice / have the last word**. He gives no interviews and needs no publicity as his reputation is all through **⁴a way with words / word of mouth**.

Banksy's back at school!

In Banksy's home town of Bristol people **⁵don't hold back / sit up and take notice** from singing his praises or from shining **⁶the light on / a spotlight on** his work. Recently a primary school named a school house after him. Banksy secretly painted a mural in the playground as a 'present', leaving a note saying 'it's always easier to get forgiveness than permission'. When the children found it the following day they couldn't **⁷put / place** into words how surprised they were. Banksy always has **⁸the last word / a lasting word**!

Extend

3 Complete the text with these words.

accessible   articulate   convoluted   eloquent
short and sweet   verbose

Tips for getting your message across

Graffiti, poetry or prose are all forms of communication; about getting your message across to your audience. People don't like long, rambling messages, so be ¹.......................... . Messages which use too many words and are ².......................... are tedious to listen to. So be concise: less is more. Arguments that are ³.......................... can be difficult to follow, so be ⁴.......................... and make your speech easy to understand. Choose your words carefully, be ⁵.......................... , as if you were creating something beautiful. Finally, be careful to pitch the level right because it should be ⁶.......................... and easy to understand.

4 Choose the correct answer (A, B or C) to complete the sentences.

1 I think that Mary should be the one to present our argument as she is so ...., she expresses things so well.

   A articulate   **B** wordy   **C** verbose

2 I think I must have offended him because he was very .... with me this morning.

   A inarticulate   **B** curt   **C** wordy

3 You should make some cuts. The argument's well expressed, but it's far too long and ....

   A inarticulate   **B** convoluted   **C** wordy.

4 The plot to this film is so complicated and .... that I just can't follow it.

   A verbose   **B** convoluted   **C** short and sweet

LISTENING

1 You are going to listen to three different extracts. Read the questions and answer options and underline the key words in the answers.

Extract 1

You are going to listen to a conversation between a lecturer and a design student about a project on the originality of fashion.

1 How did the girl feel about being given clothes by her grandmother?

A relieved to have fashionable clothes

B inspired to create her own clothes

C pleased to be able to share her love of fashion

2 According to the lecturer, originality in fashion is being devalued because designers

A only know how to make minimal changes to existing products.

B have to compete with large brands.

C don't have enough time to come up with new ideas.

Extract 2

You are going to listen to a conversation between two friends about electronic devices.

3 How does the boy react to his friend's new phone?

A He complains that it looks just like his.

B He argues that cheaper phones last longer.

C He explains that his friend could have saved money.

4 How does the girl feel about copycat products?

A annoyed that they are so easy to produce

B sad about their impact on originality

C frustrated that nothing is done about them

Extract 3

You are going to listen to a conversation between a girl and her brother about books.

5 What is the girl doing?

A complaining about the predictability of stories

B worrying about finishing reading a book for school

C defending her favourite story genre

6 What do they both emphasise about good stories?

A the individuality of the writer's voice

B the ability to recognise the writer's influences

C the memorable characters

2 e ◀)) 7.2 Listen to the three extracts. For questions 1–6 in Ex 1, choose the answer (A, B or C) which fits best according to what you hear.

3 ◀)) 7.3 Replace the highlighted words in the sentences (1–6) with the correct form of these words. Listen to the recording again and check your answers.

blatantly   ploy   push   shell out   swipe   tweak

1 Shops are always encouraging .... consumers to buy their new products.

2 I guess it's just a trick .... to get us to spend more money.

3 I can't believe that you spent .... so much money.

4 It involved copying a plot and altering .... a few minor details.

5 It wasn't obviously and intentionally .... copying a plot.

6 He was advocating stealing .... other writers' ideas.

time out

Throughout history, inventions have been ripped-off or copied from other people. So much so, that sometimes the inventor of the object is disputed.

Below are some people/businesses connected to well-known inventions. Match the inventions (1–6) with the people/businesses (A–F).

1 the radio

2 the lightbulb

3 the telephone

4 the smartphone

5 the search engine

6 the car

A Nikola Tesla / Guglielmo Marconi

B IBM / Apple

C Archie / Google

D Henry Ford / Karl Benz

E Thomas Edison / Joseph Swan

F Alexander Graham Bell / Antonio Meucci

Choose two of these inventions. Research the contributions of the people/businesses.

USE OF ENGLISH 1

1 Complete the text with the correct form of the verb in brackets.

So what if it's a forgery?

1 Expert, Ian Charusse alleged that forgery of famous art .... (increase) year on year, over the previous decade.

2 Last night on the news it was announced that a famous German art forger .... (release) from jail.

3 He swore that he .... (know) the gravity of his crime.

4 Art critics claimed that Michelangelo .... (create) forgeries.

5 Eighty percent of people interviewed regretted .... (buy) a forgery.

6 Twenty percent of people interviewed said that they .... (decide) to buy a copy rather than the real painting.

2 Complete the reported statements using the correct past form of these verbs.

complain convince encourage estimate hope
recommend regret worry

1 'I am so very sure that the painting I bought is an original.'
He ....

2 'You should buy art from a reputable dealer.'
She ....

3 'It doesn't bother me if it's a forgery.'
He ....

4 'This painting is far too expensive.'
She ....

5 'We think that the German artist copied about fifty European artists.'
They ....

6 'We want to believe that our painting isn't a forgery.'
They ....

7 'I wish I hadn't bought the painting'
He ....

8 'You should go to the exhibition, you'll enjoy it.'
She ....

3 Choose the correct words to complete the sentences.

1 They asked us **on / of / for** our opinion.

2 She said that she hoped **for / on / that** a miracle to happen.

3 He insisted **about / on / with** the authenticity of the painting.

4 We asked people **how / which / what** their opinions were.

5 She claimed **for / that / in** the painting was an original.

6 The woman objected **to / for / with** completing the survey.

4 ⓔ Complete the second sentence so that it has a similar meaning to the first sentence using the word given. Do not change the word given. Use between three and six words.

Fake or designer?

1 We think that the first forgery dates back to the High Renaissance.
IS
The first forgery .... back to the High Renaissance.

2 'If you sell me counterfeit goods then I will report the company to the police,' he said.
THREATENED
He .... to the police if the goods were counterfeit.

3 'Do you think buying fake designer goods affects the original designer?'
WHETHER
We were asked .... buying fake designer goods affects the original designer.

4 It is thought that the three men were selling fake goods.
HAVE
The three men .... selling fake goods.

5 He thought it would be a good idea for me to check the authenticity of the painting.
ADVISED
He .... painting was authentic.

6 This painting is authentic because it has a signature on the back, she said.
REVEALED
She .... because it had a signature on the back.

USE OF ENGLISH 2

1 Write the noun form of the verbs (1–7). Use the clues to write the last verb and then its noun (number 8).

1	duplicate	....	Clue: the third letter
2	break	....	Clue: the second letter
3	defend	....	Clue: the fourth letter
4	close	....	Clue: the fourth letter
5	offend	....	Clue: the seventh letter
6	confuse	....	Clue: the last letter
7	treat	....	Clue: the last letter
8	....	....	

2 Match the suffixes (1–8) with the verbs (A–H) according to the nouns they make.

1	a/ence	**A**	commit	treat
2	ication	**B**	defend	offend
3	ment	**C**	dismiss	approve
4	al	**D**	decide	confuse
5	ure	**E**	depend	dominate
6	(t)ion	**F**	close	press
7	ce	**G**	elect	substitute
8	sion	**H**	qualify	identify

3 **e** Use the word given in capitals at the end of some lines to form a word that fits in the gap in the same line.

Extend

4 Make nouns from these verbs using the correct suffix (1–6).

criticise   disturb   impress   involve   relate   survive

1	-ship	....	**4** -ment	....
2	-ism	....	**5** -ion	....
3	-ance	....	**6** -al	....

5 Complete the sentences with the nouns from Ex 4.

Tips for client presentations

1 The audience's first .... of you is important, so dress appropriately and smile as they walk in!

2 Don't get flustered by .... during the presentation.

3 Thank the members of audience for contributions to the presentation, even if their .... was minimal.

4 Don't take .... personally; use it to improve future presentations.

5 Talk to members of the audience after the presentation; this helps to strengthen your .... with potential clients.

6 For more tips, check out my free e-book, which is a .... guide for first-time presenters.

Don't let bad habits ruin your presentation

We know that lack of preparation and a sloppy appearance is guaranteed to make a bad impression, but even with careful preparation, you can still make mistakes.

For example, when something goes wrong, such as an equipment
¹..................... or typos in the handouts, you'll be tempted to   **FAIL**
²..................... , but you shouldn't. Saying sorry could create a   **APOLOGY**
bad start and portray you as someone lacking in ³..................... .   **CONFIDENT**

Keep your cool – it's not your fault so don't make it seem like it is. Likewise,
don't make excuses even if you feel like your ⁴..................... isn't   **PERFORM**
your best, especially as your audience probably hasn't noticed anything
wrong with your ⁵..................... .   **DELIVER**

No matter how you are feeling, you should appear ⁶.....................   **SUITABLE**
enthusiastic – you can't expect other people to be interested in your
presentation if you don't seem to be.

Finally, remember there is ⁷..................... nothing more   **ARGUE**
distracting in a presentation than constant ⁸..................... .   **MOVE**
Shuffling your notes, playing with a strand of hair or rocking backwards and
forwards draws the audience's attention away from the content.

SPEAKING

1 Choose one of the topics below. Use a timer or record yourself and talk about the topic for a minute. Don't worry about the content, just try to guess how long a minute of talking is. Check the timer to see how close to a minute you were.

- a famous leader
- a hobby you love
- some work you've done recently that you're proud of
- a documentary you've enjoyed
- an interesting recent news item

2 Read the long turn task and complete the sentences from a student's talk (1–6) with these words.

---

because first having moving obviously personally
regarding whereas

Your pictures show items from a news broadcast.

Compare two of the pictures and say how relevant the events might be to the television viewers' lives and how the people in the news items might be feeling.

A

B

1 .... of all, of course the people at the rocket launch must be very excited, because it's .... something that you don't see every day.

2 .... the weather – it's a cold snowy day and I guess the people are cold.

3 It's important to show what the weather is like on the news .... people need to know what to expect.

4 ...., I don't always believe in the weather forecasts, but .... said this, pictures of current weather situations are interesting.

5 .... on to comparing these pictures, both pictures show things we can sometimes see on the news.

6 The differences are quite big, one shows an event which is quite unusual .... the other …

3 🔊 7.4 Listen to the talk and check your answers to Ex 2. Which of these pieces of advice has the student not followed?

1 It's always good to say which pictures you're going to talk about.

2 Try to structure your talk logically – first compare, then deal with the first question and finally the second question.

3 Use discourse markers and linking words to organise your talk.

4 Give justification for your opinions where possible.

4 Look at the pictures in Ex 2 again. Read the new task and think about what you are going to say. Try to plan it in your head without making notes.

Your pictures show items from a news broadcast.

Compare two of the pictures and say how the people in the news items might have prepared for these situations and how memorable the situations might be.

5 🄴 Record your response and listen to your recording to check if you followed the advice in Ex 3.

C

WRITING

1 Are these comments about reports and proposals True (T) or False (F)?

1 A report deals with a current or past situation, but a proposal needs to consider a plan for the future. ....

2 A report is usually objective and deals mainly with facts. ....

3 A proposal only uses persuasive language in the conclusion. ....

4 A proposal uses more formal language than a report. ....

5 A report uses headings whereas a proposal just has paragraphs and bullet points. ....

6 In both a report and a proposal the writer needs to give an opinion. ....

2 Tick what the summary section of a proposal should do.

1 contain detailed information ☐

2 refer back to the objectives of the proposal ☐

3 use different phraseology from the rest of the proposal ☐

4 contain strongly expressed opinion ☐

5 repeat the same information as before ☐

3 Read the writing task and the sections from a model answer. Match the headings (1–5) with the sections (A–E).

> You and some students at your school would like to set up a school radio station to broadcast during breaks and lunchtimes. You decide to write a proposal to the principal of your school making suggestions about a possible school radio station.
>
> In your proposal you should outline how the station could be run, suggest what type of items it might broadcast and explain how it would benefit the students at your school.
>
> Write **220–260** words

1 Introduction ....

2 Reasons for having a radio station ....

3 What the station would broadcast ....

4 How the station would be run ....

5 Summary ....

A We would suggest that the station is manned by student volunteers from different year groups. There could be a school club dedicated to the station where students meet, plan and record different items to be broadcast.

B We strongly believe that a radio station such as this would bring students together and involve them more in school life as well as giving students the opportunity to be involved in organising a very exciting project. We really hope that this proposal will be given consideration.

C Students like to be involved in school life and keep updated with school news. They can currently do this through the school website and newsletters, but a radio station would be more immediate and also entertaining at the same time.

D The purpose of this proposal is to present the idea of setting up a school radio station which students could listen to during their breaks and free time in the school day.

E We believe that students would enjoy listening to class discussions or debates and hearing students talk about their achievements and trip experiences. There could also be interviews with teachers and local people. For example, we could invite local businessmen to give interviews about work prospects and careers advice. Other ideas would include phone-in programmes where students can discuss school issues and song-request sections with music by school bands and groups.

4 Read the writing task and plan your proposal.

1 Decide which headings you will use.

2 Make notes about what you will include in each section.

3 Think about style and the functional language you might use.

> You and some students at your school would like to make a weekly video report about school news to post on the school website. You decide to write a proposal to the Principal asking for some free time from lessons and funding for the equipment needed to continue with the project.
>
> In your proposal you should outline the purpose of the weekly report, explain what the project would involve and clarify what you would need to set the project in motion.

5 e Write your proposal in 220–260 words.

UNIT CHECK

1 Complete the email with these verb phrases.

could have had   could have phoned   had needed to see   might just as well
ought to have known   should have   shouldn't have been waiting   will have heard

Hi Melanie

I hope all is well with you. I guess you
¹ .... from Lucy about my blazing
argument with Mike. He is being so unreasonable. I got here
three days ago and he phoned me for the first time yesterday!
He ² .... me earlier! He said that
he ³ .... his mates and that I
⁴ .... for him to call. What a cheek!
I ⁵ .... an accident for all he knew.
Thinking about it I ⁶ .... just ignored
his call yesterday.

He wouldn't listen to my point of view and I
⁷ .... have been talking about
anything. I ⁸ .... that this holiday
was going to be difficult because he has been really down recently.

Anyway, enough about me. How are you getting on?

2 Report the statements using these verbs.

announce   encourage   expect   grumble   reassure   recommend   swear   warn

1 'Don't worry you will pass the exam,' she said.

....

2 'I promise that I will look after it,' he said.

....

3 'You should be very careful because it's hot,' he said.

....

4 'Go on, try it,' she said.

....

5 'I think that they will arrive at about 7 p.m.,' he said.

....

6 'If I were you, I'd buy an electric one,' she said.

....

7 'I am going to have a baby,' she said.

....

8 'The lessons are so boring,' he said.

....

3 Match the sentence halves.

1 I won't go back on my word,

2 I can't put into words

3 I don't need to do any publicity because

4 You always have to have the last word

5 At moments like this

6 In a word,

7 You have a way with words as

8 The business owners were worried about, for want of a better word,

A competition.

B you always seem to know what to say.

C no matter what we argue about.

D I promise.

E it's all word of mouth.

F words fail me. I can't think what to say.

G how grateful I am for your help.

H appalling.

4 Choose the correct words to complete the sentences.

Tips for speaking in public

1 Don't talk for too long. Keep it short and **simple** / **sweet**.

2 Try to **put** / **turn** what you are feeling into words.

3 If you include some real questions, then your audience will **sit** / **stand** up and take notice.

4 Even if you don't have a way with **phrases** / **words**, you can still give a good public speech.

5 If you have something that you think is worth saying, then don't **handle** / **hold** back. Say it!

6 Make your arguments clear and to the **dot** / **point**. Don't complicate matters.

7 If you are angry about something, then **say** / **tell** it as it is.

8 When dealing with audience questions, don't let the audience **walk** / **run** all over you. Be assertive.

8 Healthy body, healthy mind

READING

1 Complete the text with these words / phrases.

> brevity   laudable   no-holds barred
> time constraints   vilify   wordy

Notes from health campaign workshop

A health campaign is a ¹.. project, but you need to think carefully about the aims for it to be successful.

Avoid making printed information too ².. — simplicity and ³.. are key.

Don't ⁴.. people's habits or actions, this sounds too authoritarian. Keep it upbeat!

Remember the ⁵.. you have, especially for nationwide campaigns — implementing them can be a lengthy process.

If launching a social media campaign with a comments section, be prepared for people making comments with ⁶.. . Think about who will moderate this.

2 Read the questions (1–4) in Ex 3 and underline the key information. Then scan the text for similar information. Remember that the opinions will be phrased in different ways to the question.

3 🅮 Read the texts again. For questions 1–4, choose from the commenters (A–D).

Which commenter:

1 expresses a similar opinion to A about the intentions of health campaigns? ....

2 holds a different opinion to the other commentators about the effectiveness of health campaigns? ....

3 has the same opinion as D about more practical ways of dealing with health issues? ....

4 holds the same view as C about the way campaigns address certain age groups? ....

4 Match the expressions in bold in the text with these meanings.

1 listen to a piece of advice: ....

2 focus your energy on something: ....

3 copy what other people are doing because you want to feel a part of it: ....

4 not look at something again because you don't think it's important: ....

5 avoiding: ....

6 repeating the same mistakes: ....

7 very similar to something else: ....

8 the idea something is based on: ....

5 Complete the sentences with the correct form of an expression from Ex 4.

1 The campaigners didn't .... about cultural sensitivities and their campaign was a flop.

2 If I were you, I would .... of that topic because it's too controversial.

3 They have a new marketing team to avoid the campaign .... as previous campaigns.

4 I used old photos in my ads and now everyone is .... and doing the same.

5 I'm sure we can make this campaign a success if we ....

6 The .... behind the campaign was that teenagers listen more to their peers.

7 The poster was so subtle that no one ....

8 Putting together a health campaign is .... telling a story.

Health Campaigns: Do They Work?

A Miguel

When you're a teenager like me, it can sometimes feel like you are being bombarded with information on how you should live your life, as if you aren't capable of making your own decisions. There are already so many people in your life trying to guide you on appropriate behaviour and imposing rules, that it's tiresome to encounter the same sort of thing on social media. I understand that social media is an easy way to reach people and it makes sense that health organisations have a responsibility to make information available to people, but too many of them are taking out social media ads for their campaigns. They all seem to preach warnings about supposedly inappropriate behaviour: don't eat this, avoid drinking that, under no circumstances should you do this, but that is acceptable. I do agree with the **principle** behind public health campaigns and recognise that in some cases this may be the only way of ensuring that information reaches the masses. However, it would be no bad thing to limit them. Surely the more we are exposed to hard-hitting messages, the less effective they become?

B Gemma

Campaigns need to be backed up with some real help, otherwise they are just pointless. I remember a pretty shocking video last year about the effects of second-hand smoke on children that quickly went viral. Even though it broke viewing records online, I don't think it stopped people smoking. Think about it; disturbing images of the health problems smoke can cause have been on cigarette packets for years and yet people continue to smoke, most of them **don't** even **give** the images **a second glance**. To me, this is because the focus is simply on stopping whatever harmful action is the focus of the campaign, rather than offering alternatives. Consider someone who smokes because they are incredibly stressed; perhaps if the campaign centred on reasons for the unhealthy behaviour and provided support on ways to better manage this, people would be more likely to **heed the warning**.

C Irina

Although it's died down slightly recently, I don't think it's any surprise that social media campaigns have taken off in a way that more traditional campaigns have struggled to achieve. People, especially young people, don't like feeling like they are being talked down to and can usually see through something pretty quickly so sometimes, no matter how well you try to dress it up, a quirky billboard advertisement encouraging teenagers to drink more water becomes less appealing once the audience catches onto the objective behind it. Conversely, social media campaigns get people involved, whether it's throwing a bucket of water over you, taking a silly selfie or striking a ridiculous pose. These exploit society's modern obsession with sharing to raise awareness in a natural way more **akin to** word of mouth promotion. There's always a risk that people will just **jump on the bandwagon** without realising the context behind the trend, but it's usually only a small percentage. Overall, I think that these types of health campaign create a feeling of togetherness, which is crucial.

D Nicolas

As I see it, although the rationale behind health campaigns is admirable, the trouble is that they are often too little, too late. There are a lot of social media health campaigns that target people aged in their late teens, like me, about eating healthily. I know that I eat too much fast food, but it's become a habit over the past few years and so it's more difficult to change it. The same applies to all of my friends. I'm not saying that I can't change my habits, of course anyone can change if they really **put their mind to it**, but I think that health campaigns would be more effective if they looked more at preventing unhealthy behaviours before they start. I struggle with my weight and I'm sure that wouldn't be the case if I hadn't got used to grabbing a burger or chips after school with my friends. When I noticed my younger brother **falling into the same pattern**, I talked to him about **steering clear** of too many fatty foods and I think that health campaigns should mirror this kind of model.

GRAMMAR

the passive

1 Match the examples (1–5) with the uses (A–D). For one use, there are two examples.

What do we know about stress?

1 Time constraints and hectic lifestyles are **believed to be** the main causes of stress.

2 Although little talked about, both good and bad stress **are known to** exist.

3 Knowing your own stress threshold **is said to be** important in controlling stress.

4 Techniques such as yoga **are widely used** to combat stress.

5 **It is said that** stress changes the neurochemical makeup of the body.

A the agent is unknown, unimportant or assumed (or to be diplomatic)

B the agent is too wordy or complex to front the sentences / the agent is new, interesting or surprising and the end position gives it more impact

C fronting a sentence with *it* to draw a conclusion, be more tentative, or avoid giving more specific information about the agent

D an alternative impersonal passive form instead of the 'it' fronting structure

2 Complete the text with these phrases.

> are said to increase   be put off   have been shattered
> having jobs done   need to be   thought to be
> weren't made to be   will be halved

Life hacks to cope with stress

1 Don't .... from making mistakes. They may be vilified, but it can be a positive experience.

2 If your dreams .... , then look to the future. Don't dwell on the past. '

3 Living outside your comfort zone is .... a positive experience — so embrace it.

4 Problems .... if you talk to your friends about them.

5 If you .... supported by friends at times, this is completely normal. We all need our friends.

6 Procrastination and putting off jobs .... stress levels.

7 It may be laudable to want to be perfect, but the truth is we .... perfect.

8 Remember that there is nothing wrong with .... for you. Accept help from others.

3 Rewrite the sentences in the passive, omitting the agent.

1 The doctor asked me to answer some questions related to anxiety.

....

2 Our teacher told us to think of ways to deal with stress.

....

3 My friends gave me a weekend away for my birthday.

....

4 The editor of the magazine asked readers to send in ideas for relaxation.

....

5 A helicopter took the guests to a spa retreat for the day.

....

6 The camera crew are filming the event later today.

....

7 Experts tell us that knowing our stress threshold is important.

....

8 The judges are giving him an award this evening.

....

VOCABULARY

expressing emotions

1 Use the clues to complete the crossword.

Across

4 speak or shout at length in an angry, impassioned way (4)

5 make a high-pitched piercing cry or sound (6)

7 laugh lightly and repeatedly, from amusement, nervousness, or embarrassment (6)

8 extremely strong reaction of anger, shock, or indignation (7)

Down

1 extreme anger (5)

2 smile in a self-satisfied way (5)

3 half-suppressed, typically scornful laugh (7)

6 express grief by shedding tears and crying (4)

2 Choose the correct words to complete the texts.

What makes you feel happy?   → follow

My best friend. He's always offering to do things for me. He's really **¹considerate / compassionate** in that way.

Helping others. I can really **²empathise / sympathise** with people who choose to work in the caring professions. We all **³groan / moan** far too much about trivial things in life rather than showing **⁴compassion / consideration** for people who really do need help.

Making videos. If I feel depression coming on, I do something creative like making videos and it really lifts my **⁵gloomy / grumpy** mood.

3 🔊 8.1 Listen to people talking about what makes them angry and complete the sentences.

What makes you feel angry? → follow

When people borrow my things without asking it drives me insane, and I just can't help letting
¹ ....

When I have to re-take exams in the summer when my friends have holiday, I just have to
² ....

When I feel that someone is not treating me with respect then I have to ³ .... and tell them how I feel.

I can't stand cruelty to animals and if I catch people doing it, then I really lose control and
⁴ ....

If people change my plans without my permission, then I am not happy, and you can tell by my
⁵ ....

4 Complete the text with these words.

---

chuckling   fed up   groan   laugh   let rip   outraged   ranting
shaken up   sympathise   weep

Happiness is no laughing matter

I ask the question, 'What makes you happy?' and I can hear you ¹ .... with despair because you have heard this question *so* many times before. I do ² .... with you because I feel the same. We are ³ .... with hearing about it.

OK, so we've had a ⁴ .... about it, now let's be serious. Life can be hard at times and we can get stressed. Ask yourself the following. Over the past week, have you been so ⁵ .... by something or someone that you have to just ⁶ ....? Or have you been so ⁷ .... by a tragic news event that it makes you want to ⁸ ....? We don't need to be relentlessly cheerful, but a little less ⁹ .... about the bad stuff, and more ¹⁰ .... about the funny stuff may be a good start.

LISTENING

1 You will hear a nutritionist, Rebecca, talking to a group of students about food. Look at the gapped sentences, which summarise the talk. Think about what type of word (verb, noun, adverb, etc.) might go in each gap.

1 Rebecca claims that most people are .... that food plays an important role in our lives.

2 Rebecca describes the amount of plastic used to wrap food as ....

3 Rebecca uses the word .... to describe her feelings about global food distribution.

4 Rebecca finds it amusing that people refer to cultural starvation practices as ....

5 Rebecca feels that Rob's claims are ...., and this worries her.

6 Rebecca believes that people's diet requirements are influenced by their ....

7 Rebecca is particularly worried about liquid meals being available to the ....

8 Rebecca advises people who follow extreme food practices that negative .... aren't immediately apparent.

2 🔵 🔊 **8.2 Listen to the talk. For questions 1–8 in Ex 1, complete the sentences with a word or short phrase.**

3 Complete the sentences with these words / phrases.

---

ailments   fasts   manifests   scepticism   susceptible
trial and error   upcoming   wreaked havoc

---

1 Francis has been complaining to the doctor about her various ...., even though she has no treatable symptoms.

2 Sam is preparing for his .... talk on food preparation techniques in ancient cultures.

3 Despite the .... surrounding his diet plan, the nutritionist has sold thousands of copies of his book.

4 Surely there must be a better way to work out a solution than by .... ?

5 Not drinking enough water causes dehydration, which quickly .... itself with headaches.

6 Many cultures take part in yearly ...., in which people can only eat after a certain time.

7 The import ban .... on the food industry, causing many companies to lose millions.

8 Not getting enough protein can make athletes more .... to injury.

USE OF ENGLISH 1

1 Match words from A with words from B to make compound nouns.

A balanced fire-proof five-year-old fussy growing increasingly dangerous long-standing long-term slowly cooked sweet

B amount boy diet eater food problem relationship tooth tradition vest

2 Put the compound nouns in Ex 1 into the correct place in the table.

adjective + noun	compound adjective + noun	compound adjective with adverb + noun

3 Decide whether these words apply to ingredients (I), food (F) or vegetables (V).

1 freshly-picked ....
2 processed ....
3 frozen ....
4 reliably sourced ....
5 convenience ....
6 local ....

4 Replace the highlighted phrases with compound nouns.

If we eat ¹food cooked slowly, the food is more tender and has more taste.

....

²Food cooked at home is healthier than ³food which is processed.

....

Most ⁴problems with health can be improved with ⁵exercise on a regular basis.

....

5 e Read the text and complete the gaps with one word only.

Foods to make us smile

We all remember how as children we used to be criticised for eating too much chocolate and sweets and then praised ¹........................... eating our greens. It makes sense when we ²........................... back, because the danger of sugar is a growing problem ³........................... has a long-lasting effect on our health. Most people love chocolate regardless of whether they have a sweet tooth or ⁴..........................., but it's not such an innocuous treat. The happy buzz that we feel after eating chocolate is short lived and after we are left in a grumpy mood. But don't ⁵........................... depressed, as experts have come ⁶........................... with a list of foods that can put a smile on our faces. Not ⁷........................... are they healthy, but they also boost our endorphins leaving us feeling happier. Some foods are endorphin-releasing foods which means ⁸........................... by eating them we feel happier.

Extend

6 Complete the text with these words / phrases.

best-kept far-reaching guitar hectic high-performing hour and a half's little-known serious updated well-trained

─ live smarter ─

Try to juggle a ¹........................... social life with studies, homework, exams, ²........................... practice ... and you'll end up with a ³........................... loss of sleep. The next day you'll struggle to keep awake during the tedious ⁴........................... journey to college, and then it all starts again! Sleep is essential and ⁵........................... students, who are studying hard, need to sleep.

Follow our smart life hacks if you want to achieve ⁶........................... change in your life.

* It's a ⁷........................... fact, but sleeping in a cold room can boost your metabolism.
* The ⁸........................... secret for great skin is to use face cream with UV protection all year.
* Get organised! Make sure that you have ⁹........................... software, which will correct the latest bugs.
* Join a gym and find a ¹⁰........................... instructor to put you through your paces.

USE OF ENGLISH 2

1 Complete the lists of collocations (1–6) with these words.

> acquaintance   adherence   break   contact   gold   reliance

1 close: call, range, ...

2 heavy: fine, rainfall, ...

3 tough: luck, call, ...

4 solid: build, concentration, ...

5 strict: law, control, ...

6 casual: glance, observer, ...

2 Correct the highlighted mistakes in the sentences.

1 My Pilates instructor bears such a casual .... resemblance to my mum!

2 If you use someone else's gym pass, you risk getting a solid .... fine.

3 Training for a marathon is close .... going at first.

4 There is no tough .... evidence to back up the scientist's claims.

5 To the strict .... observer, Polly looks fragile, but she's really very strong.

6 Following a tough ...., protein-based diet helps repair muscles after training.

3 Read the text and decide which answer (A, B, C or D) best fits each gap.

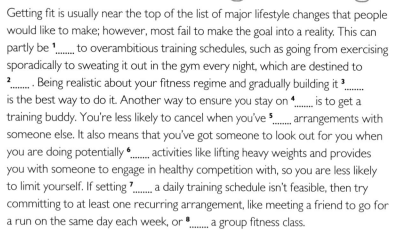

Why you shouldn't train solo

Getting fit is usually near the top of the list of major lifestyle changes that people would like to make; however, most fail to make the goal into a reality. This can partly be **1**...... to overambitious training schedules, such as going from exercising sporadically to sweating it out in the gym every night, which are destined to **2**...... . Being realistic about your fitness regime and gradually building it **3**...... is the best way to do it. Another way to ensure you stay on **4**...... is to get a training buddy. You're less likely to cancel when you've **5**...... arrangements with someone else. It also means that you've got someone to look out for you when you are doing potentially **6**...... activities like lifting heavy weights and provides you with someone to engage in healthy competition with, so you are less likely to limit yourself. If setting **7**...... a daily training schedule isn't feasible, then try committing to at least one recurring arrangement, like meeting a friend to go for a run on the same day each week, or **8**...... a group fitness class.

1 A blamed   **B** put   **C** allocated   **D** attributed

2 A fail   **B** fall   **C** miss   **D** lose

3 A up   **B** on   **C** into   **D** around

4 A track   **B** path   **C** route   **D** way

5 A did   **B** made   **C** met   **D** caused

6 A unhealthy   **B** tiring   **C** risky   **D** tedious

7 A out   **B** back   **C** in   **D** up

8 A attending   **B** going   **C** participating   **D** assisting

Extend

4 Match the sentence halves to make the correct adjective + noun collocations.

1 The media think that the cyclist is **fair**

2 Although he tried not to show it, Eric's **suspicious**

3 These bright orange T-shirts are **standard**

4 A serious ligament tear meant that getting fit came at a **high**

5 Despite coming a **poor**

6 What we need is someone with a **steady**

A nature meant that it took him a long time to feel comfortable with his personal trainer.

B issue so the instructors are easily identifiable.

C price for Alex.

D second, Sam was just happy to have been able to take part.

E hand to take over the project.

F game because he has a high-profile sponsorship deal.

5 Complete the definitions with the adjective + noun collocations from Ex 4.

1 a tendency to be distrustful of situations or people: ....

2 given to everyone, regardless of preference, size, etc.: ....

3 finishing long behind the person ahead of you: ....

4 someone / a situation open to reasonable criticism: ....

5 have self-control / be calm: ....

6 negative consequences of an action / a choice: ....

SPEAKING

1 Read the comments about turn taking and decide which is correct (A or B).

1 **A:** You should give your opinion about a prompt or a question and then pause to allow your partner to add theirs. If your partner says nothing, then continue yourself.

B: If you are paired with a student who is less confident about speaking than you are, you should try to encourage him/her, for example by asking another question.

2 **A:** If you have a lot of things to say in the collaborative task, keep talking as long as you can as this is your opportunity to show the examiner your language skills.

B: If you have a lot to say about a prompt, limit the length of time you speak to show that you understand turn taking.

3 **A:** If you are paired with a strong student who has a lot to say, allow him/her to give an opinion and then interrupt politely.

B: If your partner doesn't stop talking, just start talking yourself as you need to show the examiner your language skills, too.

2 🔊 8.3 Listen to the extracts. Which comments in Ex 1 do they illustrate?

Extract 1 .... Extract 2 .... Extract 3 ....

3 Put the words in the correct order to make expressions for interrupting politely and asking for clarification.

1 sorry / I'm / to / interrupt, / but / really / …

....

2 me, / say / excuse / can / just / that / I / …

....

3 mean / not / I / you / I'm / understand / what / sure / .

....

4 was / what / that / sorry, / ?

....

5 you / on / like / to / I'd / go / before / say / …

....

6 please / you / that, / could / rephrase / ?

....

7 sorry, / I'm / didn't / that / catch / I / .

....

8 to / just / that / add / like / I'd / …

....

4 Read the collaborative task about how valuable different things are to staying healthy and think about what you would say about each prompt.

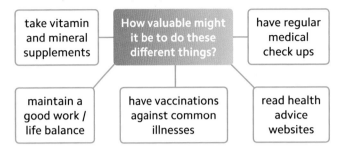

take vitamin and mineral supplements	**How valuable might it be to do these different things?**	have regular medical check ups
maintain a good work / life balance	have vaccinations against common illnesses	read health advice websites

5 e 🔊 8.4 Listen to a student giving his opinion about three of the prompts. Record your own comments after his. Remember to refer to his comment and finish by either moving on or inviting further comment. For one of the recordings you will need to interrupt politely.

6 Listen to your recording. Did you remember to refer to the student's comment and to finish in one of the ways given in Ex 5?

WRITING

1 Read the task and the model answer (without an introduction). Which ideas has the writer used?

> You have listened to a radio discussion about how to teach children about healthy eating from an early age at primary school. You have made the notes below:
>
> **Ways of teaching children about healthy eating at primary school**:
>
> * invite professionals to give talks
> * give easy practical cookery classes
> * watch age-appropriate informational programmes
>
> **Some opinions expressed in the discussion:**
>
> 'Specialists know exactly the right information to give.'
>
> 'Learning by doing is always a good thing.'
>
> 'Animated easy-to-follow documentaries would be a fun way of learning.'
>
> Write an essay for your teacher discussing two of the ways in your notes to teach children about healthy eating at primary school. You should explain **which way you think is more effective**, giving reasons to support your opinion.
>
> You may make use of the opinions expressed in the discussion, but you should use your own words as far as possible.

[Introduction ....]

One way this could be done at primary school would be to ask professionals such as chefs and nutritionists to the school to talk to the children about food and health. As long as the speakers can engage the children with the topics, this could be a good option as children enjoy a break from the normal classroom routine. However, boring formal speakers might well be demotivating, so the speakers should be chosen with care.

Another option that could be both educational and enjoyable for the children would be basic practical cookery classes linked to nutrition. For example, a project on the importance of fruit and vegetables in our diet could lead to a competition to make the healthiest sandwich.

The problems associated with unhealthy eating certainly need to be addressed at an early age and options such as these could easily be put in place. Getting children practically involved in cooking would be my preferred option as actually doing something teaches us much better than simply being told about it. Children who engage with food in this way are far more likely to eat healthily in their later lives.

2 Match the points (1–3) with the introductions (A–C). Which would be best for the essay in Ex 1?

1 It includes the writer's choice of option. ....

2 It is short and to the point. ....

3 It presents an argument that can be referred back to in the essay. ....

A It is high time that we taught children about healthy eating in primary schools. There are lots of ways to do this.

B Parents don't teach their children about healthy eating so the schools have got to do it. It will cost a lot of money, but there's no alternative. I think getting the children to do cookery is the best answer, but there are others.

C Eating healthily has undoubtedly become an important issue today. The health implications of eating the wrong types of food are significant and it is believed that the earlier children are taught about the importance of eating well the better. While parents have the main responsibility for this, primary schools definitely have an important role to play.

3 Read the essay in Ex 1 again and underline four phrases that link back to the argument in the introduction.

4 Read the exam task and plan your essay.

> You have had a class discussion about why people get into bad eating habits. You have made the notes below:
>
> **Why people get into bad eating habits**:
>
> * eating patterns in childhood
> * advertising of unhealthy foods
> * lack of time to prepare or eat healthy meals
>
> **Some opinions expressed in the discussion:**
>
> 'You can easily get used to having sugary snacks between meals when you're at school.'
>
> 'If you don't see these 'amazing new chocolate bars' in the ads you won't want one, will you?'
>
> 'Fast food is so convenient when you're on the go, but it isn't that good for you.'
>
> Write an essay for your teacher discussing two of the reasons from your notes. You should explain **which is the most important reason why people get into bad eating habits,** giving reasons to support your opinion.
>
> You may make use of the opinions expressed in the discussion, but you should use your own words as far as possible.

5 e Write your essay in 220–260 words.

UNIT CHECK

1 Rewrite the sentences in the passive form, using the verb in bold.

1 We **know** that Vitamin E good for the skin.

....

2 Years ago, people **thought** that salt was good you.

....

3 We now **think** that salt is related to high blood pressure.

....

4 The USA **exports** the majority of walnuts that we eat.

....

5 Mexico **grows** a large amount of the avocados that we eat.

....

6 People usually **encourage** children to eat plenty of fruit and vegetables.

....

7 A few years ago doctors **claimed** that green tea was a miracle drink.

....

8 Scientific discoveries have **shattered** many health myths.

....

2 Complete the sentences with a word from A and a word from B.

A balanced   freshly picked   fussy   growing   home-cooked
   long-standing   processed   sweet

B diet   eater   food (x2)   problem   tooth   tradition   vegetables
---

1 .... is usually better than food which is cooked in restaurants.

2 I love eating chocolate and cakes. In fact, I have a really ....

3 For a healthy diet, cut down on .... which has lots of added sugar and salt.

4 In our village we have a .... of baking plum pies in August.

5 It's important to eat a bit of everything to have a ....

6 My brother is a really .... – there are lots of foods he won't eat.

7 I'm a keen gardener. I think that .... taste better than those in the shops.

8 Obesity is a .... in the Western world and it is a serious health hazard.

3 Choose the correct words to complete the sentences.

1 I was a bit shaken **up / down** by the terrible news. I couldn't believe it.

2 When he heard the news he was furious. He just **lost / found** it and really **let / made** rip.

3 What's wrong with you? You've had a **short / long** face all day. Are you OK?

4 Oh no! My great aunt is staying for two weeks! I'll just have to **grin / smile** and bear it.

5 I need to talk to you. It's something that I just have to get **on / off** my chest.

6 Don't just shoot your **tongue / mouth** off when you are angry. Calm down and relax.

4 Complete the sentences with these words.

---
compassion   consideration   depressed   empathise
gloomy   groan   grumpy   moan   stressed
sympathise
---

1 Just recently I've been feeling very down. I think I might be feeling ....

2 When I told him that he would have to do it again, he let out a ....

3 That's really bad luck. I do .... with you. You poor thing.

4 The room looks so dark and .... You need brighter colours in it to cheer it up.

5 After careful .... , I have decided to apply to the university.

6 Show a bit of .... for other people. You're not the only one with problems, you know.

7 My sister often has a .... to me about her boss. He doesn't treat her well.

8 To be a good social worker, you need to be able to .... with other people.

9 I have so much work to do. I'm feeling quite .... by it all.

10 My father is often in a .... mood in the morning. Later he gets more cheerful.

Leaders and followers

READING

1 Complete the quotes with these words / phrases. There are two words / phrases you do not need.

by default   charisma   draining   get his head round   head up
ideally placed   sizeable   sought out   squabbles   up-and-coming

---

✉¹ 👤 ⚙

'I wouldn't hesitate to recommend Alana. From the very first day, when she was asked to
¹.. a team of her peers, she proved to be confident and talented. Her natural
².. meant that she was a motivating and approachable leader, and she handled minor ³.. in a calm and fair way.'

'Tiago's positive attitude meant that, although he had a ⁴.. share of the responsibilities on a challenging project, he quickly managed to ⁵..
the details. He ⁶..
permanent employees to get advice and as a result was one of the strongest participants on the leadership programme.'

'The demands of her project placement could have been
⁷.. , but Petra handled everything with constant optimism and a refreshing level of professionalism considering her age. I strongly believe that she is ⁸.. to take on a leadership position.'

---

2 Read the article about teenagers who have participated in youth leadership schemes. Which teenagers didn't have a positive experience overall?

1 A, B and C

2 only D

3 C and B

4 only B

3 🄴 Read the article again. For questions 1–10, choose from the teenagers A–D. The teenagers may be chosen more than once.

Which teenager:

1 has kept in contact with the other participants? ....

2 found the experience frustrating? ....

3 enjoyed being given some control? ....

4 mentions developing skills directly
related to working life? ....

5 felt the need to make some plans
after the leadership academy? ....

6 feels that the activities were inappropriate
for the age group? ....

7 gives specific details about the course's program? ....

8 uses examples to emphasise the
negative parts of his/her experience? ....

9 makes a comparison between the
program and everyday life? ....

10 is unenthusiastic about the course content? ....

Youth Leadership Academies

This forum is for exchanging experiences on youth leadership academies. Please follow all rules regarding forum conduct.

A MadelineM

Spending two weeks of my summer holidays at a youth leadership academy wasn't high on my wish list of activities at the end of the term; I've definitely **outgrown** summer camp! That said, right from the very first day, the program exceeded all expectations! The time flew by and I was sad to leave. Without a doubt, the best thing was meeting people from all over the country, exchanging ideas and learning new ways of doing things. Constantly working as a team meant that things **got heated** at times and there were more than a few arguments between different members of the group. It showed us that we have to get on with each other and make the best of each other's skills; after all, we can't just walk out of a job after an argument! Before taking part in the programme, I'd felt reasonably confident about leaving school and starting work, but now I realise just how far I have to go before I'll really be ready for the workplace. So, this term I'm going to join the events committee at school to help out with the student-led events that take place throughout the year.

B GTP01

Towards the end of the last term I'd been feeling the pressure of university applications and was concerned that I hadn't been as involved in extra-curricular activities as I should have been. Nowadays, it's not enough to have an **outstanding** academic record. A lot of universities want you to demonstrate other skills as well, not to mention the fact that these are a requirement for the world of work, too. I was looking forward to the youth academy programme when I signed up for it, but after a couple of days I was already wishing that I hadn't bothered. The tasks that we were given were supposed to **equip** us with real-life skills, but they were all intentionally 'wacky' to appeal to people in my age group. Unfortunately, this just had the opposite effect as it felt like the organisers were trying too hard and were completely out of touch with people my age. Everyone in my group was on the same wavelength as me; we wanted to work seriously and be challenged by something that we might encounter in the future. To be perfectly honest, I came away feeling disappointed and cheated.

C SammyX

I only signed up for the youth leadership academy programme because my parents thought it would be beneficial as something that I could add to my CV, especially because my cousin, who's two years older than me, did it once and it helped her to get her first job. They didn't push me into it, but they strongly recommended it! The programme itself was nothing special; the highlights were getting the chance to improve my coding skills, which I've wanted to do for a while, and the mountaineering team challenge was **a blast**. Apart from that, the biggest impact that the experience had on me was the people that I met. Each participant gets a mentor who is someone that took part in the programme the year before; coincidentally, my mentor had been mentored by my cousin! We **hit it off** straight away and, since the program finished, we've kept in touch. In fact, the three of us have been messaging each other non-stop about a youth academy app, to help young people develop the kinds of skills that the programme practises, but without the costly price tag!

D Me123

Attending a youth leadership summer programme is almost a rite of passage at my college; there are two major universities in our city so there's always a little bit of **rivalry** amongst students as to which one is the best, according to the one you choose to go to. After looking forward to the programme all year, I was thrilled that it didn't disappoint – in fact, I'd probably say that it **surpassed** all of my expectations! It was very full-on as the schedule was packed; every day we were there for eight hours, with at least three different sessions per day. The first few days were less flexible as we did a variety of experiential-based lessons to develop different leadership skills, such as fostering relationships and ethics. Then towards the end of the week we moved onto a group action project, which I preferred because it meant that we could be in the driving seat! At the end of the week, we presented our projects during a day-long event that was sponsored by various companies. Receiving applause from business leaders made me feel really proud, and all the freebies were an added bonus!

---

4 Find words / phrases in the text which mean the following.

1 a feeling of competition between two people ....

2 provide someone with something they need ....

3 became full of angry feelings ....

4 felt too old for something ....

5 was greater or better than ....

6 of very high, impressive quality ....

7 a lot of fun ....

8 like someone as soon as you meet them ....

GRAMMAR

emphatic structures

1 Underline the emphatic structure in each sentence. Match the structures (1–7) with the descriptions (A–D). Some descriptions can be used more than once.

The benefits of joining a club

1 Never before had I spoken in public, but in the debating society I'm getting used to it. ....

2 It's the charismatic people that I have met that make the drama club so amazing. ....

3 What I love about clubs is that I meet people that I wouldn't otherwise have met. ....

4 Not only are they fun, but it's useful because it looks good on my CV. ....

5 It does sometimes feel draining playing sport every week, but I do feel in great shape. ....

6 It's the fact that I am always learning something new that I love.

7 In no way would I say that I am creative, but in this club I am developing creative skills. ....

A inversion after certain negative adverbs or phrases.

B cleft sentences introduced with *it* using relative pronouns.

C use of auxiliary verb when we would not normally use it.

D cleft sentences introduced with *what*.

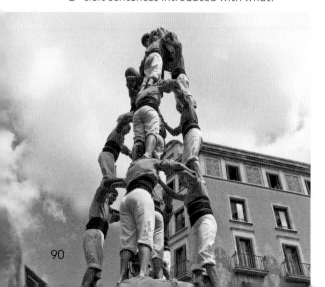

2 Complete the text with these words / phrases.

never   no circumstances   no sooner   no way   not once   not only   what (x2)

The **teamwork** of building human towers

Add comment | Report

I usually find traditional cultural activities boring. However, the Catalan tradition of 'castellers' or competing to build human towers can in ¹ .... be labelled as dull. Groups of people use their bodies to literally construct human towers. The people at the bottom form a solid base upon which the others climb, so ² .... are they incredibly strong, but also very agile. It all happens with clockwork precision and ³ .... has one person got into their position that the next person then climbs up. ⁴ .... impressed me about the spectacle was not only the physical dexterity, but also the synergy. ⁵ .... before had I seen such an example of real teamwork. ⁶ .... also amazed me was the fact that the activity attracts all types of people and all ages. It may sound like a very dangerous activity, but surprisingly ⁷ .... did I witness an accident. I'm sure they must happen, though, and under ⁸ .... should you try this yourselves. But do see them if you can, because they have the edge when it comes to a traditional event!

3 🔊 9.1 Listen to three people talking about 'castellers' and complete the sentences.

1 **A:** What I love about 'castellers' is ....
  B: No way would I ever .... !

2 **A:** Never have I .... 'castellers'.
  B: Under no circumstances would I recommend this to .... heights.

3 **A:** Not only .... I've joined a second group!
  B: Only once ...., when I was ill.

4 🄴 Read the text and complete the gaps with one word only.

A SENSE OF **BELONGING**

I love social media and social media groups. However, usually no sooner have I joined a group ¹ .... I am criticised for wasting my time, and no ² .... would I expect to hear my parents or teachers promoting them. In fact, ³ .... do we hear about the benefits of these groups and under ⁴ .... circumstances would I have imagined that scientists would support them! ⁵ .... may surprise you is that doctors are saying that social groups are important. Apparently, for most people, it is ⁶ .... when we identify with likeminded people ⁷ .... we feel truly secure. They say that a sense of belonging is crucial for happiness and that being a part of a group really ⁸ .... give us the security and sense of purpose that we all crave for.

VOCABULARY

managing and teamwork

1 Complete the text with these words.

collaboratively   ideas   lead   respect   responsibility   stifled   take   tasks

REASONS WHY VOLUNTARY WORK COULD BENEFIT YOU

You learn to be responsible

Each project consists of different jobs and you may find that you have to delegate ¹............................ to others.

Other times you may have to ²............................ the initiative and make decisions for the group.

You learn about teamwork

Teamwork is about working together towards the same goal and working ³............................ . As a team member you may have to look after others to assume ⁴............................ as part of the group.

You do something creative

Sometimes it may feel like our creativity is ⁵............................ by routine. Volunteering can be a way of doing something different and of bouncing ⁶............................ off others in a creative way.

You gain respect from others

It can be an enriching experience in which we can ⁷............................ by example and in doing so can earn the ⁸............................ of others.

2 Choose the correct words to complete the tweets.

#Group projects

→ follow

1   I love working in a group, but I prefer to **take** / **have** a back seat and let others take the lead.

2   We all work on different projects during the morning then we **hold** / **touch** base at lunchtime and decide what is left to do.

3   It's not always easy to make decisions, but we all put our **thoughts** / **heads** together and come up with solutions that we all agree on.

4   I'm the leader of the project. I have complete responsibility and the buck **stops** / **ends** here.

5   It's quite intense working in a group and you need to be a team **player** / **competitor** to really enjoy the experience.

6   One member of our group does next to nothing. Someone should put him in his **position** / **place**.

3 Complete the text with one word in each gap. You have been given the first letter.

Volunteering abroad

We have various types of voluntary work, all with the aim of improving conflict ¹r............................ in countries around the world.

Conservation and the environment
We need teams of people to work ²c............................ in small groups at a marine conservation project in Croatia. The basic ³r............................ is lots of energy – an interest in marine wildlife would be desirable.

Teaching

If you have good ⁴c............................ skills, then you may be interested in teaching young children in India. They need help with simple mathematics and spelling to improve their ⁵p............................ at school.

Building
In Borneo and in Ghana we are looking for people to work on building projects. You don't need finely ⁶h............................ skills or to be trained in construction.

Animal protection
Baboons are in danger of extinction and despite their innate ⁷s............................ strategy in the wild, they need our help. Working at the baboon sanctuary in South Africa is a rewarding experience and the animals trust their helpers ⁸i............................ .

LISTENING

1 You will hear five people talking about taking breaks while working / studying. Look at the two tasks below and make notes about possible synonyms for each of the options.

Task 1

For questions 1–5, choose from the list (A–H) what each speaker says is difficult for them about taking a break.

A recognising the right moment	Speaker 1	**1** ☐
B completing tasks	Speaker 2	**2** ☐
C appearing to be lazy	Speaker 3	**3** ☐
D losing time	Speaker 4	**4** ☐
E dealing with unexpected events	Speaker 5	**5** ☐
F having too much responsibility		
G feeling unproductive		
H feeling pressure to conform		

Task 2

For questions 6–10, choose from the list (A–H) the possible consequence of not taking a break each speaker mentions.

A cause an accident	Speaker 1	**6** ☐
B weight gain	Speaker 2	**7** ☐
C physical pains	Speaker 3	**8** ☐
D poor memory retention	Speaker 4	**9** ☐
E difficulties with colleagues	Speaker 5	**10** ☐
F inability to concentrate		
G lack of energy		
H desire to give up		

2 e 🔊 9.2 **Listen to the speakers and complete the two tasks in Ex 1.**

3 Choose the correct word to complete the definitions.

1 **make a point:** do something in a way that is **deliberate / accidental**
2 **intense:** extreme / very difficult
3 **striking a balance:** giving two things the **same / right** amount of attention
4 **stroll:** a walk at a **quick / relaxed** pace
5 **slump:** something that has gone **down / up** suddenly
6 **unavoidable:** cannot be **seen / prevented**
7 **overruns:** takes longer than **expected / usual**
8 **a quick fix:** a **temporary / permanent** solution

time out

Relaxation is an important ingredient in your efforts to get the most out of studying. There are also other, more bizarre study skills that people use. A few are listed below.

Have you ever tried any of the following while studying?

1 Shouting out the mark you want to get at the top of your lungs.
2 Listening to classical music.
3 Taking regular naps.
4 Connecting information you want to learn with popular songs.
5 Binging on carbohydrates.

Which of these study skills do you think would work for you? Choose one to try next week.

USE OF ENGLISH 1

1 Decide if the statements are formal (F) or informal (I).

1 One of the key factors for success is proof of academic success. ....

2 You should make a list of all your exams that you've passed in a CV. ....

3 In a competitive job market it should never be assumed that academic achievements alone are sufficient. ....

4 What may have been a forgone conclusion a few years ago, does not necessarily hold in today's climate. ....

5 Include stuff like hobbies on your CV. ....

6 Additional information will provide employers with a better insight into your personality. ....

7 For example, if you've done voluntary work it shows that you care about others. ....

8 So think about all the interesting bits that you can add. ....

2 Complete the text with these words.

---

acquisition   importance   increase   performance
re-evaluation   refusal

What do we think about soft skills?

Over the past few years, due to the poor ¹............................ of some countries in global testing there has been a ²............................ of the desired skills for our graduates. This has led to an emphasis on the ³............................ of soft skills, such as communication skills or empathy. In education, we have seen an ⁴............................ in problem-solving tasks and a general understanding of the ⁵............................ of soft skills. However, we have also seen a ⁶............................ from some employers to take soft skills on board.

EMPATHY

TEAM SPIRIT

3 Rewrite the sentences using these nouns to replace the words in bold.

---

argument   complexity   development   difficulty   increase   refusal

---

1 Experts **argue** that soft skills such as empathy and negotiation skills are essential for recruitment.
There is ....

2 The **complex** skill sets needed for twenty-first century jobs are challenging for students.
Students are challenged ....

3 People's understanding of the importance of soft skills is **increasing** rapidly.
There is ....

4 Our knowledge of soft skills has **developed** over the past five years.
There has been ....

5 Some people **refuse** to acknowledge the relevance of soft skills in the workplace.
There is ....

6 It is **difficult** for some people to identify soft skills.
Some people ....

4 ⓔ Complete the second sentence so that it has a similar meaning to the first sentence using the word given. Do not change the word given. Use between three and six words.

1 Interviews tasks are often designed to test how creative a person can be in resolving problems.
CREATIVITY
Interview tasks are often designed to test .... in resolving problems.

2 Some educationalists don't accept that soft skills are important and this puts candidates at a disadvantage.
FAILURE
The .... of soft skills by some educationalists puts some candidates at a disadvantage.

3 The candidate worked hard for the interview and this was evident in her presentation.
WORK
The hard .... the interview was evident in her presentation.

4 Some people are confused as to what the format of skills-based interviews consists of.
CONFUSION
There .... to the format of skills-based interviews.

5 Skills-based interviews aim to assess how candidates perform in different situations.
PERFORMANCE
Skills-based interviews aim to assess the .... in different situations.

6 People are competing more than they used to for jobs in the digital marketing industry.
COMPETITION
There is .... used to be for jobs in the digital marketing industry.

USE OF ENGLISH 2

1 Match these suffixes and prefixes to the groups of words (1–6).

---

en-   -en   mis-   over-   re-   under-

---

1 .... length   loose   light
2 .... hear   align   pronounce
3 .... look   flow   run
4 .... estimate   stand   take
5 .... trap   danger   sure
6 .... wind   fresh   do

2 Replace the highlighted sections of the sentences with the correct form of words from Ex 1.

1 Think about possible difficult interview questions in advance to be certain that .... you are prepared.

2 Stay focused and give the group task your best; remember that you won't be able to take it again ....

3 Don't panic if you understand incorrectly .... Ask if you can start your answer again.

4 Don't allow the extra waiting time to make you more nervous if the interview before yours takes longer than expected ....

5 Take care not to minimise .... the importance of a good first impression.

6 Most interviewers will forgive .... nervousness during an interview, but not lateness.

3 **e** Use the word given in capitals at the end of some lines to form a word that fits in the gap in the same line.

Why are some interview questions so tough?

In our interviews, we always include questions that are not traditional, such as 'How would you describe this job to a five-year-old?'
¹............................ , candidates were surprised by these questions, but now the ²............................ is for interviewees to expect to be asked something out of the ordinary. Contrary to the
³............................ that these strange questions are designed to catch students out, they're actually a way for interviewers to get a better feel for their
⁴............................ .

ORIGIN
TEND

ASSUME

PERSON

Interviews have a tendency to be ⁵............................ , with neither the student nor the interviewer acting how they would normally act in the workplace. Most students are so well prepared that an unexpected question is one of the only ways to be sure they react naturally. These questions also
⁶............................ the interviewer to see how the person thinks and responds to new ideas.

NATURE

ABLE

There are no correct answers and often the most
⁷............................ answers are the simplest ones. The only way to prepare for these questions is to
⁸............................ your critical thinking skills, perhaps by using logic puzzles and brainteasers. But, really, the best advice is just to go with the flow!

IMPRESS

SHARP

Extend

4 Add a suffix or prefix to these words to complete the definitions.

---

fast   force   pay   react   take   train

---

1 .... : give someone less money than they deserve / should be given

2 .... : respond to something with too much / unnecessary emotion

3 .... : learn new skills in order to get a job in a different area

4 .... : confuse something / someone with something / someone else

5 .... : join two sides together to close them

6 .... : cause something to happen by not offering another choice

SPEAKING

1 Are these statements about the LCQ (the listening candidate's question in the long turn task) True (T) or False (F)?

1 The student who is not doing the long turn (the one-minute talk) is asked a question by the other student. ....

2 When answering the question, the student must choose one of the two pictures chosen by the other student. ....

3 The question should be answered in detail. ....

4 If your answer repeats something the other student has already said, try to rephrase your opinion. ....

5 You need to relate the picture to your personal experience or preference. ....

2 🔊 9.3 Read the long turn task questions and listen to a student giving a long turn. Which two pictures is she talking about?

What might be the advantages of working in these ways?

How might the people be feeling?

3 🔊 9.4 Listen again and tick (✓) the things the student talks about.

1 the similarities ☐
2 the differences ☐
3 the advantages related to the first picture ☐
4 the advantages related to the second picture ☐
5 how the people in the first picture might be feeling ☐
6 how the people in the second picture might be feeling ☐

4 Which of these questions would be most suitable for the LCQ?

1 Which situation would you prefer to be in?
2 Which people are likely to finish their work quickest?
3 Which situation is the most relaxing?

5 e 🔊 9.5 Listen to the correct question and record your response.

6 e 🔊 9.6 Look at the pictures again and listen to two different questions about them. Record your response.

7 Listen to your recording and check that you:

1 compared the pictures
2 answered the two questions
3 talked for about a minute.

A

B

C

WRITING

1 Read the task. Tick (✓) the points you might expect to find in a report.

1 an opening 'Dear Sir' ☐
2 an introduction detailing the purpose of the report ☐
3 headings for each section ☐
4 some facts about the school ☐
5 quotes from the teachers at the school ☐
6 a detailed list of tasks you did ☐
7 comments about the good and bad points of the experience ☐
8 suggestion(s) for improvement ☐

> You recently spent a week doing work experience at a primary school. This included observing teachers, assisting the school secretary with administration and helping small groups of children with their reading.
>
> Your college principal has asked you to write a report evaluating the success of the work experience and making recommendations about whether it is worthwhile for college students to be placed here again next year.
>
> Write **220–260** words.

2 Read a student's answer, ignoring the gaps, and underline examples of the points in Ex 1.

The aim of this report is to evaluate my recent period of work experience and make recommendations as to whether ¹........ .

The placement

My work experience was from 15–26 May at Blackfield Primary, which is a relatively small school with 120 children. I am considering a career in teaching and ²........ . The staff here are all passionate about their work and gave me a warm welcome as well as a great deal of good advice.

The work

My time was divided between the classroom and the school office. On the whole, ³........ . I saw a range of levels and a variety of different teaching methods. However, as far as developing my own skills is concerned, I would have preferred to have more involvement with the children, other than simply listening to them reading. Regarding the administrative work, ⁴........, which was both useful and enjoyable.

Recommendations

For anyone thinking about becoming a teacher this placement is very good indeed as, for the most part, ⁵........ . In the light of my fortnight at the school, I would suggest that future students visit the school prior to the start of the work experience to discuss what would be most useful for them to do during the time.

3 Read the report in Ex 2 again and complete it with the phrases A–E. Is the information in the phrases A–E general (G) or specific (S)?

A it provides excellent opportunities for both learning and practice ....
B the time spent in the classroom was extremely valuable ....
C this was an excellent opportunity to see experienced teachers in the classroom and to learn about what they have to do ....
D I helped with the production of the monthly online newsletter ....
E this particular placement should be offered to students next year ....

4 Complete the expressions for introducing information with these words.

exception far part point rule whole

1 As a ...., I went through the lesson plans with the teachers before class.
2 With the .... of Wednesday afternoons, when I listened to the children's reading, I had little direct involvement with their learning.
3 From the .... of view of my own personal development, I have to say that it was a positive experience.
4 For the most ...., the lessons were engaging.
5 As .... as discipline was concerned, I saw no problems at all.
6 On the ...., I would recommend a placement at this school to any potential teacher.

5 Read the writing task. Plan your report.

> You recently spent a week doing work experience at a leisure centre. The experience included observing a variety of training sessions, helping with administrative tasks and teaching beginners a sport you are proficient at, under supervision.
>
> Your college principal has asked you to write a report evaluating the success of the work experience and making recommendations about whether it is worthwhile for students to be placed here again next year.

6 ⓔ Write your report in 220–260 words.

UNIT CHECK

1 Complete the text with these words / phrases.

in no way   never   no circumstances   no sooner   not only
not until   only once   what

Choosing team members

Choosing the right people for your team is important.
¹................................. am I saying that you should be elitist, but
²................................. I have learnt is that choice is important.
Generally, teams require a balance of abilities, and
³................................. should you think about ability, but also
attitude. ⁴................................. have I found an exception to this
rule, which was a women's football team. Strangely, all the
team members were excellent goal keepers! ⁵.................................
had I come across anything so bizarre! ⁶................................. we
had been playing for a few months, did I realise that they all
shared a similar talent.

Consider the temperament of your team members –
under ⁷................................. should you choose players who
are all ultra-competitive. You would probably find that
⁸................................. have you started the match than an
argument breaks out. So, choose your team with care.

2 Complete the second sentence so that it has the same meaning as the first sentence.

1 I had just accepted the role of team leader when I started
   to regret it.
   No sooner .... than
   ....

2 I have only been chosen once to be team captain.
   Only once ....

3 I hate being the leader and I am also very indecisive.
   Not only ...., but I am
   ....

4 When I was in the band I never wanted to be the lead
   singer.
   At no time ....

5 I wouldn't say I am a sporty person, but I do like running.
   In no way ....

6 I will never buy a lottery ticket because I think it's a waste
   of money.
   Under no circumstances
   ....

3 Rewrite the sentences using these nouns.

argument   competition   complexity   development
success   suggestion

1 Relationships are complex, but that's what makes them
   interesting.
   The .... what makes them
   interesting.

2 Some people suggest that you should choose friends who
   are different from you.
   There is .... friends who
   are different from you.

3 How friendships develop depends on many factors.
   The .... many factors.

4 It isn't healthy for friends to compete with each other.
   .... is not healthy.

5 Some people argue that friendships are our most
   important relationships.
   There is .... our most
   important relationships.

6 Most friendships succeed if both people invest time and
   emotion in them.
   The .... how much time
   and emotion we invest in them.

4 Complete the gaps with these phrases.

lay down   put our heads together   put (somebody) in (their) place
take a back seat   team players   the buck stops here

Team talk!

Be diplomatic with members of the other team. If you feel that
you have to ¹.. , then do it
with tact.

It is not always necessary to be at the centre of the action.
Sometimes it is best to ²..
and just watch.

Remember, above all, that you are
³.. and that you are not
playing alone. The group must come first.

I don't want to sound arrogant, but I am your manager and
I ⁴.. the law, and so
please remember that ⁵.. .
If there is anything that we disagree about then we can
⁶.. and find a solution to it.

PART 1

For questions 1–8, read the text below and decide which answer (A, B, C or D) best fits each gap.

WHAT'S IN A SMILE?

According to Darwin, all smiles are a universal human expression and the cause and the ⁰result of smiling doesn't vary from culture to culture. However, there are different types of smiles and not all are what they seem.

First there is the genuine smile of happiness, which when words ¹....... , is a way of transmitting your happiness, joy or gratitude. Then there is a 'grin and ²....... it' smile, which means things are not alright, but you are going to put on a brave face. There is the smile which is not really a smile, which shows contempt, a ³....... . When we feel obliged to smile, where we haven't ⁴....... up any trust with the other person, we offer a fake smile.

Smiling ⁵....... an atmosphere of goodwill and if all those around you are looking straight-faced and gloomy, then go ahead and flash them a smile. ⁶....... the initiative whether it be for friends, family, colleague or strangers on the street. Don't take a ⁷....... seat and don't be shy. It doesn't matter if you are the first one; it's good to ⁸....... by example.

0	**A** reflection	**B** end	**C** result	**D** final
1	**A** fail	**B** leave	**C** crumble	**D** depart
2	**A** support	**B** have	**C** bear	**D** accept
3	**A** sob	**B** smirk	**C** laugh	**D** giggle
4	**A** built	**B** constructed	**C** caught	**D** got
5	**A** constructs	**B** warms	**C** creates	**D** opens
6	**A** Take	**B** Hold	**C** Hand	**D** Deal
7	**A** front	**B** middle	**C** side	**D** back
8	**A** lead	**B** stand	**C** show	**D** guide

PART 2

For questions 9–16, read the text below and complete the gaps with one word only.

Amazing under-water vision

Some years ⁰.............ago............. it was reported by various media sources ⁹................................ the children of the Moken tribe, living on an island off the West coast of Thailand, had exceptional vision when swimming under water. A Swedish scientist, Anna Gislen, heard about the tribe and insisted ¹⁰................................ going to see their amazing ability for herself. Anna was delighted with ¹¹................................ she found on the island; a group of young children who spent their days playing and hunting for fish and seemingly ¹²................................ to swim with their eyes fully open. Anna assumed that the children must have ¹³................................ born with a different type of vision, but what was challenging for her was to come ¹⁴................................ with a scientific explanation for the phenomenon. She carried out an experiment with a group of European children in the same location. The children needed to ¹⁵................................ supported in the task, but findings revealed that their underwater vision did improve. Anna concluded that this ability might ¹⁶................................ been due to years of practice and familiarity with the water.

PART 3

For questions 17–24, read the text. Use the word given in capitals at the end of some lines to form a word that fits in the gap in the same line.

A well-paid job that no one wants

Most employers advertising a job with an annual salary of almost half a million dollars and a beautiful **0**.............setting............... would	**SET**
understandably expect that the advert would attract **17**............................ interest from potential	**CONSIDER**
candidates. Unfortunately for one doctor who owns a practice in rural New Zealand he has so far been unsuccessful in his **18**............................... of	**PURSUE**
a second doctor to work alongside him. Despite being offered more than twice the average wage for a doctor in the area, the job advert is still to attract **19**............................ applicants.	**ENTHUSE**
Prospective candidates may be put off by the **20**............................... of the practice's remote	**ISOLATE**
location and its lack of a high-speed internet connection. This **21**............................... of many	**WILLING**
professionals to accept less than ideal working conditions in exchange for excellent financial compensation adds another interesting dimension to the **22**............................ controversial debate	**TYPE**
on money versus **23**............................ . As	**HAPPY**
for the doctor's practice in New Zealand, the only **24**............................... they have is to extend	**OPT**
the campaign online in the hope of finally securing someone to occupy their vacant post.	

PART 4

For questions 25–30, complete the second sentence so that it has a similar meaning to the first sentence, using the word given. Do not change the word given. Use between three and six words, including the word given.

0 The organisation wants to make people aware that these social issues exist.

RAISE

The organisation wants .... to raise awareness of ....these social issues.

25 I was too afraid to let him know that I crashed the car.

DARED

I .... him that I crashed the car.

26 I can't think of any word to describe the documentary other than appalling.

WANT

For .... word, the documentary was appalling.

27 People in many cultures say that the key to a healthy body is a healthy mind.

BELIEVED

In many cultures, ... that the key to a healthy body is a healthy mind.

28 Sam's boss recommended her for the promotion because she works really well in groups.

PLAYER

Sam is a .... so her boss recommended her for a promotion.

29 In the end, we weren't allowed to enter the executive lounge at the airport.

PERMISSION

In the end, we were .... enter the executive lounge at the airport.

30 The interviewers were impressed by Joan's performance in the group task.

IMPRESSION

Joan's performance in the group task .... the interviewers.

READING AND USE OF ENGLISH

Part 1

For questions 1–8, read the text and decide which answer (A, B, C or D) best fits each gap. There is an example at the beginning (0).

How unique is your body?

With the increase in identity **0**theft , experts are looking for ways to replace passwords, which are essentially fallible as they rely on people **1**_____ numbers to memory. Biometric identification has so far been a(n) **2**_____ success with banks. Biometrics measures the **3**_____ of a person through voice and fingerprint recognition. It is not entirely infallible, but it has **4**_____ the respect of scientists. There are, however, some body parts which may be more reliable than fingerprints. Whilst two people may well be the **5**_____ image of each other, in reality they are quite different. **6**_____ twins may appear to be the same, and you may think that they are **7**_____ from each other, but in fact this is just not true. Our distinctive body parts include our ears, eye movements, the shape of our skulls and our nails. So, in terms of originality, our bodies really do have the **8**_____ word!

0	**A** fraud	**B** theft	**C** robbery	**D** copying
1	**A** remembering	**B** committing	**C** putting	**D** sticking
2	**A** burning	**B** stunning	**C** resounding	**D** endearing
3	**A** difference	**B** individuality	**C** peculiarity	**D** profile
4	**A** earned	**B** collected	**C** received	**D** acquired
5	**A** spitting	**B** cutting	**C** double	**D** duplicate
6	**A** Alike	**B** Similar	**C** Equal	**D** Identical
7	**A** indistinguishable	**B** unequal	**C** indifferent	**D** unalike
8	**A** last	**B** ultimate	**C** definitive	**D** end

Part 2

For questions 9–16, read the text and and complete the gaps with one word only. There is an example at the beginning (0).

The benefits of a good cry

The act **0**_____of_____ crying usually involves the shedding of tears and a change in our facial expressions, similar **9**_____ that of laughing. Our breathing is shorter and the shallower our breathing the **10**_____ we gulp for breath. Tears can be provoked **11**_____ a whole variety of reasons and the cause is most commonly due to sadness, but **12**_____ always so. Our reasons for a good weep could be for a whole host of reasons. Having said **13**_____ , the most common reason for crying is grief. Crying can be seen as a cry for help, in **14**_____ to draw attention to ourselves as babies do; a way of communicating when words fail us; or it could be as a way of relieving stress or anxiety. Most people claim to feel better after a good cry and some studies claim that crying at a film can **15**_____ a genuine mood booster. So, don't be embarrassed by your tears, let **16**_____ flow.

Part 3

For questions 17–24, read the text. Use the word given in capitals at the end of some of the lines to form a word that fits in the gap in the same line. There is an example at the beginning (0).

The mother of all demonstrations

In today's ⁰ ....competitive....... work of job hunting, remember that the   **COMPETE**

¹⁷................................. alone on your CV may not be enough to impress in a job interview.   **QUALIFY**

Managers and employers nowadays are ¹⁸............................. interested in your interpersonal   **INCREASE**

skills or your soft skills. So, let me ¹⁹............................. you as to what employers are looking for.   **LIGHT**

Essentially, they are looking for a CV which contains more than just academic ²⁰.............................;   **ACHIEVE**

one that includes voluntary work or something involving teamwork and initiative. Be

²¹............................. and prepare for the interview, and think of examples of how you   **CONSCIENCE**

have developed or are developing soft skills. An ²²............................. to demonstrate   **ABLE**

interpersonal skills both on the CV and in the interview room can result in a poor interview

and evidently no job offer, so do not ²³............................. their importance. A candidate   **ESTIMATE**

who doesn't demonstrate effective communications skills in the first interview may well

not be invited for a second interview. So, let this be a ²⁴............................. tale for those   **CAUTION**

of you preparing for interviews.

Part 4

For questions 25–30, complete the second sentence so that it has a similar meaning to the first sentence, using the word given. Do not change the word given. Use between three and six words, including the word given. Here is an example (0).

0 'Shall I open the door for you?' Angela asked me.

OFFERED

Angela ....offered to open the door........ for me.

25 You are not to speak during the exam.

NO

Under .... you speak during the exam.

26 I thought that you had been given the job.

UNDER

I was .... that you had been given the job.

27 According to recent reports, our general health is better than last year.

REPORTED

Our general health .... than last year.

28 'I will give you extra homework if you are not quiet,' the teacher said.

THREATENED

The teacher .... extra homework if they were not quiet.

29 We have agreed to try harder in class.

WILL

It has .... try harder in class.

30 It's possible that Tom didn't turn off the computer.

MIGHT

Tom .... computer on.

Part 5

You are going to read an article about the psychological effects of new economies. For questions 31–36, choose the answer (A, B, C or D) which you think fits best according to the text.

....

New economies

When deciding which career path to follow, most people try to get the best balance between a secure job and something that they get genuine enjoyment from. Traditionally, this hasn't been easy to achieve, as personal circumstances such as family responsibilities and living costs, the need for job security and a lack of opportunity often force most people to settle for either the former or the latter. However, changing consumer and employment demands combined with the expansion of easily accessible digital platforms have opened up space for the emergence of the gig and shared economy. These are slowly changing the face of employment and the way in which people earn a living.

The gig economy is characterised by short-term or freelance work contracts. The most well-known examples of these are delivery services in which motorbike or car owners are sent assignments through a third-party app to deliver takeaway food on behalf of a variety of restaurant establishments. The worker does not have employment ties to either the app-based company or the restaurants for which it delivers meals. On the other hand, the sharing economy involves renting out possessions that you aren't currently using or don't use often, such as your apartment or private parking space, or by inviting people to share things with you in order to cut down the costs, such as offering spaces to additional passengers in your car when going on a long journey.

Although founded on different principles both the gig economy and the shared economy represent forms of flexible income that differ from conventional methods of employment. Of the two options, the shared economy is the least stable. However, despite the superficial differences, these economies could be linked by their apparent dependence on certain conditions that permit success – the ability to cope with the uncertainties and setbacks that are an inevitable side effect of working alone and without the security of a traditional employment contract. For those working on temporary contracts, despite the possible financial benefits and ability to pick and choose which jobs you accept, disconnecting from work can prove a challenge as time away often means missed opportunities. The distinction between work time and leisure time becomes blurred, and you need to exercise a lot of discipline to commit yourself to taking time off. Furthermore, while skills, qualifications and networking can give you a competitive edge in traditional employment, in the gig economy employers can cherry pick from thousands of faceless contractors with apparently identical skills sets. Standing out from the class usually comes down to one denominator: price. Being able to hold firm and charge the price you feel is fair for your services in the face of competitors who undercut you by large percentages causes internal conflict that easily transforms to stress and despair if you watch opportunities getting swallowed up by others while you sit twiddling your thumbs. On the other hand, giving into the temptation to lower your price in order to secure a job can lead you into a cycle of low prices that is difficult to get back out of.

If you try to make a living from the shared economy, then you are vulnerable to the needs and whims of other people, offering you little security, which in turn makes it difficult to control time and finances. Whereas an employment contract with a fixed number of working hours clearly establishes a monthly or annual salary, workers on an hourly rate with no guarantee of regular hours struggle to plan financially and may feel pressured into working to irregular and erratic schedules in order to make ends meet. Some people struggle with feelings of panic and a fear of destitution that can stem from such a lack of control. In the gig economy, there is uncertainty over how much work you will be offered and in the shared economy you are vulnerable to other people's demands, such as when they want to make bookings to rent your property or possessions. It's easy to feel that you'll never work again if your projects dry up or that you've unknowingly received some bad reviews if interest in whatever you are sharing slows down. Dealing with these feelings can be incredibly difficult and some people end up recognising that they actually need to belong to something to boost their self-esteem. In this case, it is advisable to maintain permanent employment and lean on the gig and shared economies only to supplement your main income. As in any job, taking care of your emotional health is most important, and just because something looks like an easy way to make money with minimal effort doesn't mean that there aren't hidden side effects.

31 In the first paragraph the writer says that people usually
    A do not take great pleasure in their jobs.
    B struggle to divide their time equally.
    C look for alternative ways to make money.
    D have to choose between their finances and their happiness.

32 According to the writer, the new economies
    A are equally risky ways to earn money.
    B are preferable to traditional employment.
    C aren't as different as they seem.
    D allow people to earn regular salaries.

33 In the third paragraph, the writer says that people in the gig economy
    A are responsible for their professional development.
    B have to decide between taking a holiday or earning money.
    C should stay motivated to do physical activity.
    D sometimes lack self-motivation.

34 The writer warns that
    A earning enough to live on is rare.
    B accepting less money for a job is not advisable.
    C negotiating on price is the only way to get work.
    D prices should be determined based on experience.

35 The writer says that success depends on
    A being able to cope well with unpredictable circumstances.
    B taking opportunities when they present themselves.
    C knowing how to market yourself to other people.
    D having skills the employers are looking for.

36 The writer concludes that the gig and shared economies
    A shouldn't be the only way people make money.
    B don't allow people to make money as easily as regular employment.
    C are suitable for everyone who doesn't want to work for a company.
    D have a negative impact on most people's emotional health.

Part 6

You are going to read four opinions on an article called *Paying for essays,* which is about giving criminal records to students who pay for academic essays. For questions 37–40, choose from the extracts (A–D). The extracts may be chosen more than once.

A

In my opinion, paying for essays is a practice that has been around for years; however, the article showed me that those selling essays operate on a much larger scale nowadays than I had realised. As the article states, these students have perhaps become more blatant in their advertising and are certainly much easier to locate thanks to mobile technology. Of course, students who resort to this measure are to blame, but if you are going to hand out potentially life-changing, and to my mind unnecessarily severe, consequences to students, then surely the same rules need to be applied to people involved with writing these essays. They also need to be held to account. While the article presented sufficient reasoning for and against giving out criminal records to students, I would like to have seen more reference to dealing with those benefiting from the operation.

B

While I find the whole practice of paying for an academic essay wholly unacceptable and I agree that it should definitely be a punishable offense, this article didn't convince me that students who are caught should be given criminal records. It didn't give us a full picture; the article simply listed a series of facts and, although the numbers involved are appallingly high, for me this wasn't enough to justify her suggestion of such unnecessarily extreme measures. Facts only present the situation itself and what I felt was missing in this talk was possible hypothesis for the reasons why students don't feel confident enough to produce their own work. Blaming laziness and a lack of drive is too easy and is a poor excuse to justify giving students criminal records. I would have appreciated a fuller overview of the whole issue.

C

Overall, I found the article highly informative about many aspects of the issue of paying for essays. Perhaps I had been a bit naïve, but I was unaware that paid-for essays were so prevalent in higher education nowadays. Although the writer is completely right in her affirmation that technology has facilitated it, I distinctly remember a scandal at my university after a student was caught charging others in exchange for writing essays for them, and that was over twenty years ago! Contrary to the article's claim that current consequences are too soft and don't do enough to discourage students, I don't believe that giving criminal records is the best route to go down. There is no need to ruin young people's futures for making a foolish mistake.

D

I am pleased that this topic has been given such a large platform, as it's something that academics, in particular university lecturers like myself, have been debating for quite some time. However, while I applaud the writer's efforts in trying to get cheating to be taken seriously, I don't think that the article was objective enough. It seemed to present the students negatively and it was obvious that the writer felt personally offended by the students' actions, although the reason for this wasn't clear. I'm sure that the writer made such a controversial statement in the belief that it was guaranteed to get attention. The article became tedious after the second paragraph, and although I believe that the writer's suggestion of giving criminal records is a valid one, I would have liked alternative punishments to have been explored more in the article.

Which person:

shares the same opinion as D about the lack of a balanced argument in the article? 37 ☐

has the same view as C about the effects of giving students a criminal record? 38 ☐

has a similar opinion to A about the popularity of paying for essays? 39 ☐

holds a different view from the others about giving students a criminal record? 40 ☐

Part 7

You are going to read an online article about fidgeting – when you keep moving your hands or feet because you are anxious or bored. Six paragraphs have been removed from the article. Choose from the paragraphs A–G, the one which fits each gap (41–46). There is one extra paragraph which you do not need to use.

Why do we fidget?

Whether it is unpicking a paper clip, tapping our foot on the floor or pinging a rubber band, most of us mindlessly fidget with something while we are working out a problem or contemplating an idea. But why exactly do we fidget, and is it just a distraction from the task at hand? PhD student Mike Karlesky, with the support of his advisor Katharine Isbister, at New York University's Polytechnic School of Engineering, carried out some interesting research.

41	

It is widely known that for specific groups of people, such as those with learning difficulties or attention deficit disorders, fidgeting can serve as a coping mechanism in challenging situations. For the general population, engaging our hands in constant movement, for example by doodling or clicking a pen, can result in increased memory and creativity.

42	

As part of Karlesky and Isbister's research, he set up a blog through which he asked people what they usually play with when they are bored at work. Using the blog submissions, he was able to determine an overall inclination towards everyday objects that allow for repetitive actions, such as folding paper into chains or repeatedly removing and replacing the lid of a pen.

43	

The study's findings go some way to explaining the explosion in popularity of so-called fidget toys in recent years, such as a small, multi-surfaced cube that can be spun, rolled, clicked and flipped and that has already attracted multi-million-dollar funding from various revenue sources. Equally popular are fidget spinners – a plastic device that can be spun around a central disc in a way similar to old-fashioned spinning top toys.

44	

Some schools in the UK have begun banning fidgeting toys unless students have an officially-recognised attention deficit disorder as teachers complain that many students were bringing in the devices with the sole purposes of annoying and showing off to their peers by doing tricks that they learnt online.

45	

For Karlesky and Isbister, their research can reach further than just the production of for-profit, market-specific fidgeting toys. Instead, it can be applied to product design as a whole to optimise work tools for productivity, such as by adding a spinning device under a desk to curb distraction or a fidget attachment for a computer that can be played with to stop the mind wandering.

46	

In short, fidgeting is no longer a quirky personal trait and is well on its way to becoming a lucrative, multi-faceted industry in its own right.

A

Another point of contention is the justification of allowing a student to use these on the premise that it helps him or her to concentrate when this comes at the expense of the concentration of other students. Peers of a student using a fidget spinner are often driven to distraction by the constant whirring and spinning. As such, teachers are faced with an ethical dilemma over whether to give priority to the needs of one student over the personal comfort of others.

B

Apparently, this is down to the fact that, contrary to popular belief, not all tasks require 100 percent focus in order to be perfectly executed. In fact, allowing part of your brain to engage in something seemingly banal and repetitive like those mentioned above can help to focus your attention on the main activity for longer. As a result, you are more likely to perform the activity more efficiently. Essentially, fidgeting keeps boredom at bay to allow you to hold your attention and over time this can increase your overall attention span.

C

The results showed that in general, fidgeting brings various cognitive benefits, such as boosting creativity and memory. However, these benefits are largely unrecognised by people who fidget. Instead, they choose their fidgeting mechanisms for reasons that are both highly personal and surprisingly passionate.

D

Through such questions it was discovered that soft and squishy materials that mould easily are among the most popular. Similarly, small objects that possess sentimental value are often preferred as they can be comforting and reassuring in stressful or uncertain circumstances.

E

Among the benefits of these tools is the fact that it is more sanitary than some common fidgeting habits. Chewing on a pen lid or biting your fingernails, for example, can cause a build-up of germs that could lead to a skin infection. However, not everyone is convinced that these are just harmless tools to distract idle hands.

F

Taking this one step further, understanding the science of fidgeting can have an impact on the design of digital interactions. For example, it may be possible to enable computers with a sensor to detect fidgeting that triggers an automatic five-minute shut down for the user to take a break.

G

While this may be true, it is no surprise that many well-known companies have launched their own product ranges. These are not only marketed to children who can't keep still in the classroom, but also to office workers who may also need distraction to carry out challenging tasks or to cope with stressful situations.

Part 8

You are going to read a magazine article in which five careers advisors give advice about writing a CV. For questions 47–56, choose from the advisors (A–E). The advisors may be chosen more than once.

Which advisor makes the following statements?

Choose words carefully as some may be crucial for employers.	47
Use your CV to sell yourself.	48
Your CV should be aesthetically pleasing to employers.	49
Get rid of redundant information.	50
It is fine to exaggerate your strengths.	51
You should be systematic when reading the job specifications.	52
Your CV is similar to a photo of yourself.	53
The majority of employers don't look kindly on a generic CV.	54
Don't aim to include an extensive list of achievements.	55
Your abilities and expertise are more important than academic achievements.	56

Writing the perfect CV

Writing a good CV is crucial when applying for jobs. We've asked five careers advisors to give some tips on how to write the perfect CV.

Advisor A

Think of your CV as a snapshot of you. Think of it as a visual image of yourself, but created by words rather than colours and shapes. Your CV should be enticing to the eye, and a joy to behold for the reader. Needless to say, the content needs to be top notch, but it is essential that the CV engages the reader. So, I'm thinking quality paper, tasteful design, clear layout and a well-chosen, professional photo. Think about the layout, use bullet points and don't cram the page. Be coherent in your design choices, make perceptive decisions and always bear in mind the target audience. Finally, don't forget to think very carefully about your choice of colour scheme, think of the effect that colours can have and make a judicious choice.

Advisor B

Even if you have a specific career path, every job that you apply for to some degree is going to be slightly different and each company prioritises different skills. A blanket CV quite frankly looks sloppy and is not going to bowl over most bosses. Your CV should mirror the job which you are applying for and I firmly believe that you should tailor your CV to each job, and it needs to be unambiguously and unequivocally suited to the particular job you are aiming at. An in-depth analysis of the skills set and tasks inherent in the job needs to be done and then reflected in the CV. Make it easy for employers to see why you are the ideal student. Include your achievements which are particularly pertinent and remember that the information must be up-to-date.

Advisor C

We live in a highly competitive world and people who thrive in business are the ones who naturally market themselves in the right way. Self-marketing does not have to be an onerous process. In fact, it should be an enjoyable and creative one. You need to review your core strengths, define your competitive edge, know your USPs and go out and brand yourself Keep your finger on the pulse of what is happening in the marketplace and make sure your CV portrays your unique marketing message which sells you and your brand. There is nothing wrong with boasting; remember you are the CEO of your own company and the company's success depends on you. Use language which oozes confidence, assertiveness and authority.

Advisor D

There is nothing more tedious for a company than having to wade through lengthy CVs which go into irrelevant detail about every award and exam taken. Your CV is certainly not meant to be your autobiography and so two pages of A4 is the maximum you should be aiming for. Remember it is you who is approaching the company and not the other way around, so don't bore them with information which needs to be sifted through. Don't use ambiguous language, be precise and concise so that employers can see at a glance what they are looking for. Be ruthless about eliminating all superfluous information or wordy language. Don't leave gaps in your experience as this looks suspicious. Finally, proofreading is essential, so double check for mistakes.

Advisor E

As opposed to the traditional chronological CV you should be writing a competency-based CV based on transferable skills. A competency-based CV allows employers to see at a glance how your experience and skills match those of the job. The central core of your CV should be your competency profile as opposed to a list of exams you have passed. You should include a range of skills sets which encompass languages, IT and soft skills such as problem-solving, effective communication and negotiation skills. Refine your keywords and make sure your CV is keyword rich. Many companies use software to scan CVs for keywords, so be keyword savvy if you don't want to miss out on that perfect job.

WRITING

Part 1

You must answer this question. Write your answer in 220–260 words in an appropriate style.

....

1 You have recently listened to a radio discussion about the best ways of approaching the environmental problems facing the world today. You have made the notes below.

> **Best ways of approaching environmental problems:**
> - actions of individuals
> - cooperation of different countries
> - scientific research
>
> Some opinions expressed in the discussion:
> 'People can't make a difference on their own – the problems are too big.'
> 'Working together always gets more done than working apart.'
> 'Scientists can do a lot of things, but they can't perform miracles!'

Write an essay for your teacher discussing **two** of the points in your notes. You should **explain which is the best way of approaching environmental problems, giving reasons** to support your opinion.

You may, if you wish, make use of the opinions expressed during the discussion, but you should use your own words as far as possible.

Part 2

Write an answer to one of the questions 2–4 in this part. Write your answer in 220–260 words in an appropriate style.

....

2 You have been asked by the principal of your school to suggest ideas to promote cultural awareness and understanding among the students. You decide to write a proposal for an international food week, offering meals in the cafeteria from a different country each day.

   In your proposal you should explain your idea, describe what it would entail and say why you think it will help promote cultural awareness among the students.

   Write your **proposal**.

3 Your college website is asking for reviews on outstanding television documentary series that have both thrilled and informed viewers. Write a review of a series you think will interest others, outlining the content and explaining its entertainment and educational value.

   Write your **review**.

4 You have heard about a proposed building development on an area of land close to your college, and you feel that this development will not be beneficial to the area. Write a letter to the editor of the local newspaper outlining the proposed changes, explaining your feelings about them and saying what action should be taken about the proposed development.

   Write your **letter**.

LISTENING

Part 1

🔊 10.1 **You will hear three different extracts. For questions 1–6, choose the answer (A, B or C) which fits best according to what you hear. There are two questions for each extract.**

....

Extract 1

1 In the man's opinion, Escape Rooms
   A are too expensive.
   B could have limited appeal.
   C develop useful team-building skills.

2 What is the woman doing?
   A explaining how Escape Rooms work
   B persuading the man to try one
   C identifying a problem with them

Extract 2

3 The man's opinion of the houses built as part of the Tiny House Movement is that
   A they offer a really practical solution for some people.
   B they use extremely innovative designs.
   C they are a good financial investment.

4 Why does the woman think that the Tiny House Movement doesn't make financial sense?
   A People won't be able to sell on their houses in the future.
   B They are not a cheap alternative to normal sized houses.
   C They are not built in popular locations.

Extract 3

5 What point is the woman making about doppelgängers?
   A The press invent stories about them.
   B Some people are making a lot of money from vulnerable people.
   C The fact that coincidences happen is not very interesting.

6 How does the man feel at the end of the conversation?
   A curious about doppelgängers
   B naïve for believing all he reads in the press
   C interested in signing up with an agency to work as one

Part 2

🔊 10.2 **You will hear a student called Richard Stuart giving a presentation in his biology class. For questions 7–14, complete the sentences with a word or short phrase.**

Lessons from nature

Richard says it's common knowledge he is not naturally good at **7** ....

Richard uses the word **8** .... to describe his final decision about the delivery of his presentation.

He states that he doesn't need to give an **9** .... about why we need trees.

He uses an example of collaboration among **10** .... to describe how we can do things that seem too big for us to do.

Richard understands that not everyone will agree with the **11** .... that he is making.

Richard describes the fact that we ignore nature as **12** ....

He uses the word **13** .... to praise some attitudes to nature.

Richard believes that we should turn to nature for **14** .... rather than the internet.

Part 3

🔊 10.3 **You will hear an interview with a man called Mike Lemmington, who started his own gelato business, and a woman called Samia Johnson, who runs a marketing agency. For questions 15–20, choose the answer (A, B, C or D) which fits best according to what you hear.**

-----

15 How did Mike feel about opening his own café?

    A passionate about working for himself

    B uncertain about starting a business

    C doubtful about his financial expertise

    D enthusiastic about having a new challenge

16 What did Mike feel was his largest barrier to success?

    A the initial investment needed

    B the difficulty in mixing the ingredients

    C the demand for gelato in the UK

    D the low profit from a gelato stand

17 What's Samia's attitude towards her business?

    A She is in the right place at the right time.

    B It is perfectly matched to her personality.

    C It is worth spending all her money on.

    D She sometimes considers going back to university.

18 What does Samia enjoy most about her business?

    A doing a variety of work

    B being able to help other people

    C having the opportunity to travel

    D using her social media skills

19 What do Mike and Samia both think about their success?

    A It sometimes takes the fun out of their work.

    B It took longer than they'd hoped.

    C It happened naturally.

    D It is due to their dedication to their first customers.

20 What does Mike say about his ambition?

    A It drives him to make more money.

    B It is impossible to control.

    C It is part of the process, not the result.

    D It influences the decisions he makes.

Part 4

🔊 10.4 You will hear five short extracts in which people are talking about their attitudes to luck. While you listen, you must complete both tasks.

....

TASK 1

For questions 21–25, choose from the list (A–H) the reason each person gives for feeling fortunate.

A finding something important   Speaker 1   21 ☐

B taking a trip abroad   Speaker 2   22 ☐

C making a lot of money   Speaker 3   23 ☐

D getting a good deal   Speaker 4   24 ☐

E signing a business contract   Speaker 5   25 ☐

F realising a dream

G winning a competition

H selling a business

TASK 2

For questions 26–30, choose from the list (A–H) the advice each person gives about how to be lucky.

A be more careful   Speaker 1   26 ☐

B read self-help books   Speaker 2   27 ☐

C don't always take people's advice   Speaker 3   28 ☐

D meet new people   Speaker 4   29 ☐

E have faith in your first choice   Speaker 5   30 ☐

F avoid asking other people for help

G try new things

H don't get distracted

SPEAKING

Part 1

🔊 10.5 The interlocutor will ask you and the other student questions about yourselves. Listen to the recording and answer the questions.

Part 2

🔊 10.6 The interlocutor will give you three different pictures and ask you to talk on your own about two of them for about a minute. You will also have to answer a question about your partner's pictures after they have spoken about them.

Listen to the recording and answer the questions.

Student A

• How important is practice in developing these skills?
• How long might it take for the people to make an improvement?

Student B

- Why might the people be trying to change their appearance?
- How might they be feeling?

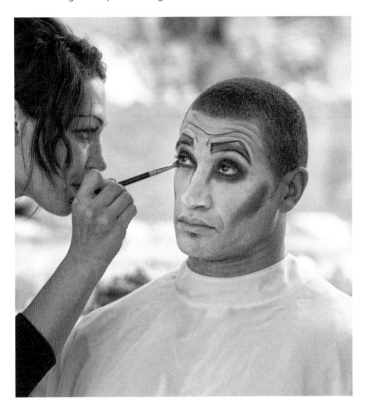

Part 3

🔊 10.7 The interlocutor will ask you and the other student to discuss something together. Read the task and listen to the interlocutor's instructions. Discuss the task.

Here are some aims governments and scientists have for the future.

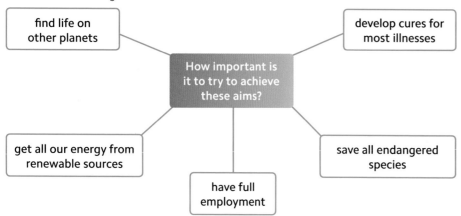

Part 4

🔊 10.8 The interlocutor will ask you and the other student questions related to the topic in Part 3. Listen to the recording and answer the interlocutor's questions. Discuss the questions with the other student.

AUDIOSCRIPT

1.1

Miranda

When I look back on my childhood, I think now that my parents were really quite unconventional. They were, and still are, both writers. We didn't have a TV because they didn't believe in TVs and so it was actually quite boring. I used to plead with them to get a 'normal' job, but they had been writing all their lives so I wasn't going to change them. I guess they have always been a bit hippyish in their thinking. You know, no rules and we were able to express our feelings and all that. Looking back, it seems that most of my childhood consisted of chilling on the sofa while my parents were working away writing. From a six-year-old's viewpoint, their work seemed awesome, and my parents used to be very laid back about stuff. What was there not to like!

Sally

I guess that as a child I always took it for granted that we would always be a large family. Having two older sisters was fun even though I would complain about them most of the time. When Beth left home I didn't really think about it. I felt fine I think. But it was only after Charlotte had left that it really hit home and I realised just how lonely I was going to feel. After both of them had left home it dawned on me that the youngest gets a raw deal. I had been sharing a bedroom with my sister Charlotte for years and then the next thing I knew it was just me. Charlotte and I would talk about our plans for the future for hours. Mum and Dad were great and they did tell me that I was going to feel a bit lonely for a while. But I don't think I really listened to them and it all just seemed to change so quickly.

Lucas

Our family is from another culture and I think that as I was growing up I noticed the cultural difference more and more. You know, when friends came round and we used to eat different food from them. Sometimes my mates would comment on it. Now I look back and think that's really positive because the more you look around you and see how other people live, the better you understand your own background. Our parents moved here when I was eight years old, but I think my parents had been considering the move for ages. Our parents were special. They took the time to talk to us and see how we were getting on and if we had been having a tough time at school they would give us a special treat. They didn't spoil us though! Quality time with us mattered to them. That felt good.

1.2

C = Carla   J = Jim

C: Do you know I think that I've got a really bad memory. At least a bad long-term memory. I can remember the stuff I need to remember on a day-to-day basis, but when it comes to remembering my childhood … it's another matter.

J: But I understood that we can all remember back as far as three and a half, or at least that's what I've read anyway. Is that not your case?

C: Well, to be honest, I can't remember anything from before I was six. I think I blocked out some memories from early childhood, perhaps because my mum was quite ill and she was in and out of hospital. She did get better, in fact she recovered fully, and now she's fine. But I think that I had a hard time of it seeing her ill and I just wanted to forget.

J: The mind is very clever that way. It protects us from pain. I agree there are things we just choose to forget. I guess that's what we call having a selective memory.

C: I think that once I started school I felt much better, you know, more confident. Those first days at school were quite memorable. I remember very clearly what my first teacher at primary school said to me though. Word for word. I can hear her as if it were yesterday.

J: Ha ha. That's amazing!

C: Yes, it is! I was really tearful and found the whole experience of leaving Mum really traumatic. She came up to me and said 'Carla, I can't guarantee that you are going to enjoy today. In fact, I can't guarantee that you are going to enjoy school at all. But I can guarantee that you will make some very good friends here.'

J: And did you?

C: Yes of course. You know me. Miss sociable. How about you?

J: I can remember much earlier than school. At least I think It's my memory and not just because of my parents reminiscing.

C: Go on.

J: I know it sounds weird, but even as far back as three years old I have a vision of my father playing the guitar. It's still as clear as day. I can see him now with his long hair playing away!

C: I love it!

J: I think my long-term memory is probably better than my short-term because I have a vivid recollection of both images and smells from my childhood. Often I'll come across a scent that triggers a memory from way, way back. Doesn't that happen to you?

C: No. I wish it did though. I have no recollection of those sorts of things. My brother has got a phenomenal memory though, much better than mine. Loads of times he has to jog my memory because for me it's all a blur. He goes on about when we were little and I can never remember the half of what he talks about.

J: I'll swap you then. I'd love a better short-term memory for when it comes to revising for exams!

1.3

Speaker 1

I think I started developing my technique for memorising lists when I was around ten years old. As the class monitor at school, I was responsible for giving out the art materials. I had to remember how many pencils and paintbrushes had been given out and collected back in. With forty pupils in the class, it wasn't easy! Remembering lists isn't as simple as just looking at the words – I have to make a visible link between each word in the order they appear in the list. I never imagined that I'd be able to use it in my job as an events coordinator, but my skill for memorisation means I assist the host and make sure they greet all of the attendees appropriately.

Speaker 2

When I was at school, my teacher taught us an acronym to remember the order of the planets to help us prepare for a test. Since then, I've always come up with a quirky acronym for a list of words I wanted to remember – my family and friends are bemused by how I can rattle something off, but the method helped me get through college and it makes life as a history student much easier! I don't need to spend as long studying dates and facts now that I have a system for remembering them. This means that I have more time to train for the World Memory Championships – I want to beat my personal best of ninety-five words!

Speaker 3

My family moved around a lot as I was growing up so I didn't have many friends. I took up memorising card tricks so I didn't get bored on my own, and I soon got hooked on challenging myself to memorise the order of the cards in the deck. Eventually, I started trying to remember as many decks as possible. The world record is thirty-one decks in an hour, so that's the one to beat. I've now got a large social group because of memorisation. Last year, I was ill and couldn't go to the World Memory Championships. My friends livestreamed it just so I could feel involved – it was a great feeling after being so lonely when I was younger.

Speaker 4

Throughout my teens, I was on my county's swimming team and trained every day, which was intense. I used to keep my focus while I was swimming up and down the pool by counting as high as I could – this helped me ignore the building pain and fatigue in my legs, too. I realised that it could be a good way to memorise things I needed to know for school. Once I ran out of things to memorise, I started compiling long lists of numbers and silently reciting them from memory as I swam. I still go to the pool to train for the World Memory Championships – I lost five kilos and got so much fitter when I was preparing for the last competition.

Speaker 5

I remember a list of information by picturing a journey around my house. I know it's difficult to understand, but I spent most of my childhood recovering from a minor brain injury after being in an accident and for a time this was the only way that I could remember things. As I couldn't attend regular school for a while, I had plenty of time to develop the technique and I now have a knack for remembering all kinds of things. These days I give talks at universities about how to use this technique and I've even released a web series about it.

1.5

A: OK. Shall we look at education first?

B: Sounds like a good place to start!

A: Right, well my view is that history books of the future will probably highlight the fact that today methods of teaching are changing. We're not all sitting at desks and listening to teachers talking. We learn by doing things and discussing in groups and teams. What's your opinion?

B: You're SO right. And add to that the fact that now lots of schools have their students working on computers and doing research in class and at home – it's a really big change.

A: Right – kids from five years old are using computers in class – it's amazing! They even start learning programming very early on. So good for their future education.

B: I couldn't agree more. Ways of educating are changing very quickly at the moment. There's a lot of research into how we learn and that's changing everything.

A: That's a really good point, and it leads us on to this prompt 'scientific progress'. I guess people in the future are going to remember us for all the advances in technology, don't you agree?

B: That's true, but on the other hand I don't think technology is going to stop advancing in the future. Everything will continue to get faster, smaller, easier to use …

A: Yes, I didn't mean that progress will stop in the future – just that we'll be remembered for when it first started to really speed up, and for being the first digital experts.

AUDIOSCRIPT

B: Absolutely. That's an excellent way of putting it. And I think we'll also be remembered for when space tourism started in earnest – the whole 'Fly me round the moon' thing!

A: Of course! When people in the future read about that, space tourism will probably be perfectly normal and natural …

B: But still expensive!

A: You can bet on that!

1.6

1

OK, let's move on to 'social issues.' Well, for me one of the biggest social issues today that I think will go in the history books is the housing problem that young people face. There are lots of young people looking for houses and very few houses that they can afford! So more and more young people – even those with babies and young children – are having to live with their parents for a long time. That can put huge strains on relationships. I can't believe that this problem has just been allowed to get worse and worse! Have you got any thoughts about that?

2

Right – so, 'popular culture'. I'd imagine that history will remember us for the explosion in reality TV shows. Personally, I don't watch many – just some of the talent series. But I think people in the future could well look back and think – wow – what on earth did they see in those shows? Don't you agree?

1.7

1

I usually get an idea and then start writing straight away. I think I write better like that. One thing leads to another, you know? I don't like to spend time over thinking and writing a plan – that's boring and not very creative. Most of the time I end up with a pretty good piece of writing!

2

I start off by underlining bits of the task that I must remember to include. Then I make some notes and group them into paragraphs. I find this really helps me structure my answer.

3

I think the more time you spend planning the better, and I always try to read it through again afterwards and look out for mistakes. Sometimes I add an extra adjective here or there.

4

I make a couple of notes, not many really, just a guide sort of thing. Then I write it up. I must admit I don't read it again. I've tried, but it usually seems OK to me, so now I don't bother. Your first thoughts are usually correct I find.

2.1

Hi, my name's Lisa and I'm here today to tell you my story of turning failure into success. As you're getting ready to graduate, you're probably all thinking about your future in some way. So, I'd like to ask you a question: what does success sound like to you? I bet you could all visualise success – fancy cars, designer clothes, an office door with your name on a gold plaque, but, to me, it's the public recognition that comes with sporting achievement. The sound of the crowd chanting my name resonated in my head when I was training. It made me dig deeper even when I was so exhausted that I felt I couldn't go on. For years, all I did was train, study, eat, sleep and repeat. Until one day, when I was in the final stages of making the junior Olympics team, I took a hard fall during a training match and tore a ligament in my knee so severely that it ended my dreams of being a professional athlete. Although they were all encouraging, I could tell that my family and my coach were upset, so I tried to be optimistic even though I was devastated.

Recovering from my knee injury took a long time. While being made to go to painful physiotherapy sessions three times a week was difficult, I struggled the most with being forced to rest indoors far more than I've ever done. Suddenly, after years of braving the elements on the hockey pitch, I was spending hours hunched over my laptop surfing the internet all day. I started to become skilled at recognising security flaws on websites and I soon found that I was dedicating my time to it in the same way I had done to my hockey training. I realised I could still be successful. I'd always know that being a world-class athlete took hard work and commitment, so I just needed to redirect my determination. Working in the tech industry is the opposite of sports, but I'm actually really enjoying it, and being out of my comfort zone has only pushed me harder. The knock-back in hockey became new inspiration.

Of course, it's not all been easy – I didn't just decide that I was going to be successful and it happened overnight. While I'm fortunate to have a good support system and I've benefited from a couple of lucky breaks, it has still been a long process and it's my self-belief that's been vital in helping get me here. I still face challenges and adversity every day. But, you know what? When I was fifteen I thought the worst thing in the world would be if I couldn't play hockey. I haven't played hockey for twenty years, yet I still think I'm doing pretty well as the first female CEO of a well-respected data security firm whose innovative solutions are trusted around the world – for me I'd say it's an honour. Failure happens to everyone, it's a part of life. I know that some of the things I've said today sound like clichés, but the message I want you to take away from this talk is that we *need* setbacks to give us the strength to achieve what we really want.

Now, I'd like to hear from you – how many of you here have been knocked back recently? How are you going to use that experience to build yourself back up?

3.1

I know that I shouldn't knock charities or charity workers as they do such valuable work, but I do sometimes feel that they are a bit behind in the way that they go about their work. It seems to be a sector which hasn't really evolved as fast as it could have done over the past few years. I think it's about time that they upped their game in terms of using more entrepreneurial ideas and much more creative ways of raising money. Banging a bucket for coins in shopping centres is sadly out of date. But if you want to hear about some real blue-sky thinking, then look no further than the Blue Cross. They have started this zany idea of using dogs as a way to help boost donations. The dogs wear specially-designed jackets with credit-card readers allowing people to donate without having to dig in their pockets for change. The dogs come from a guide-dog centre and so they are already trained and ready to work.

I'd read about something similar recently, but this was by far the more impressive idea. Organisations such as Blue Cross are changing the way we think about charities, and the faster this happens the more money they will be able to raise.

I think that this is a really cool way of tapping into the latest technology and at the same time making it easier for people to give money. People usually want to give money to charity, even if it's a token gesture. If people have to look for spare coins when they are asked to give money, it can put them off. Not everybody carries cash on them, runners and joggers probably don't. After all, cash is becoming a thing of the past.

3.3

I = Interviewer   C = Carol   J = Jason

I: Good morning and welcome. Today we'll be looking at community development programmes. First, I'd like to welcome Jason and Carol from the project Community Kitchen. Now, Carol, I understand that the whole idea for the Community Kitchen was yours. What motivated you?

C: I wouldn't say the whole project was my idea! But it was started by myself and two friends when we started to host 'community dinners' at the community centres. We'd make huge batches of simple, nutritious meals like fish pie or spaghetti Bolognese and charge people a small amount for them. So many people in the community worked at the supermarket warehouse, but lots of them lost their jobs or had their hours dramatically reduced. It had a big impact on a lot of people round here and it became more difficult for people to pay their bills, for groceries and things like that. Some parents couldn't afford to buy fruit and vegetables for their children. We held a meeting about it at the community centre, and it was unsettling to hear that so many people were left without enough money to buy proper food for their families.

I: Can we just touch on how much people have to pay for the meals?

C: Oh, we don't charge a lot, around thirty or forty pence per person. Because we buy ingredients and cook in bulk, the costs are much lower than the equivalent meal for, say, a family of four. All we ask for was enough to cover the cost of ingredients. Most people want to make a contribution, too. At one point, the demand got so high that we had to go to the council for financial help so that we could get proper catering equipment and expand the kitchen at the community centre. And that's when we met Jason, who has been an incredible support to us all. We still have to charge in order to keep the project going – funding from investors only covers major investments, not the day-to-day running costs, like ingredients.

I: Could you give us a bit of insight into your job as a community outreach worker, Jason?

J: Of course. Essentially, I liaise between local government and the local community, to deliver educational programmes and help both sides understand each other better. Having a positive impact on people's lives and empowering them to demand the services that they need is very rewarding, especially on a project like the Community Kitchen. Working on a project and seeing it come to life is definitely the best part of my job.

I: How long have you been involved in the project?

J: Well the Community Kitchen project has been running for just under a year – we're actually in the process of organising a big street party to celebrate its one-year anniversary, but the local government has been on board for around nine months. In addition to meeting a basic need in the community, by providing cheap, nutritious meals, as its expanded we've been able to get young people involved as volunteers, which is vital to the development of the community. Not only does this engage them in the community, but also equips them in skills such as team work as well as more practical qualifications in food hygiene – all of these help them become more employable. I get a great sense of pride in seeing the achievements that the young people we work with make.

I: How do you both feel about the future of the project?

J: One of the fantastic things about this project is its sustainability. Really, I think that this is the key to its current and future success. It generates enough income to cover its expenses. Now that the community centre kitchen has been turned into a functioning catering kitchen that meets regulations standards, we're planning on carrying out a series of workshops on healthy eating for children in the area, as part of the government's commitment to reducing childhood obesity.

C: I agree – we are able to buy ingredients from the money charged for each meal and we have recently started making a small profit, too. We are saving that money to use in the future to purchase larger items. Personally, I'd like to expand into home delivery. Although the dinners at the community centre have strengthened relationships between people in the community, I think it's important for families to spend mealtimes bonding and talking about their day. Plus, logistically, it's not always possible for people to come to the community centre during serving hours. Having recyclable containers and a couple of bikes for the volunteers to deliver meals around the community would help us expand and benefit more people.

I: Well, that sounds just …

3.4
1
It's hard to make a decision about this and the main reason I say that is because there are pros and cons to all the options.

2
We can't change the planning laws! You've just got to look at what happens if people are allowed to extend their houses without any consultation! It's a nightmare.

3
People need to eat less sugar. If you think about it, one biscuit contains huge amounts.

4
Buying from websites you don't know can be dangerous. My point is that you don't know how secure your payments are.

5
In my opinion it's important to save money every week. For a start, you never know when you might really want to buy something big.

6
There are lots of benefits of sharing a flat. A good example is that there's always someone to chat to or to ask advice from.

3.6
To be honest, I would say that most of these would take a lot of getting used to! It's a pretty big step. You're leaving behind your comfort zone, aren't you? I guess it would depend on the individual – but I would say that it might be having more learner independence. It's not going to be a quick change, like maybe getting to know new people – it's going to take time to get used to not having as much support as we're used to. What do you think?

4.1
I = Interviewer   V = Vicky   N = Noah

I: Today the sun is out and I am at the University of Southampton to interview some students to find out what fashion really means for them. A subject which has caused much debate from students so far. First, I'd like to start with Vicky, a student from the faculty of Ecology and Marine Conservation. Vicky, can you tell us about what fashion means for you please?

V: I have to admit that I enjoy choosing my clothes and combining different ideas. Why not? For me it's something creative and I get a lot of enjoyment from it. I choose my clothes carefully though, none of those synthetic fabrics that are so bad for the skin. I wear clothes which are eco-friendly and consistent with my beliefs. My clothes are an expression of who I am.

I: That's great. And so you think that your look is different from that of your friends?

V: I think so. Fashion is an expression of our individuality. It's our way of making a statement about who we are. My clothes reflect my choices and my unique taste.

I: Would you say then that you follow the latest fashion trends?

V: No, I don't think so. I never take any interest in high street fashion. Fashion doesn't have to be all about following the latest trends. All trends are repeated and they all become indistinguishable from each other. I don't know why we keep trying to re-invent the wheel.

I: Thanks very much, Vicky. Now let me turn to Noah, a second-year student. Noah, you mentioned to me earlier that you're not interested in fashion. Is that true?

N: Absolutely! To be honest there are so many other areas which are worthy of our attention. Just look around you – politics, science, the arts – take your pick. By comparison, fashion really is such a meaningless thing. Also it's so ephemeral, what is fashionable now will be forgotten very soon.

I: So there are no fashion trends that you follow?

N: Certainly not. Right now a lot of people look the spitting image of scarecrows! You know, with that trend for wearing their jackets halfway down their backs.

I: I take it that fashion doesn't occupy much of your thoughts or time.

N: Absolutely not! Talking about fashion is equivalent to a conversation about biscuits. I'm not interested in the slightest in trends. What is more important in life I think are values which are constant and which are eternal as opposed to something so meaningless and transient.

I: I suppose I should have predicted this response from a philosophy student!

N: In all honesty, I feel sorry for fashion victims at times because I think that they're just being brainwashed by the media to think a certain way. Fashion victims are carbon copies of each other. They just want to follow each other like sheep and fit in with the crowd.

4.3
Extract 1
You are going to listen to two presenters talking on a radio show about names.

A: Today, we're going to be talking about how your name gives you a sense of identity. Our name can greatly influence the shaping of our personality. Some cultures believe that strong names will prepare their child for success. If we feel negatively about our name, we can transfer those feelings to our sense of self. Take a recent court case in the USA of a boy who took his parents to court because he was being ridiculed by his peers about his non-traditional name. He was desperate to change it and his parents wouldn't let him, even though it was affecting his self-esteem.

B: And did the judge overrule his parents?

A: Yes, I was glad to read that the judge allowed him to change his name to one that both the boy and his parents are happy with.

B: And quite rightly, too. After everything that he has been through with his original name, it would incredibly unfair to give him another name that he wasn't happy with. If you think about it, choosing a name for a baby is a huge responsibility and I'm sure most people don't even realise it – I have some friends who decided on their child's name on the spur of the moment in the hospital room! I know that sometimes the name has a special meaning to the parents, but they should really consider the way it could affect their child in the future.

Extract 2
N: You are going to listen to a teacher talking to a new student.

A: How have you been settling in?

B: All of the teachers have been really understanding about giving me a chance to get to grips with the way school works here. There is one thing that has been bothering me, but I haven't been sure about how to bring it up before. I don't want to make too much of a fuss and I'd rather not have to mention this, but I think it's important. The thing is, a lot of teachers seem to have trouble pronouncing my name. Some of the teachers try, but they just end up getting flustered and so they don't ask me anything else for the rest of the lesson, and a couple of teachers have even gone as far as saying that they'd rather pronounce it the way that is easiest for them, or have asked if they can call me by an English name.

A: And how does that make you feel?

B: At first, I didn't think too much into it. I know it's not a common name here, but, in some classes, it's causing some awkwardness and I don't like being singled out. Also, as time goes on I've realised that, actually, it isn't fair to be called something different. Yes, my name is difficult to sound out phonetically for people who only speak English, but is just as much a part of me as anything else, and I feel like I'd be losing my sense of identity and my heritage if I adopted an English-sounding name.

Extract 3
You are going to listen part of a radio interview between a chat show host and a blogging expert.

A: I'm going to pass over to Nab Jenkins, aka Fab Nab, to tell us a little bit about his success as a blogger.

B: You may be surprised to hear that the key to my success is my name. I used to resent having such an obscure name when I was younger, and sometimes people didn't even believe it was my real name! When you're a blogger or influencer, however, a memorable name increases the chances of sticking in people's head. The most impressive social media or blog content is useless if your name is forgettable or is too complicated for people to remember.

A: What advice would you give a budding blogger on choosing a catchy name?

B: Before anything else, try working with what you have. Take me. Nab is a pretty well-known classical name in Scotland. My mum gave me this name because she wanted me to keep a bit of her Scottish heritage. However, I've never met anyone else called Nab in the USA and there probably aren't any other bloggers with the same name. Plus, it rhymes so easily with 'Fab'. So, before you start racking your brains trying to come up with something wonderfully original, write down your own name and think of associated words, words that rhyme, plays on words, etc. That way, you can come up with something unique, but still retain your identity.

4.4
OK, so if we're looking at how important it is for good friends to have common experiences, then I'd say it depends! On one hand, yes, it's great to have shared experiences – like when you're growing up, at school and so on – there's always that common ground between you. But it's not the be all and end all … I mean, if you've got a new friend, then you don't have those shared experiences, but you'll probably share future ones, won't you? And that's just as important. What do you think?

4.5
T = Teacher   A = Student A   B = Student B
1
T: Some people say that the friends we make when we're very young remain our best friends. Do you agree? Why / Why not?

2
T: People often expect children to have similar personalities to their parents, but they don't. Why might this be?

A: That's tricky! I think a lot of parents think that their children will turn out to be mini versions of themselves! In particular, I think they expect them to be good at or interested in the same things, maybe not so much the same personalities. I know my dad thought I'd want to be a doctor like him – but I don't! The thing is, children are influenced by so much – not just their parents. I mean – indirectly – like what their friends think and so on. Don't you think that's true?

3

T: Do you think you can make really good friends online, without ever meeting them? Why / Why not?

B: There's no one answer to this question, really. I'd have to say yes and no! On one hand, I think you can make good friends, for example, in other countries, online, but part of me thinks you can't really get to know another person well without meeting them and talking face to face. You learn a lot about a person by doing things together, like we said before.

5.1

1

I wouldn't say this is my favourite department store because it is a bit pricey. But the design of the shop pushes all the right buttons because it's such a lovely place to wander around. So it's worth a visit even if I come out empty handed.

2

I'm looking for one of those Persian-style rugs for my lounge and this morning I checked them out at the market. But the salesman was so insistent that it really put me off buying it; I hate it when they give you the hard sell. I did see one which I thought would be perfect though … perhaps I'll venture back and try again.

3

I've been chatting to Jude about organising a weekend away at the end of the month. We're thinking about glamping in Wales. You know glamorous camping. However I've already spent most of my allowance this month, so I'm going to have to watch my money. I reckon if I don't go out at all, or buy any coffees, that I'll just about manage it.

4

It's my grandparents' wedding anniversary next month. They've been together for sixty years. Can you believe it!? Jackie and I are going to get them one of those weekend packages away. That's if I can convince her … you know Jackie. My sister is really mean when it comes to spending, and never wants to part with money.

5

Look at this rose bush! Isn't it just wonderful? OK, I know that you are going to ask me what on earth I'm going to do with it and why I bought it … I just couldn't resist buying it at such a knock-down price, and it will look stunning on the terrace. I've even got the spot for it. Come with me and I'll show you!

6

I know I said that I wasn't going to have any junk food this week, and I'm not. Just saying. I haven't ordered any takeaways at all. Not even when Kevin was round the other night. He suggested a Chinese, but I stood firm. But now … I have this insatiable desire for a pepperoni pizza. What's wrong with me? Tell me I shouldn't, please. I shouldn't, should I?

5.3

Speaker 1

When I moved from France during my teens, there were so many things I had to learn culturally that I kept a log of them in my journal. My French friends insisted that I should turn it into a business opportunity, but I wasn't convinced there was a market for it until I started interning at the French consulate and heard stories from kids who were struggling like I'd been. Using my teenage scribblings to make a business plan was tough, especially when my internship had ended because I didn't have anything on the backburner in case it didn't work out. In the end, though, that was both terrifying and liberating. That fear definitely pushed me harder.

Speaker 2

Never forget the moment you had your original idea, that one that inspired you. Mine was on a drive home from work on another stressful day, just before I drove past the remains of a roadside accident. It seemed like a sign, so I quit my job the next day. I would definitely encourage all young entrepreneurs to seek out mentors, but be careful not to let this take over. Expertise can make your product or service better, but it's easy to fall into the trap of trying to please everyone. No one knows your idea better than you so trust your own intuition and what you are trying to achieve.

Speaker 3

Something that I learnt to accept early on was that building a start-up isn't just a job, it's a way of life. It sounds like a cliché to say that you live and breathe it, but that's how it can feel. After I began working on my business idea, I came close to quitting so many times, but my mates convinced me to keep going. I was so grateful for that support when I finally opened my company and started trading. Working so intensely on something can have a negative impact on your personal life and it's essential not to lose sight of other aspects of your life.

Speaker 4

Learning to embrace your mistakes is an important skill for any entrepreneur. So many things went wrong in the beginning that I was tempted to just retreat and give up, especially when I accidentally deleted all of my notes for my first prototype. My university professor told me to keep going, but I'd almost had enough. It wasn't until I travelled to South Africa to listen to a talk by an industry leader that I realised that I was holding myself back. His talk reminded me how much I enjoyed the area I was working in and that maybe I purposely chose it over working for someone else. Now that my company is finally trading, I try to keep it fun.

Speaker 5

Ironically, most start-ups fail in the beginning because the founders have too much to do and get overwhelmed, not because they are poorly-received or are huge failures, so it's important not to lose your passion for your idea. After getting my original idea during a charity trip to Indonesia, I could have easily fallen into that trap. I knew there was a need for my product in rural communities all over the world, but turning the idea into a business was difficult, even though a local factory offered to help me with the initial manufacturing. Going to a networking event for entrepreneurs with similar business models helped me move forward. I learned how to simplify my goals and focus on small achievements so I could stay motivated.

5.4

OK, I'm going to talk about these pictures – the students in the classroom and the one where the children are playing shops. I would say that both pictures were taken in an educational environment, but whereas the first shows teenage students in a formal classroom or lecture situation, the second could well have been taken at some sort of playschool. Clearly the ways of learning about money are very different because in the first, information is being given maybe as part of a course. The children in the second are learning through play. Thinking about the usefulness or effectiveness of the two methods, it's hard to say, but I think I'm right in saying that learning through play or learning through doing something is usually better than listening to theory. However, both groups are learning different things about money. In all probability the children will be learning about the value of money, whereas the students could well be learning how to manage their money when they're working or studying at university. In that case, both ways of learning are likely to be very useful. When it comes to how they're feeling, it's highly likely that some of the students are a bit bored! I may be wrong but their body language shows that to me. The kids, however, look as if they're having a great time.

5.6

Your pictures show people dealing with money in different situations. Compare two of the pictures and say why the people might be dealing with money in these different situations and what difficulties they might face.

6.1

J = Journalist   P = Patrick   M = Melanie

J: Today I'm talking to a children's illustrator, Patrick Hampton, and a child psychologist, Melanie Rowles. Patrick, you've been selling soft toys of Oscar the Owl to help parents support children with their emotional development. How did you come up with the idea?

P: A few years ago, my little sister had to spend a month in hospital, and even though I spent hours with her every evening, it broke my heart to see her look so afraid and lonely every time we left the hospital at night. So I drew her a picture of an owl and called it Oscar. I told her that owls are night animals so it would stay awake to look over her. By the time she was discharged, all of the children on the ward had asked for pictures of Oscar the Owl next to their beds. For some reason, it really resonated with them. I'd been struggling to get noticed as an illustrator, and it was the most artwork I'd had commissioned! Although I've always drawn doodles for my sister, I'd never thought about children's illustration as a career, it seemed too silly and I thought of myself as more serious. But I figured that I had nothing to lose so I developed the character of Oscar the Owl more and invented a short back story, then started selling different versions of the illustration on a peer-to-peer e-commerce site.

J: How long did it take you to start making regular sales?

P: It actually gained momentum pretty quickly, and I was able to set up my own website dedicated to Oscar the Owl. Eventually, I was able to raise enough capital to start producing and selling soft toy versions of Oscar. I realised that I'd tapped into something special when I got a call from a children's author, telling me that she'd been inspired to turn the idea into a series of storybooks and asking me to illustrate it. I've also had emails from teachers about ways they've used Oscar in the classroom. I honestly had no idea that it would be used by so many people in so many different ways, but given that the premise is uncomplicated, I suppose it makes sense that people could connect with it and use it as a springboard for development.

J: Melanie, from a psychological point of view, what benefit can something like Oscar the Owl have for children?

M: Actually, Oscar the Owl can be used to exploit some very serious issues, such as bereavement and abandonment. Children often feel more comfortable sharing their feelings with imaginary creatures, and the owl is traditionally seen as a wise, solid creature. While I wouldn't recommend allowing children to become too reliant on Oscar the Owl, or indeed any other physical substitute for human contact, being able to open up about things that are troubling or upsetting them can help process difficult feelings. This is especially useful for children who are more withdrawn or children who may be developing emotionally at a slower rate than normally expected for their age. Children are known for having very active imaginations and believe that Oscar the Owl is real. This can also be exploited by parents as a tool for reinforcing positive behaviour, for example by writing notes from the owl thanking the child for tidying up their bedroom.

J: Do you think it's dishonest to encourage children to believe that something is true when it isn't?

M: Not necessarily. While some psychologists believe that leading children to believe that certain things exist when they don't can inhibit their imagination, I think that it feeds their imagination. It's possible that children may feel let down to learn that something isn't true, but make-believe isn't about tricking children into believing something. It's about presenting them with a situation and then letting them take it from there. Children actually learn to differentiate between fiction and reality at a much earlier age than many people realise, so they are able to understand that what they imagine isn't necessarily possible in the real world.

J: Finally, how important do you think imaginative play is in the age of technology?

M: Oh, incredibly important. I can't stress just how important it is! Children benefit enormously from games of make-believe as it stimulates the learning process. If you ask me, there's no harm in indulging children's naturally inquisitive natures, especially when real life can be so bleak sometimes and some children have to deal with tough situations at a young age. I grew up in the countryside having adventures in the woods fighting battles with sticks and making friends with the people who lived in the river. It makes me uncomfortable to think that a generation might miss out on the simple pleasures of running around on a made-up quest in favour of an electronics-based one.

P: I see the difference in the way that they play and the games that we used to play when we were younger. Children spend so much time on screens nowadays and while I recognise that there are some fantastic interactive games out there, for me, nothing beats traditional play. Even the most advanced electronic games are limited to the specifications of the software, whereas there are no limits on what a child can create using a cardboard box!

6.3

Oh yes, this is really interesting. You think you're getting the full truth from someone but what's to say that you are? They could say almost anything, make up stories just to get us interested. And to be perfectly honest, perhaps their memories aren't that clear! For me, it's not that important – unless they tell fibs about other people I guess. What do you think?

6.5

You know, as far as I'm concerned, there's a lot of mistrust about all of these things, but most people, I would say, have lost faith in the honesty of advertisements, not only food ones. It's cynical, I know, but advertisers have a terrible reputation for being very careful with the truth! Don't you agree?

7.1

1 Mark

Social media has really changed our lives and the way that we can get things done. I can't imagine what it would be like to live without it really. It's so easy to get your message across to people and to ask them for help. I know that some people think that people my age are too reliant on social media, but I think that nowadays it's really essential for any business. Looking back a few years, we ought to have known that social media would be the key to success.

2 Alexia

I had been toying with the idea of doing something different before going to university. My parents wanted me to go straight to university, but I wasn't

so sure. I guess I just saw this time as an opportunity to do something for myself, and for others as it turns out. I suppose that they imagined that after university I would get a job straight away. I wouldn't have even thought about doing voluntary work if it hadn't been for my friend Sam. He went to Thailand and had such a great time that I couldn't resist copying him.

3 Simon

I'm outraged at the way that cyclists are treated in our town. I cycle to college every day and I have been doing so for years. I think that cycling is a way of reducing carbon emissions and it's a way of keeping healthy at the same time. The amount of cycle lanes in the centre of town is pathetic. Near to James Square I have to get off and walk because there just isn't enough space for cyclists. If I'd written to my political representative, I could have put a stop to this earlier. I just didn't think about it.

4 Sally

I've been trying to raise awareness about the amount of rubbish on the beach in our town. I go walking on the beach every morning and just recently it seems to be getting worse. I think it may be because people have parties on the beach. That's fine, but I don't think that people should be allowed to leave their rubbish behind. I started an online campaign to get people to think about the problem and to sign a petition. The response from the public has been amazing and I realise now that at the beginning I was needlessly worried that people wouldn't take me seriously.

5 Joanna

My friend Amanda and I believe that we get too much homework to do at school, especially over the weekends. We both play volleyball in the school team and it's just getting impossible to do sport and the homework. So we went to the students' union and asked them for advice. They suggested that we could start a petition to see if other students feel the same way. But the petition was a failure; we only got one response so we might just as well have not bothered.

7.2

P = Professor   E = Erica

Extract 1

P: Erica, I was very impressed with your project proposal. You're obviously very passionate about this topic; I felt that came across very strongly in your proposal.

E: Thank you. My family didn't have much money and I used to get upset about not having the latest fashions like my friends. Then, my grandmother gave me a lot of her old clothes – she loves fashion, too. I loved going to her house and talking about fabrics and patterns as we adjusted the clothes to make them look more modern. It also showed me that many trends are just a replica of other people's ideas from years ago, with a few twists.

P: Yes, I noticed that you feel very strongly about the commercialisation of fashion and exploiting past trends for profit.

E: I think it really suffocates creativity, as it's almost impossible to produce original designs on the kind of scale that large chains use. It frustrates me that clothes shops are always pushing consumers to buy their new products when they've only used a different pattern or textile. I know it's a ploy to get us to spend more money, but it sets a really high standard for smaller shops and lesser known designers to follow, and consumers start to expect new products regularly.

Extract 2

M: I can't believe that you shelled out so much money for a smartphone. It looks almost identical to mine and I paid much less. There's really no need to spend a lot of money on electronic goods nowadays because as soon as a flagship model comes out from a well-known brand, you can guarantee that a cheaper copy will be on the market a few weeks later.

F: Yes, but the quality isn't the same. I agree that there's no originality in the design of electronics, but they fall down on durability and functionality.

M: Maybe that's why the market leaders don't go after the firms that sell imitations of their products, because they know that their quality speaks for itself.

F: I don't think that's the reason, I think it's just that they simply can't keep up with the fast turnaround times. Sometimes copycat versions of gadgets go on sale on cut-price wholesale websites for a much lower price than the original before entrepreneurs have even managed to manufacture their first batch. It's just a reality nowadays that good ideas will fall victim to copycats, which is a shame because it means that people with genuinely good ideas that could become quality products don't stand a chance. Unfortunately, though, I really don't think that a lot can be done to stop it.

Extract 3

M: What do you think about the choice of novel for this term, Sandra?

F: I'm not very pleased with it. I understand that Mr. Parsons is trying to engage us more in reading by choosing young adult novels, but personally I've had enough of alternate universe novels. I used to really like them, but the only ones I truly enjoy are the ones that sparked the trend, mainly because they really were original and there were so many twists and turns. Lately, I've given up on so many books a few chapters in because it's blatantly obvious what is going to happen.

M: I know what you mean. Writing is supposed to be about creativity, not blatantly copying a plot and tweaking a few minor details.

F: True, although there's always been an overlap between stories. I don't mean swiping other writers' ideas, but the more you read, the more likely you are to be influenced by other writers. Personally, I think that the best writers have their own unique style; you know who is writing it instantly.

M: I agree. The novels you remember are the ones that stand alone and have the strongest personal identity. I wonder how many of the stories that are being churned out at the moment will have the sort of legacy of a classic like *To Kill a Mockingbird*?

7.4

T = Teacher   F = Female

F: Fine – yes – I'd like to talk about these two. First of all, of course the people at the rocket launch must be very excited, because it's obviously something that you don't see every day, and it's important for all of us because it's … like … progress – and science needs to advance and also it can give everyone a good feeling, a boost because it's a good news story. Regarding the weather – it's a cold, snowy day and I guess the people are cold and a bit fed up, particularly if they've got to get somewhere on time. They might be worried that they're going to slip over, too. It's important to show what the weather is like on the news because people need to know what to expect and what clothes to wear! Perhaps, also, the weather is different in your part of the country and you need to know what's happening to people in other areas. Personally, I don't always believe in the weather forecasts, but having said this … pictures of current weather situations are interesting. Moving on to comparing these pictures, both pictures show things we can sometimes see on the news which are relevant to our lives in different ways. The differences are quite big, one shows an event which is quite unusual whereas the other …

T: Thank you.

AUDIOSCRIPT

8.1

Speaker 1

I share a flat with Emily and Dan and it does get a bit chaotic at times. But I like to know where my stuff is and I suppose I'm actually quite tidy. I have the occasional clear up and throw out things I don't need. I like sharing a flat, but when people borrow my things without asking it drives me insane, and I just can't help letting rip.

Speaker 2

This year I've passed all my exams and so I'm off on holiday, without a care in the world! But it hasn't always been like this and I sometimes have to study in the summer. What I really hate is having to study alone. When I have to re-take exams in the summer when my friends have holiday I just have to grin and bear it.

Speaker 3

I like to treat people with respect and be polite. I expect the same back from people, it's only normal, I think. Some people tend to think that they are the only ones in the world and that everything revolves around them. When I feel that someone is not treating me with respect then I have to get it off my chest and tell them how I feel.

Speaker 4

I've always been an animal lover from a very young age. I just think there are so many cruel people around or people that treat others badly. Then there are animals. They are innocent creatures and we should treat them with respect and care. Some people don't look after animals in the way they should do and it infuriates me. I can't stand cruelty to animals and if I catch people doing it, then I really lose control and shoot my mouth off.

Speaker 5

I like to know what I'm going to be doing in advance. I suppose I'm extremely organised, but I like it that way. Every morning I make a list of things that I have to do during the day and then I cross them off as I go through the day. It may seem strange, but I like it that way. If people change my plans without my permission, then I am not happy, and you can tell by my long face.

8.2

Hi everyone. I'm Rebecca and I'm a dietician. I studied Food Science and Nutrition just like you, so I'm very excited to be here today to tell you a little bit about the relationship between food and energy, which I've been researching as part of a new TV documentary that will air later this year.

Now, let's begin with the basics. Food's essential to life, everyone's aware of that. It gives us energy and protects our bodies from becoming susceptible to a whole host of ailments, by boosting our immune system. However, while there's no denying that food is the cure for many problems, it's also the cause of others. The most well-known of these is overeating, which can lead to obesity. Increased demand for and production of industrialised food has wreaked havoc on the natural environment, mainly due to the packaging which companies think is mouth-watering and attractive, but in my opinion is excessive. When it's non-biodegradable plastic, it poses threats to wildlife and complicates waste disposal. In contrast to this shocking waste, there are a vast number of people around the world who still don't have access to the quality food they need – this situation seems shameful to me.

So do we really need to rely completely on food for fuel or should we be looking more closely at other alternatives?

Throughout history, there have been many documented accounts of people claiming to live without food. In my documentary, I spoke to followers of different cultural practices who claim not to have eaten for years. Some spend hours looking at the sun each day in the belief that this will remove the desire to eat or drink because their body will absorb all of the nutrients it needs from the sun, while others believe that the body can be sustained by transforming spiritual energy into nutrients. Honestly, I don't believe referring to starving yourself as an eternal fast makes it meaningful or worthwhile!

More recently, an engineer called Rob Rhinehart has embarked on an ambitious project to create a drink that contains the optimal balance of nutrients that the body needs, in an attempt to reduce dependency on buying food. After a long period of trial and error, he finally settled on what he considered to be the perfect combination of thirty-nine ingredients, which included vitamins, minerals, carbohydrates and oil-based fats. Rob has received heavy criticism, which is understandable. I am concerned that his claims even seem dangerous. The amount of food that a person needs to consume is different for each person. It's not only based on their weight or age, it depends more on his or her lifestyle, so there's no magic formula.

There's still heavy scepticism around and criticism of claims of living without food, and quite rightly so. Looking directly into the sun can cause blindness. Although natural sunlight is a proven source of vitamin D, the body depends on a combination of different vitamins in order to function properly. What concerns me the most is the possibility that a miracle meal-replacement drink could be sold to the mass market. Although diet shakes and liquid diets are nothing new, they're usually medically controlled and are never presented as a long-term solution, which is exactly what Rob Rhinehart is proposing.

In my upcoming documentary, I investigate the scientific principles behind ancient and modern practices that cut out food in order to prove that they're potentially life-threatening. Although claimants may not immediately feel any harmful side effects, they're putting their bodies at substantial risk as not all ailments immediately manifest themselves physically; many health problems may only come to light after some time, when it could be too late. There are no two ways about it: food is essential for survival.

8.3

Extract 1

So, looking at whether doctors should be paid more than teachers, I would say definitely yes. If you think about it, doctors have to study for years and years at university and they are essential to society. I'm not saying that teachers aren't, but to become a doctor you must be really dedicated.

Also look at the number of hours they work. They have very long days and work at weekends, too – a lot of them. They certainly earn their money.

OK, let's look at the next prompt …

Extract 2

A: Well, as far as I'm concerned, the government definitely needs to invest more money than they already do in healthcare facilities. And, quite honestly, that's because we're all living longer so there's a real drain on the current resources. In my case, our local hospital is too small to deal with all the patients – there just aren't enough beds! So they have to send people to another hospital a long way away – which isn't good because their families can't visit them. I also feel that there need to be more doctors' surgeries closer to people's homes …

B: Governments have already invested a lot of money in healthcare facilities – it just isn't managed very well. There's enough money in the system, but it isn't going to the right places – there must be more efficiency, not more money.

Extract 3

There's been a lot on the news recently about food labelling. It's all about manufacturers being legally obliged to put detailed information about their products on the packaging. I'm not really sure how important that is. I guess, on one hand, it's good that people can read about what's in their food, like too much salt or sugar … or even nuts for those people who are allergic, but I'm not convinced that having it there means people are going to bother to read about it. I'd say the people who read the details are the sort of people who know a lot about food and health anyway and know what they should or shouldn't eat. Most of us are just pretty lazy, I would say, and couldn't be bothered to …

8.4

1

For me, this is one of the most important things people can do to help keep healthy. These days most of us work long hours and students like us study all day and then have loads of homework or assignments to do once college has finished. I think this can cause a lot of stress and that leads to all sorts of problems. Trying to ensure that you get enough time to relax is really important, and one way of doing this is to …

2

I'm not too sure about this one. How much of these extra supplements that you can buy now – well, how much is necessary or just part of a growing big business – people spend lots of money on vitamins every month and I'm pretty sure that most of these things we get from a well-balanced meal anyway. Don't you agree?

3

This is an interesting one – how valuable are health websites? Mm – I know my mum is always on those. She gets a pain somewhere and straightaway she's online checking it out. Sometimes I think they do more harm than good – you know – she'll get stressed out, eventually go to the doctor and find out she got the wrong end of the stick online! But, I don't know, I guess some of them help people.

9.1

1

I've been a member of a 'castellers' group since I was about ten years old. My brother took me along one day to a group that he belonged to. I fell in love with it immediately! What I love about 'castellers' is being part of a team.

Nowadays my position is on the fourth layer up. When I was smaller I used to climb higher up, but not terribly high as I'm not that brave. No way would I ever have gone right to the top!

2

I know that some people think that we are mad and that doing this is a very risky way to spend our weekends. In fact, we practise every Tuesday evening, too, so it's quite a few hours a week. It's really not as dangerous as people think, though. Never have I hurt myself when doing 'castellers'.

It's true that in order to be safe we have to really be in form, practise regularly, concentrate on what we are doing and above all trust the rest of the team. If one person falls then we often all fall. Under no circumstances would I recommend this to anyone who is afraid of heights.

3

I love being a part of our local 'castellers' group. We meet twice a week between June and November. I know it must sound like a big commitment, but there are a lot of us and we don't have to go every week. I'm really obsessed with it, though. Not only do I go every week, but I've joined a second group!

Usually people join because it's a family thing. But not in my case. In fact my family thinks I'm crazy because I often miss out on weekend breaks if it's the season for 'castellers'. Only once did I miss a Sunday last year, when I was ill.

9.2

Speaker 1

I make a point to schedule in regular studying breaks so I can keep hold of the content I'm studying. Taking a break sounds simple, but it sometimes makes me feel like a failure. I'm so determined to do well in an exam that I want to take advantage of every spare second and so it's frustrating when my body won't cooperate, even though I'm well aware that it's counterproductive to try to force yourself to work or study. I'm definitely guilty of devising revision timetables that are too intense and I usually ask my flatmate to take a look at it and give me a reality check.

Speaker 2

My job requires me to be creative, and, unfortunately, creativity doesn't always come when I want it to. Sometimes I can struggle all morning to come up with a realistic dialogue between characters, and then I have a sudden burst of inspiration and I'm afraid to stop in case I lose it and have to start again. I have to force myself to take some time out because I know that I'll pay for it later. It isn't productive if it means that I can't work properly for the next day or two because I can't focus on the task. Striking a balance can be tricky,

Speaker 3

Working in an office-based job means it's easy to fall into the trap of spending the whole day indoors. Most of my colleagues have lunch at their desks and meetings are often scheduled for during the lunch period because people take it for granted that you'll be in the office. I wish I could go for a proper walk every lunchtime, but I can usually only fit in a quick stroll around the block. At least it clears my head and I go back to my desk feeling refreshed, which means I don't get tired and avoid the typical mid-afternoon slump that I'd get if I didn't get any fresh air.

Speaker 4

I work in customs at the port, and taking regular breaks is pretty impossible. If a ship arrives ahead of or behind schedule, or doesn't have the correct paperwork, it can cause everything to go off schedule. It's not uncommon to spend the whole shift sorting out a problem and because of the logistics involved I can't just take time out. I'm going to speak to my supervisor about this, though, because the other day I had to check two huge shipments and did a double shift without a break. Driving home feeling so tired felt dangerous, and I was terrified I'd crash into another car.

Speaker 5

I have to attend a lot of meetings, but I make sure not to schedule more than two meetings back to back, otherwise I start getting awful headaches. Sometimes this can be unavoidable, especially when a meeting overruns or head office sends me more tasks to do. The company has just been taken over and I'm really keen to impress the senior management team. I want to present myself as hardworking and proactive, so I don't feel like I can ignore emails or phone calls because I'm taking a break. Sometimes I just have to keep myself hydrated, make a quick fix with subtle exercises like flexing my feet and hope that works!

9.3

I = Interlocutor   C = Student

I: Your pictures show people working in different ways. Compare two of the pictures and say what the advantages of working in these ways might be and how the people might be feeling.

C: OK, I'd like to talk about these two pictures. Clearly, both pictures are of people working and getting a job done, and both situations are meetings of some sort. However, they show two completely different ways of working. Whereas the people in the video meeting are in an office or a meeting room, the ones sitting on the floor are in a much more relaxed setting. The purpose of both types of meeting could well be the same – that is, to bring together people's ideas, but in the first picture the people involved are linked by screens and the interaction is not quite as spontaneous as it should be in the picture of the other much more informal meeting. In the formal meeting, the people give

their opinions or contributions politely, in turns, whereas I'm sure the others interrupt each other or talk over each other at times! Because of the relaxed setting, I'm sure they get a lot more actually done – a big advantage! As to how they're feeling, I would say that the people in the informal meeting are really engaged with what they're doing and are quite excited or enthusiastic about the brainstorming or activity they're involved in. Regarding the other picture, although they're smiling I guess the people might be a bit bored!

9.5

Which people are likely to finish their work quickest?

9.6

Your pictures show people working in different situations. Compare two of the pictures and say why the people might have chosen to work in these situations and what might prevent them from working efficiently.

10.1

1

N: You overhear two friends discussing Escape Rooms, the physical adventure games.

F: Hey, have you seen they've opened an Escape Room in town? You know, one of those places where you go in a group to resolve a puzzle and escape. Fancy it?

M: Yes, I heard about it. I don't reckon it will take off, though. People are not really fussed about video games any more. Well, apart from the geeky ones. Also, I'm not sure that most people are that interested in resolving mysteries. It sounds more like a niche idea and may take off on a small scale. I can't say I'm keen.

F: Well, I'm not into video games either, but I reckon it would be fun on so many levels. You know – the problem solving, negotiation, teamwork and all that. Like taking a video game to another level and making it much more interactive and dynamic. It would do you the power of good to really switch off with something so immersive.

M: I can see the appeal in terms of doing something together and I suppose it could be a laugh providing it's not too expensive. But the idea of resolving a physical puzzle or analysing group dynamics does *not* sound like my idea of fun, and I really don't think it's going to be a crowd pleaser in our town.

F: You can be so difficult to please at times …

2

N: You will hear part of a discussion between two architects about the Tiny House Movement.

M: I've just come back from a conference about the Tiny House Movement. You know, the social movement that encourages people to downsize the space they live in. Really thought-provoking stuff.

F: I reckon it's a fleeting phase. Addressing a problem we have at the moment: lack of dwellings in popular locations and soaring house prices. I'm sceptical about whether it's here to stay.

M: But I think that all sorts of people stand to benefit. Students, single people, single-parent families, first-time buyers. The nuclear family is becoming something of an anomaly and the housing we offer needs to reflect this.

F: Well, I've read that these houses are an inexpensive alternative, but the expense of building them is not really cutting the costs. The smaller pieces need to be custom-built which is a costly business, and hence counterproductive. Also, they are so impractical! The idea of having children in something so small is simply not viable. As for the actual living together …

M: OK, the initial costs are higher, but as they become more commonplace, this should have a knock-on effect on the costing *and* people will save on high rents and mortgages.

F: Well, I'd be very reluctant to advise my clients to go down this route. It just doesn't make financial sense as we just don't know if people will eventually get a return on their equity.

M: Time will tell.

3

You hear part of a conversation between friends about look-alikes, doppelgängers.

M: Did you read that article about that guy who met his double on a plane? You know the one who went to find his seat and there was someone who looked incredibly like him. Freaky!!

F: Oh, yes, you're talking about doppelgängers, look-alikes. I did, but I don't really believe all the hype about that. According to stuff I've read, we all have a double somewhere in the world. I just think – so what?

M: But you're so cynical about it. Where's your curiosity? I think it would be amazing to meet your own double.

F: Not really. Perhaps if you look far enough, it's bound to happen. You know, fortuity. Quite frankly I like to spend my time and money on more intellectually challenging stuff!

M: Talking about spending money, I heard about these agencies that you can sign up to and they do searches to find your match.

F: For goodness sake! If you believe the press, the whole issue has caused no end of problems with people having DNA tests, etcetera, to prove that there is or there isn't a link between them.

M: I guess I did take the article at face value and I was really taken in by it. When you put it like that, I suppose you have a point.

10.2

Hi everyone. I'll begin with a confession; I really struggled to come up with a topic for this presentation. Deciding on a topic that I found truly interesting was more difficult than I had anticipated. It's no secret that my talent lies in arts-based subjects, rather than science, and so I decided to draw upon my creativity for my presentation today. I considered going for a dynamic presentation using impressive slides and audio cues, but, in the end, I decided to concentrate on a more straightforward approach. So, with Mrs Hobbs' permission, I began to investigate a more alternative view of biology. Traditionally, we expect to apply biology to our lives in a straightforward, factual sense. To begin with, I will propose that we can gain much more from trees than oxygen. While their importance to our existence needs no explanation, I suggest that we can learn important lessons from the observation of the cycle of the production of and shedding of leaves. During the springtime, it seems impossible that the blossoms and leaves will wither and fall in a matter of months. Yet, still the tree remains rooted in the same place, and, to my mind, this can be interpreted as a form of resilience – we can deal with anything that life throws at us. Seemingly impossible processes are happening every second in nature; a leaf absorbs the sunlight and turns it into energy, ants work together to carry things that are twice their size, caterpillars transform into butterflies. Thinking about nature puts your own life into perspective and can be used as a mantra to realise that anything is possible. I realise that not all of you will share my outlook on nature and that these connections may appear to be weak to some, but, to my mind, we don't spend enough time studying the lessons that nature can teach us. You may think that our obsession with trying to produce new ways of thinking and resolving problems is praiseworthy. I've heard it described as unnecessary, but everyone agrees with the idea that it's puzzling. This is because we

AUDIOSCRIPT

rarely think to stop and look at what is, and always has been, around us. The teachings of many indigenous cultures are deeply rooted in the wonders of nature. While people around the world are often dismissive of nature's importance or are uncaring towards it, some indigenous cultures are respectful of nature and take care to observe and interpret changes in weather patterns and forestry. Returning to my earlier topic of trees, did you know that in some cultures old trees are seen as wardens who protect the household? An ancient tree in a family's garden would never be cut down for fear that this would expose the family to potential harm by removing their protection. Our tendency is to look to empowering quotes on social media for inspiration, but next time you are feeling down or confused I recommend going to any wide open field or the heart of a forest and take the time to really open your eyes to what is around you.

10.3

I = Interviewer M = Mike S = Samia

I: Today, as part of our series on successful young entrepreneurs, I'm talking to Mike Lemmington, who started his own gelato business, and Samia Johnson, who runs a marketing agency. Mike, you first. What made you start your own business?

M: Well, I've always loved desserts. As a child, I would ask my parents if I could have two desserts rather than a main course! Several years ago, I considered opening a café, but I wasn't sure about my abilities to make a success of it so soon after completing culinary school. I thought it would be more sensible to work as a *sous* pastry chef for some years. As it happens, six months later the restaurant I was working for closed and I lost my job. That same day a friend forwarded me information about the Gelato University in Bologna in Italy. I applied and, during the three months I was there, I couldn't help but find the Italians' enthusiasm and passion for gelato contagious, so when I came back to the UK I set up my own café, called it Mikalatto and began selling my own gelatos there.

I: What was your biggest barrier to success once you got started?

M: The shop itself has only been up and running for eight months. Although I returned from Bologna full of ideas and dreaming of my own gelato empire, I knew I had to be cautious and take things slowly. Getting the right flavours was incredibly important to me, so I invested heavily in equipment and devoted a couple of months to experimenting with flavours to get the perfect balance. Then I started selling on a small scale in local markets in my local towns, before opening the shop at the beginning of the year. Gelato is an integral part of Italian culture and there are gelato shops on every street, but it's not eaten by as many people in the UK so I began by building up a community of customers by selling from a portable stand at summer festivals and events, as well as at local markets. Once I realised that people loved my gelato, I opened up the shop. So far, the response has been incredibly positive.

I: Fantastic. Samia, how do you feel about the way you opened your business?

S: Well, believe it or not, I've never studied marketing! Although I was enrolled on a history of art course, I only lasted one term at university. It just wasn't for me – I wanted to see the art for myself, not just in a textbook. Despite warnings from my friends and family, I decided to blow all my savings on a round-the-world trip. At the time, social media was just becoming fashionable and I posted a picture and a recommendation about each café, restaurant and museum that I visited. I like to think I'm quite an open person and I'm known amongst my friends for giving advice, so it came naturally to me! Eventually, I built up a large following and began receiving requests to visit places in exchange for promotion. I realised that I had a talent for marketing!

I: What aspect of your job do you prefer?

S: My speciality is social media strategy, teaching small businesses in the tourism industry how to set up and manage social media campaigns. Rather than promote specific campaigns myself, I help businesses to promote themselves, and I feel fortunate that no two days are the same! A lot of my clients are small businesses that have quality products and services for tourists in up-and-coming tourist destinations, but they struggle to get noticed among the large international chains in the areas. Working closely with different cultures all over the world offering such a diverse range of products is really eye-opening.

I: Finally, what early decisions do you think have had the biggest influence on your success?

S: I had never expected to follow this path and the first few businesses I helped were just for fun. If I'd started out with a fixed plan, I'm not sure that my company would have taken the shape that it has taken. Allowing it to evolve organically took the pressure off and allowed me to develop in the way that best suits me and that, crucially, I enjoy.

M: For me it's not rushing into anything. I'm glad that I took the time to get to know my customers, to be able to talk to them about the gelato, to get their ideas and their feedback. I'm almost certain that I wouldn't have been able to do that if I'd opened a café straight away because I would have been so focused on making enough money to keep it open! I'm very ambitious and I have big plans for Mikalatto's, but I know that success is slow-burning. I don't have one end goal, instead I have lots of small goals that lead up to something bigger, and that will always lead onto something else. I think, that way, I can always keep on improving, rather than trying to make large profits so quickly that I'm not able to control things properly.

10.4

Speaker 1

When a friend introduced me to bitcoin several years ago, I was instantly intrigued. My gut instinct was that it was a worthwhile investment, even though my other friends thought it was a waste of time. As it gained in popularity, I started trading my investments and finally had the financial freedom to be able to give up my job and focus on my passion for graphic design. I was definitely in the right place at the right time. I think luck is something personal, so I don't waste time consulting other people or weighing up the pros and cons; I'm more pragmatic. You have to know yourself and trust in your intuition.

Speaker 2

I consider myself a successful person, but it sometimes frustrates me when people tell me how lucky I am to have achieved everything that I have because I've worked really hard. I started working at fifteen and made a lot of sacrifices over the years, particularly with my social life. When the opportunity came to secure a new partnership, it felt like my hard work finally paid off. I'm not sure how much luck had to do with it, but you can definitely increase your chances of something good happening by expanding your network of friends and acquaintances. You never know where one connection might lead.

Speaker 3

Luck is a psychological concept that helps us cope with the different situations that life throws at us. When my first business failed, I was tempted to use luck as a get-out card to make myself feel better rather than examine what I'd done wrong. I realised that I needed to be more independent, so it was a great feeling when I came first place in a contest for start-ups without anyone's help. Depending too much on other people doesn't always work in your favour, so I always try to remember my positive traits and feel confident in my own abilities.

Speaker 4

After reversing my car into a lamppost, tripping over a loose pavement slab and twisting my ankle and shutting my fingers in my front door all in the space of two weeks, I didn't feel very lucky earlier this month! However, I felt a bit better when I came across my grandmother's antique earring down the back of the sofa months after I lost it. I could finally relax after worrying about it for months! Although it's easy to blame the bad things that happen on being naturally unlucky, most things can be avoided if you take extra precautions!

Speaker 5

When I couldn't afford to go on my usual annual holiday last year, I decided to risk buying a secret package deal, even though I wouldn't know where I'd be going until the day before. I ended up with a five-star hotel in the Bahamas for £200 – I couldn't believe my luck! But, actually, it reminded me of something I read about the secrets of successful people – apparently, opportunity isn't influenced by luck but by how open you are to new ideas. It makes sense, actually, focusing single-mindedly on an end goal and sticking to one path to reach it is more likely to set you up for failure than being flexible to different options.

10.5

Part 1

1

What's your favourite way to spend a weekend?

2

Have you watched an interesting TV series or film recently?

3

What do you remember most about your childhood home?

4

What do you think you'll be doing this time next year?

10.6

Part 2

Student A, it's your turn first. Here are your pictures. They show people trying to improve a skill. Compare two of the pictures and say how important practice is in developing these skills and how difficult it might be for people to make an improvement

Student B, Who do you think needs help the most?

Now, Student B, here are your pictures. They show people trying to change their appearance for different reasons. Compare two of the pictures and say why the people might be trying to change their appearance and how they might be feeling.

Student A, Who do you think will remember this moment for the longest time?

10.7

Part 3

Interlocutor: Here are some aims governments and scientists have for the future. Talk to each other about how important it is to try to achieve these aims.

Interlocutor: Which of these things do you think would take the longest to achieve?

10.8

Part 4

Do you think the world in twenty years' time will be a better or worse place to live in than today? Why?

Some people say that governments only plan for the short term and not the long term. What's your opinion? Why?

Should we stop worrying about the future and focus on living today? Why / Why not?

EXAM OVERVIEW

The **Cambridge English Qualifications: C1 Advanced**, is made up of **four papers**, each testing a different area of ability in English. The **Reading and Use of English** paper is worth 40% of the marks. The **Writing**, **Listening** and **Speaking** papers are worth 20% each.

If a candidate achieves an A grade, they will receive a Certificate in Advanced English stating that they demonstrated ability at Level C2. If a candidate achieves a grade B or C, they will receive the Certificate in Advanced English at Level C1. If a candidate only achieves a B2 level, they may receive a Cambridge English Certificate stating that they demonstrated ability at Level B2.

Paper	Format	Task focus
Reading and Use of English Eight parts 56 questions 90 minutes	**Part 1:** Multiple-choice cloze. A text with eight gaps, and four options to choose from for each gap.	**Part 1:** Use of vocabulary including idioms, fixed phrases, complementation, phrasal verbs.
	Part 2: Open cloze. A text with eight gaps. Candidates write the correct word in each gap.	**Part 2:** Use of grammar, vocabulary and expressions.
	Part 3: Word formation. A text with eight gaps and a word at the end of the line in which the gap appears. Candidates write the correct form of this word in the gap.	**Part 3:** Vocabulary, particularly prefixes and suffixes, changes in form and compound words.
	Part 4: Key-word transformations. Six sentences to re-write using a given word. Candidates complete a second sentence so that it means the same as the first, using the word given.	**Part 4:** Use of grammatical and lexical structure.
	Part 5: Multiple-choice. A text with six four-option, multiple-choice questions.	**Part 5:** Identifying details, such as opinion, attitude, tone, purpose, main idea, text organisation and features.
	Part 6: Cross-text multiple matching. Four short texts followed by four multiple-matching questions	**Part 6:** Comparing and contrasting opinions and attitudes across four different texts.
	Part 7: Gapped text. One long text from which six paragraphs have been removed. Candidates replace these paragraphs from a choice of seven.	**Part 7:** Reading to understand cohesion, coherence, organisation and text structure.
	Part 8: Multiple-matching. A text or several short texts with ten multiple-matching questions.	**Part 8:** Reading to locate specific information, detail, opinion and attitude.
Writing Two tasks, carrying equal mark 90 minutes	**Part 1:** Compulsory task. Using given information to write an essay of 220–260 words.	**Part 1:** Writing an essay with a discursive focus based on two points given in the task.
	Part 2: Producing one piece of writing of 220–260 words, from a letter/email, proposal, review or report.	**Part 2:** Writing for a specific target reader and context, using appropriate layout and register.
Listening Four tasks 30 questions (around) 40 minutes	**Part 1:** Multiple-choice questions. Three short dialogues featuring interacting speakers, with two multiple-choice questions (with three options) for each extract.	**Part 1:** Understanding gist, detail, function, agreement, speaker purpose, feelings, attitude, etc.
	Part 2: Sentence completion. One monologue with eight sentences to complete with a word or short phrase.	**Part 2:** Locating and recording specific information and stated opinions.
	Part 3: Multiple-choice questions. A conversation between two or more speakers, with six four-option multiple-choice questions.	**Part 3:** Understanding attitude and opinion.
	Part 4: Multiple matching. A set of five short monologues on a theme. There are two tasks. In both tasks candidates match each monologue to one of eight prompts.	**Part 4:** Identifying main points, gist, attitude and opinion.
Speaking Four tasks (around) 15 minutes per pair	**Part 1:** Examiner-led conversation.	**Part 1:** General social and interactional language.
	Part 2: Individual long turn with visual and written prompts. Candidates talk about two pictures from a choice of three.	**Part 2:** Organising discourse, speculating, comparing, giving opinions.
	Part 3: Two-way collaborative task. Candidates discuss a question with five written prompts for two minutes, then answer a second question on the same topic.	**Part 3:** Sustaining interaction, expressing and justifying opinions, evaluating and speculating, negotiating towards a decision, etc.
	Part 4: The examiner asks questions for candidates to discuss on issues related to the topic of Part 3.	**Part 4:** Expressing and justifying ideas and opinions, agreeing and disagreeing, speculating.

Pearson Education Limited
KAO Two
KAO Park
Harlow
Essex
CM17 9NA
England
and Associated Companies throughout the world.

pearsonELT.com/goldexperience

First published 2018

Eighteenth impression 2024

ISBN: 978-1-292-19516-2

Set in Camphor Pro
Printed by Neografia, in Slovakia

Picture Credits

The publisher would like to thank the following for their kind permission to reproduce their photographs:

(Key: b-bottom; c-centre; l-left; r-right; t-top)

123RF.com: Antonio Diaz 94, Scott Griessel 117tl, happyalex 53 (C), kasto 53 (A), Dzmitry Kliapitski 63, Roman Kosolapov 95 (C), Galina Peshkova 50, Andriy Popov 95 (A), Jorg Schiemann 93, Galina Starintseva 60, Marek Uliasz 80, Mirko Vitali 51, Wavebreak Media Ltd 95 (B), Dmytro Zinkevych 5; **Alamy Stock Photo:** Christian Bertrand 75 (B), Blend Images 116tr, Hero Images Inc. 116tl, OJO Images Ltd 88, RubberBall 56, Nick Savage 68; **Getty Images:** iStock / Getty Images Plus / baona 92, AFP / Robyn Beck 75 (C), The Image Bank / Alistair Berg 21 (B), Getty Images News / Francois Durand 21 (C), Corbis / HBSS 38, Blend Images / Jose Luis Pelaez Inc 36, Getty Images Entertainment / Rabbani and Solimene Photography 24, Getty Images Sport / Andrew Redington 21 (A), Getty Images News / Eliot J. Schechter 75 (A); **Pearson Education Ltd:** 53 (B); **Shutterstock.com:** Africa Studio 46, Peter Bernik 116b, chrisdorney 73, CroMary 117tr, Magdalena Cvetkovic 72, Dean Drobot 32, Rainer Fuhrmann 18, gg-foto 27, Kaspars Grinvalds 78, iko 70, Infinity Time 82, IVASHstudio 117b, Dmitri Ma 40, Markus Mainka 83, mangostock 91, Monkey Business Images 28, Alena Ozerova 6, Wassana Panapute 85, Natthapong Ponepormmarat 12, Rawpixel.com 19, skvalval 79, Stokkete 14, Kalmatsuy Tatyana 59, Anibal Trejo 90, Blajevska Viktoria 54, wk1003mike 33

Cover images: *Front:* **Shutterstock.com:** Vladimir Hodac

All other images © Pearson Education